Dark Sides of Business and Higher Education Management

Dark Sides of Business and Higher Education Management

Volume II

Edited by

Agata Stachowicz-Stanusch and Gianluigi Mangia

BEP BUSINESS EXPERT PRESS

Dark Sides of Business and Higher Education Management, Volume II

First published in 2016 by
Business Expert Press, LLC
222 East 46th Street, New York, NY 10017
www.businessexpertpress.com

ISBN-13: 978-1-63157-566-2 (paperback)
ISBN-13: 978-1-63157-567-9 (e-book)

Business Expert Press Principles for Responsible Management Education Collection

Collection ISSN: 2331-0014 (print)
Collection ISSN: 2331-0022 (electronic)

Cover and interior design by Exeter Premedia Services Private Ltd., Chennai, India

First edition: 2016

10 9 8 7 6 5 4 3 2 1

Printed in the United States of America.

Abstract

Contemporary management studies usually concern positive and desirable solutions that increase the organizational effectiveness and performance. That is why graduates of higher business schools, equipped with idealistic views on business environment, need to face the dark side of business practice without the appropriate preparation. Their unawareness of the risk associated with management misconduct results in corrupt scandals, erosion of public trust to their organizations, or even the collapse of profitable corporations. Underestimation of unethical behaviors may lead to severe consequences.

The last decade, in fact, has been abundant in numerous examples of corruption scandals in modern organizations and instances of management misconduct that have eroded public faith (such as Enron, WorldCom, Tyco, Adelphia, Arthur Andersen, and Parmalat). These repeated misconducts have led scholars to pay more attention to the so-called "dark side" of organizations.

In the current book and journal publications, the "dark side" is pursuit as abnormal, dysfunctional, or pathological aspects of business and education. Indeed, we should say that the "dark side" is not exceptional: it is a part of the normal community of everyday organizational activities.

There are three main reasons for this book. First, since there is a highly active dark side to the organizations, which is quite unknown in management studies, this book attempts to shed the light on the practical challenges for business practice and for higher education management that come from misconduct occurring in various aspects of business and educational environment.

Second, research on the "dark side" is a new, emerging source of research in the area of business and higher education management.

Finally, it is virtually impossible to carry all the works and research on the development of positive, bright sides of business and higher education without a thorough knowledge and understanding of the destructive, dark sides of organizations that have led and still lead to the collapse of many organizations and a decline in public confidence in the corporations and their leaders.

Keywords

business ethics and integrity, business misconducts, dark side, higher education

Contents

Acknowledgments

We thank all chapter authors who met deadlines, engaged ideas, responded to feedback, and wrote magnificent chapters that make this book amazing. We are proud to have had the opportunity to work with all of them. We are indebted to our reviewers for their valuable and thoughtful suggestions that have enriched this book. We are greatly indebted to Anna Sworowska and Andrea Tomo—our research associates and colleagues—whose editorial acumen is reflected on every page of this volume.

Especially, we would like to thank Oliver Laasch, Editor of the United Nations Principles for Responsible Management Education Collection (PRME) and Rob Zwettler, Executive Acquisitions Editor, Business Expert Press, for their continuous support.

PART I

Theorizing in the Shadow (of Higher Education Management)

CHAPTER 1

Light in the Darkness of Business and Higher Education Management

Agata Stachowicz-Stanusch and Gianluigi Mangia

Contemporary management studies usually concern positive and desirable solutions that increase the organizational effectiveness and performance. That is why graduates of higher business schools, equipped with idealistic views on business environment, need to face the dark side of business practice without the appropriate preparation. Their unawareness of the risk associated with management misconduct results in corrupt scandals, erosion of public trust to their organizations, or even the collapse of profitable corporations. Underestimation of unethical behaviors may lead to severe consequences.

This book attempts to shed the light on the practical challenges for business practice and for higher education management that come from misconduct occurring in various aspects of business and educational environment.

This second volume of the book is divided into three parts.

The first part is the opening one in the form of this editors' introduction.

The second part "Shedding Lights on the Shadows" opens with Leixnering and Mayrhofer's chapter "Facebook Voyeurism: Blind Spot or Dark Side of Human Resource Management?" In this chapter, the authors analyze this phenomenon and shed light on the question whether

Facebook voyeurism is a blind spot or even a dark side of human resource management (HRM). By collecting sources from different fields of literature such as management and legal studies, sociology, psychology, and philosophy, the authors show that Facebook voyeurism in HRM is a surprisingly under-researched phenomenon and thus a particular blind spot. In particular, authors explicate what do Facebook voyeurs do wrong from a moral perspective, if and how social network sites (SNSs) content improve HR decisions and how could various concepts of privacy guide HRM.

Del Mar et al. in the chapter "University Student Plagiarism in the Digital Age and the Professors' Role in Detecting and Reporting," focus on the university professors' perceptions by examining the role they play in this phenomenon and the actions they undertake when faced with cases of plagiarism. Their study is based on the results of a qualitative study involving in-depth interviews with professors from a range of specializations within the areas of management and economics.

In his chapter "Selling Science Through University Entrepreneurship: Debates and Implications for Emerging Economies," Debabrata Chatterjee discusses about institutional changes in the field of higher education. These changes have enlarged professors' role beyond teaching and research to include faculty research commercialization and entrepreneurship in various forms—science parks, joint ventures with industry, business incubation centers, and so on. Although in some instances it has spawned hi-technology industries in certain clusters, its effect is debated. Rising importance of science-based innovations, changes in higher education and research funding policies, growing importance of global university rankings, and normative pressures on universities to spawn science-based industrial clusters are some factors that have contributed to this trend. However, the impact of academic research commercialization is debatable. While its success in developing science-based industry is doubted, evidence suggests that it might adversely impact basic research, which in turn might lead to lower innovations in the long term. The essay concludes by suggesting that brokering organizations, such as public R&D institutions, may act as intermediaries to translate university science for industry, rather than universities themselves taking on this role directly through academic entrepreneurship.

The last part of the book "Individuals: Behaviors and Perceptions" opens with the chapter "Whistling Past the Graveyard of Our Own Demise: How Neoliberalism, Corruption, Status Hierarchies, and The Imperium Threaten Higher Education." In this chapter, Duncan Waite discusses the situatedness of the professor and the professorate, his or her position as "dominated dominant." The discussion, then, is based on the focus on individual and collective actions, taking into account the organizing principles, processes, and systems that we construct, employ, and are a part of. In addition, those more macro or global forces, processes, and systems that affect us and our work are discussed, such as neoliberalism and The Imperium.

Mameli et al. in their chapter "Inside the Dark Sides: A Clinical Experience," discuss the clinical experience of training on the managerial role in public organizations through the parallel between Sci-Fi narratives and the training experience. Based on more than 1,500 hours of training over a 48-month period, this chapter also provides the possibility to explore the concept of Dark Sides from a clinical perspective. This approach is based on an understanding of the relationship between individuals and their context that gives the possibility to explore both at conscious and unconscious level the representations of the Dark Side as experienced by the participants, giving way to a reflection on what can be done to get out of these Dark Sides, or better, to act within them.

The chapter by Hinna et al. "Organizational Corruption in the Education System," is focused on the theme of corruption as a social phenomenon that decreases social and economic wealth and as dark side of human behavior in society and business. For these reasons, corruption has an obvious impact on people's daily lives, but it is also a challenging topic for the scientific debate, because of the gap in the knowledge of its causes, making possible strategies to contrast and to prevent corruption uncertain. Starting from the differences between public and private organizations and taking into account peculiarities of an education system, the article's main object is to identify antecedents of corruption within school organizations. Therefore, this article identifies a set of organizational variables that reflects the determinants of corruption within the private and public sectors, as within the education system; it then identifies specific tools that can be put in place to fight corruption in the education system.

In "Human Resource Management in UK Higher Education: Business Schools and Their Dark Side," Tom Burgess applies Palmer's novel approach that organizational wrongdoing is normal rather than abnormal. The wrongdoing arises from changes in the psychological contract and in failings in the HRM of academics in UK university business schools. To frame Palmer's theoretical perspective, the chapter uses Bauman's lens of liquid modernity to view the contextual changes in society that are buffeting universities. Key societal pressures, such as new public management and the government's research assessment exercises, are described before discussing the management of academics and wrongdoing within the business school context. The chapter uses secondary data; in particular, a case study assembled from media reports of recent events in one UK management school, to illustrate the discussion.

This book was created thanks to many authors from all over the world. They present us examples of "dark" practices in the business and in the education management environment. We hope that their theoretical and practical contribution into organizational social irresponsibility, corruption, and unethical behavior will be priceless and inspiring struggling with dark sides of business and higher education management.

PART II

Shedding Lights on the Shadows

CHAPTER 2

Facebook Voyeurism: Blind Spot or Dark Side of Human Resource Management?

Stephan Leixnering
and Wolfgang Mayrhofer

WU Vienna University of Economics and Business

Introduction

How does a beautiful naked woman on a horseback relate to human resource management (HRM)? Or, more practically: What may HRM benefit from pondering on such a situation? A lot, we think.

Image that woman—let's call her Lady Godiva—sitting on a white horse and riding through the town's streets. You—let's call you Tom—are considering a brief look at her. Wouldn't it be nice to peep just for a second? Oh, it's not what I might think, you argue: she promised to do you a great favor and to save you a lot of money. And to prove her good intentions and her honest attitude, she was willing to literally disclose her true nature. Nevertheless, Lady Godiva asked you to not peep at her in order to keep her dignity—you are aware of that! However, you now want to briefly check if she sticks to her word. But suddenly you're struggling—you feel caught, even though Lady Godiva hasn't yet recognized you. You are feeling that she wouldn't approve of you watching her. While trying to collect your thoughts, you ask yourself: If she does not want anybody to look at her, why on earth is she broadcasting herself in that way? You are weighing your options.

Figure 2.1 Lady Godiva (Collier 1897). What should you do now—peep or not?

This synopsis of the more than 600 years old legend of Lady Godiva and Peeping Tom nicely captures the very essence of a situation that more and more human resource (HR) managers find themselves in. When they have to decide on somebody's selection, promotion, or dismissal, they try to gather as much relevant personal information about the candidate as possible to support their decision. Since social media allow people to share private information online, HR managers become attracted by sources like Facebook, Twitter, and Instagram. And as soon as they are about to "check" someone online to find something that they do not know yet, they are getting close to Peeping Tom's reflections.

Academic interest in tackling the wicked issue that we would like to call "Facebook voyeurism"—the increasing danger of HR managers becoming online peepers by profession—has been rather scarce. In this chapter, we want to shed light on whether the phenomenon marks a blind spot or even a dark side of present HRM. We argue that the phenomenon of Facebook voyeurism is highly relevant to the field of HRM. Collecting and building on various sources from the fields of management and legal studies, sociology, psychology, philosophy, and arts, we develop a more comprehensive perspective and offer a multifaceted analysis of the phenomenon. We will further demonstrate that even though the phenomenon is new, it is only a present and concrete instance of a rather abstract and old problem.

Overall, this chapter urges HRM scholars to address three essential issues related to the use of social media: the benefit of the use of social media in HRM, the conceptualization of privacy, and the role of ethics. As these issues are in dire need of future research, we will conclude the chapter with suggesting avenues for future academic research and discussion.

The Emergence of Social Network Sites

After its launch in 2004, Facebook emerged as the emblem of social media and became the world's most visited website with more than one billion active users every month (Chauhan, Buckley, and Harvey 2013; Day 2013). Being the most prominent of so-called social network sites (SNSs), it provides

> web-based services that allow individuals to (1) construct a public or semipublic profile within a bounded system, (2) articulate a list of other users with whom they share a connection, and (3) view and traverse their list of connections and those made by others within the system. (Ellisonand Boyd 2013, 211)

Basically, it allows for online flows of personal information including all kind of data such as photographs, video clips, gossip, and trivia (Herbert 2011). Today, SNSs account for about 80 percent of all online content and for nearly one-quarter of the time that Internet users spend online (Comscore 2011). Those numbers indicate that individuals increasingly present themselves online and in fact, put themselves on display; and by doing so, they also demonstrate their willingness to disclose personal information, share it with others, and make it available to broader audiences. As a consequence, scholars increasingly see evidence for the fact that SNSs heavily alter our communication habits, shape our attitudes, and influence our online and offline behavior as well (Liu 2007; Mazer, Murphy, and Simonds 2007). And although people may immensely enjoy the opportunities that SNSs provide, they are also becoming more and more aware of adverse consequences that intensive online presence might entail. In a worldwide survey, 36 percent of all respondents said that they were concerned about their job prospects because of "social networking pages leaving a digital trail of information thereby eliminating plausible deniability" (Herbert 2011, 2).

The Discovery of SNSs as an HRM Tool

The Internet has made it increasingly easy to engage in amateur datamining (Zimmer 2007)—even without using SNSs. "Everybody's googling": You can find, collect, and aggregate personal details of someone's life by simply entering their name in the search engine. SNSs make it even more convenient to trace people's "friends, dates, potential employees, long-lost relatives, and anybody else who happens to arouse their curiosity" (Herbert 2011, 4). It is indeed very likely to assume that the main use of Facebook is simply social searching (Lampe, Ellison, and Steinfield 2006). In a study of 2008, users readily admitted that they used Facebook for checking up people they knew as well as others they did not. The report also says that more than 90 percent of all respondents regularly check up their friends, and 50 percent trace whom their ex-partners are dating (Foregger 2008). Labeled as "peep culture," this phenomenon was claimed to have replaced "pop culture": Instead of celebrities, people now tend to watch others they know or even complete strangers in the pursuit of entertainment and attention (Niedzviecki 2009). SNSs actively contribute to the formation of such an attitude since they encourage users to put as much of their private lives as possible online and to maximize the audience as well as its access to personal content (Herbert 2011).

It is relatively undemanding to find online information about people: Profiles are public, and privacy settings are rarely changed in many cases (Zimmer 2007). Even if access to private information is often limited to people that have been accepted as "friends," this can be overcome easily. IT-security company Sophos showcased this by setting up an online profile of a comic frog called FreddiStaur (an anagram of "ID fraudster") and asking randomly chosen Facebook users to accept Freddi as a friend in order to get access to private content. The result testifies how easy it is to obtain personal information from other users: 44% percent of all contacted users responded to Freddi, and almost all of them provided access to private data such as photos, hobbies, and employer details (Herbert 2011).

The ubiquity of SNSs and their content make them a potential target for HR managers keen on getting additional information for their individual-related decisions. To fulfill its basic task—providing the organization with the right number of people with adequate qualifications at the right time and location—HRM requires, *inter alia*, information about individuals. In particular when hiring people from outside, HR managers are faced with substantial decision uncertainty. Especially SNSs for non-business purposes such as Facebook provide plenty of personal information about individuals that cannot be gathered from conventional sources like application letters, CVs, or job interviews. Therefore, SNSs are perceived as useful for HR purposes. According to a worldwide study, three-quarter of surveyed recruiters admit online evaluation of candidates via SNS; two-third of HR managers state that they had rejected job applications due to information gathered by checking SNSs (Microsoft 2010). Another survey confirms this insight (Careerbuilder 2009): More than one-third of HR professionals surveyed say that they declined to hire applicants because of exhibitionistic content found on their SNS pages such as provocative photographs, references to drug and alcohol use, negative comments about prior employers and coworkers, and discriminatory remarks. Facebook is mentioned as the most popular destination for online checks. In addition, the study finds that the percentage of employers actively using SNSs as tools has doubled from the previous year (see also Herbert 2011). Newspapers also increasingly report on people who have lost their jobs because of intemperate posts about their employers or even broadcasting holiday pictures while they have officially been on sick leave (for some examples see, Madden 2011).

Although 70 percent of HR professionals in the Careerbuilder (2009) study report that they have a corporate policy on checking SNSs, there are no legal guidelines or at least very few legal restraints that prevent employers from gathering SNSs information for hiring decisions (Brown and Vaughn 2011; Chauhan, Buckley, and Harvey 2013; Smith and Kidder 2010). Interestingly enough and despite the vast and even growing literature that deals with social media, privacy, and SNSs in general (for literature reviews see, Chen and Shi 2009; Ellison 2007; Wilson, Gosling, and Graham 2012), the HRM literature remains almost silent on the phenomenon. It seems that efficiency as well as unintended effects of the use of SNSs in personnel selection are a widely unresearched phenomenon.

Online Watching and Being Watched

Not only is self-disclosure an important social networking communication behavior, but the willingness to disclose personal information and thereby contribute to its flow on the Web is the very condition to the rise of SNSs (Taddicken 2014). Academia has therefore already begun to apply well-known concepts such as self-presentation and impression management, self-comparison theory, or social similarity and homophily on the phenomenon of social media (for an overview see, Baruh 2010; Karl, Peluchette, and Schlaegel 2010; Su 2012). Recent literature's core explanation for people's willingness to disclose private information on SNSs is relatively simple: They do so in order to present a context-related desirable picture of themselves to the addressed forum.

Diving deeper into the phenomena of online-presentation and disclosure of the self (Belk 2013; Hollenbaugh and Ferris 2014; McAndrew and Jeong 2012), some scholars argue that such behavior may be perceived as an instance of exhibitionism as it is heavily driven by a narcissistic tendency, showing extraversion and low impulse control (e.g., Carpenter 2012; Panek, Nardis, and Konrath 2013) "to demonstrate superiority and to seek for admiration from other people in order to build a desirable self-image" (Mäntymäki and Islam 2014). It has also been argued that by their very nature, SNSs encourage endemic electronic exhibitionism as a practice of self-disclosure that makes the self known to others and attracts attention to oneself (Herbert 2011).

"Oversharing" may lead to unintended consequences (Zimmer and Hoffman 2011)—especially when sharing with the "wrong" watchers. On the one hand, SNSs appear to be a useful tool for people to stay up to date about what's happening in their social environments on the other hand, they can though be used to stalk or peep at other people (Mäntymäki and Islam 2014). In the latter case, users would typically be excited about gathering personal information about others rather than sharing data about themselves. Such a habit can be described as "online voyeurism" or Facebook voyeurism which may be defined as "the consumption of revealing images of and information about other's apparently real and unguarded lives, often yet not always for purposes of entertainment but frequently at the expense of privacy and disclosure, through the mass media and Internet" (Calvert 2000, 2).

The term voyeur (coming from voir, French for seeing) literally simply means observer. From a traditional psychological perspective, the concept of voyeurism refers to an exaggerated sexual interest in spying naked people, often engaged in sexual activities or other actions of distinct private nature (American Psychiatric Association 2013; Smith 1976). Following a broader conceptualization, voyeuristic behavior does not have to be sexually connoted (Baruh 2010; Calvert 2000). Online voyeurism is primarily nonsexual, although it seems pretty obvious how difficult it is to completely disconnect any form of voyeurism from the sexual dimension. A "Facebook voyeur" therefore is someone who tends to covertly peep into personal details of specific other people the voyeur may or may not know personally. To a *certain* extent, such a habit may indeed not be seen as abnormal, pathological, or deviant but "a common personal trait enjoyed by all 'normal' individuals to different degrees" (Baruh 2010, 203). In addition, the extent of what is widely perceived as "normal" has significantly changed since the 1970s (Metzl 2004). Behavior that a psychoanalyst in the 1960s would have denoted as voyeuristic might today be a perfect description of common TV watching habits, yellow press content, or social media use. Nevertheless, voyeurism in its present meaning refers to the deviant behavior when people are thrilled by watching others (Day 2013) and carries a particular negative connotation (Draeger 2011): This moral dimension of voyeurism makes it an even more complex phenomenon (Nathan 1990).

Despite recent but modest interest in the context of social media, the phenomenon of voyeurism has been remarkably under-researched in the past (Su 2012). A literature review from the mid-1970s states that publications related to voyeurism were scarce (Smith 1976). A more recent meta-analysis comes to the same conclusion (Metzl 2004). Apart from academia, voyeurism has nevertheless gained much interest in Hollywood with Alfred Hitchcock's *Rear Window* (1954) and Michael Powell's *Peeping Tom* (1960) being outstanding examples (Hawthorn 2003; Sabbadini 2000).

Technological achievements of the last decades obviously contributed to an increasing "voyeurization" of society and have maybe even led to a "voyeur nation" (Calvert 2000; Metzl 2004): *Peeping Tom* filmmaker Michael Powell once stated his conviction that "the cinema makes voyeurs of us all" (Hawthorn 2003, 321). Even more so, the Web provides a new kind of space where peeping is very easy and safe and potential voyeurs can come in covertly in order to consume "revealing images and information about others' apparently real and unguarded lives" (Calvert 2000, 2). Due to its use of a medium (e.g., SNSs), this phenomenon can be denoted as "mediated voyeurism" (Baruh 2010; Calvert 2000).

SNS "Prosumers" Versus Facebook Voyeurs

The overarching principle of participation in SNSs is reciprocity: Members of SNSs disclose personal information that they are willing to share with the community and thereby produce site content. In addition, they are also consumers of online content as they "gain the right" to watch sites of other people. This mechanism has been denoted as the principle of reciprocal self-disclosure (Moon 2000) where "people who receive intimate disclosure feel obligated to respond with a personal disclosure of equal intimacy" (Nass and Moon 2000, 89). SNS members have therefore been characterized as "prosumers" (Chunyan, Bagozzi, and Troye 2008) because they consume content that has been produced by other users; and in turn, they also produce content that can be accessed and consumed by others (Mäntymäki and Islam 2014). The reciprocity of prosuming also constitutes a self-control mechanism of SNSs as it shapes people's disclosing behavior. The rationale behind is that mutual disclosure and observation are the best protection of antisocial behavior (e.g., Arndt 1949). This even includes people's watching behavior insofar as every watcher could, at the same time, also be a target of the gaze of others (Calvert 2000).

The content of SNSs, which Facebook and others encourage their users to generate, is the very source of their value. Therefore, their users as content producers and consumers alike are cocreators of this value: "When sharing their experiences, reading and commenting the posts of other users, the users create value both for themselves and for other users" (Mäntymäki and Islam 2014, 5). But Facebook voyeurs violate the principle of reciprocal self-disclosure as they appropriate value from viewing others but create little content and hence value for others in return. The voyeur obtains information from other people's sites and learns about them but does not provide any in return. Yet at least some degree in self-disclosure would be necessary to contribute to the reciprocal exchange of personal information that takes place in and characterizes SNSs (Mäntymäki and Islam 2014). A mediated voyeur therefore deviates from a prosumer user as "[t]here is no reciprocal responsibility placed on the voyeur in the watching process" (Calvert 2000, 69). The SNS world has coined an own term for people who observe rather than participate in the network: "lurkers" (Day 2013). SNSs provide vast opportunity for lurkers to watch other people. Albeit lurking is widely not perceived as deviant behavior, it may be considered as an intrusion to privacy (Munar 2010).

SNSs favor a maximum of information flow to as many people as possible. Therefore, for example, in the case of Facebook, default privacy settings are as permissive as possible. Without changing those, all of a site's content (such as posts, photos, or status updates) will be available to everybody (Day 2013). However, a lot of people are unaware of that and fail in managing their privacy settings according to their actual preferences (Comer, McKelvey, and Curran 2012). A majority of users fails to use all available privacy settings, and some scholars even argue that Facebook actively tries to encourage users to maximize the potential audience as well as accessibility to personal content by automatically suggesting less strict options or making it difficult for users to manage their own settings (Chauhan, Buckley, and Harvey 2013; Herbert 2011).

SNSs are basically designed as virtual meeting places for prosumers who mutually create value for themselves and other users by both producing and consuming content. But from another perspective, SNSs may also perfectly work without obeying the principle of reciprocal disclosure, as long as there are people willing to put themselves on show on the one hand, and "lurkers" on the other hand: such a depiction of SNSs suggests that mediated exhibitionism needs mediated voyeurism (de Laat 2008), since the former requires a scene and the latter an audience: SNSs would then "provide [...] a room for users to exhibit themselves while simultaneously providing a safe, legally sanctioned venue for the mediated voyeur to meet the exhibitors" (Su 2012, 13). Such a merely analytical, nevertheless convincing position of "empowering exhibitionism" (de Laat 2008) bears the danger of neglecting the essential moral dimension of voyeurism: It rather liberates the Facebook voyeur—a label that indeed nobody wants to carry—from the term's particular negative connotation by construing it as the complementary and therefore legitimate counterpart of one-sided online disclosure of personal information.

The perspective of coexistence of excessive SNS content producers and consumers also turns our attraction to those who intentionally plan to take advantage thereof. Facebook has been "conceived of as a *collection of tools* utilized in different ways to meet different needs" (Smock et al. 2011, 2323), and as we have previously argued, HR professionals are already heavily using this toolkit. Applicants and other potential beneficiaries may therefore try to draw HR managers' attention to SNSs where they attempt to broadcast their qualities in an impression management-manner (e.g., "Linkedin," which is an SNS to manage business-related contacts: Ellison, Steinfield, and Lampe 2007). In addition, they may take advantage from high social capital due to the number of their "friends" and of the nature of their postings (Ellison, Steinfield, and Lampe 2007; Liu 2007). HR executives may in turn have a strong interest to access private information that applicants and employees wish to protect from unauthorized access and that might shed light on their "maturity, prudence[,] and responsibility" (Herbert 2011, 5)—criteria that undoubtedly are of interest from a potential employer's perspective. Such a conceptualization of professional SNS use is indeed very much in line with a Lacanian psychoanalytic view on voyeurism, as voyeurs tend to look for what they otherwise cannot see (Baruh 2010). So, are HR managers that want to take advantage of SNSs "would-be peepers [that] need a strong disin[c]entive against cultivating their passion" (Doyle 2009, 187)?

An Etiology of Voyeurism: Lady Godiva and Peeping Tom

New problems often are not really new. Instead, they may rather be a variation of an existing conflict or, more precisely, another instance of a more fundamental problem that has already been observed. Returning to our text's point of departure, the legend of Lady Godiva focuses on exactly the same problem as we do, even if the setting is very different: The story dates back to the 13th century and was most artfully put in verses by Alfred Lord Tennyson in 1840, and as it seems, there is absolutely no direct connection to "modern" mediated voyeurism or exhibitionistic tendencies of SNS users. But the legend indeed describes a setting that can be construed as essentially similar or even equal to the situation that HR managers experience nowadays. And, worth recognizing, the legend also provides the reader with a particular moral of the story.

Lady Godiva, an 11th century noblewoman, was the wife of Leofric, Earl of Mercia. The people of Coventry grievously suffered under oppressive taxes that their Lord Leofric collected. Lady Godiva took pity of her people and tried to convince her husband to ease the tax burden. In the words of Lord Tennyson (1840):

Whereat he stared, replying, half amazed,

"You would not let your little finger ache

For such as these?"—"But I would die," said she.

He laughed, and swore by Peter and by Paul;

Then filliped at the diamond in her ear,

"O, ay, ay, ay, you talk!"—"Alas!" she said,

"But prove me what it is I would not do."

And from a heart as rough as Esau's hand,

He answered, "Ride you naked through the town,

And I repeal it"; and nodding as in scorn,

He parted, with great strides, among his dogs! (par. 2)

She agreed. Lady Godiva issued an order saying that all people of Coventry must stay inside their houses and close their windows during her ride in order not to catch a view on her. Then she stripped off her clothes and rode naked through the streets of Coventry. A tailor called Tom disobeyed the order and peeped at her through a hole in his shutters. That is how Peeping Tom became the most prominent voyeur in history, and he immediately received the enormous penalty for his misconduct:

Then she rode back, clothed on with chastity:

And one low churl, compact of thankless earth,

The fatal byword of all years to come,

Boring a little auger-hole in fear,

Peeped: but his eyes, before they had their will,

Were shriveled into darkness in his head,

And dropt before him. (Tennyson 1840, par. 4)

Despite that (or even because) the story heavily alludes to a sexual dimension by the inclusion of nudity, we are very familiar with the overall situation: We are interested in glancing a bit closer at a special somebody because we think that we might benefit from what we see in one way or the other. As we know that that somebody would disapprove of us watching if he or she discovered us, we have to hide ourselves and act covertly in order not to get caught. Then we will be able to see what otherwise would be withheld from our gaze.

The story's etiology is amazingly accurate for our problem at hand: It puts the paradox of the willingness to self-disclosure and the distinct negative connotation of voyeurism at center stage and focuses on the ambiguity of Lady Godiva's message (see the "privacy paradox": Barnes 2006). On the one hand, she explicitly broadcasts her body by showing it off in public, on the other hand she states that nobody must look at her.

Despite the considerable ambiguity in the legend, the moral of the story is unquestionably clear: Eventually, Tom is heavily punished for not resisting the temptation to peep.

Blind Spot or Dark Side? Three Questions Waiting for an Answer

A look back to the recent history of HRM teaches us, again, that the problem of Facebook voyeurism is only an instance of a problem that has been witnessed before. In the 1970s, for example, HR scholars discussed whether it would be justifiable to check a job applicant's references without letting him or her know ("pre-employment reference checking": Rice 1978). Back then, the discussion focused on the unwillingness of HR executives to disclose their practices in front of the applicant. Apparently they feared that such transparency would turn the observer into the observed—an exposing situation where every voyeur would feel highly uncomfortable (Calvert and Brown 2000). This problem was perceived as even more delicate against the backdrop of employees' legal right to access their own files and discover about screening practices in the aftermath.

Based on our considerations as well as on the recent literature, we conclude that the problem of tackling Facebook voyeurism from a scholarly HRM perspective is threefold. First of all, there is a remarkable lack of empirical evidence on how the availability of personal information contributes to better decisions in HRM, in particular with regard to recruitment and selection. Second, the literature on Facebook voyeurism at hand suggests treating the issue as a privacy problem (Clark and Roberts 2010; Slovensky and Ross 2011; Smith and Kidder 2010). But not only is the concept of privacy difficult to apply to the problem of Facebook voyeurism, privacy itself seems not to be a coherent concept at all: Privacy means many things to many people and "seems to be about everything, and therefore it appears to be nothing" (Solove 2007, 479; see also Spinello 2010, and the following). And third, the relation to the moral sphere is unclear albeit undoubtedly present ("ethical problems": see the following). So, with allusion to the legend of Lady Godiva and Peeping Tom, three questions appear as yet unanswered: (1) Which advantages does Tom actually take from peeping? (2) How could a concept of privacy help to structure the widely obscure situation between Lady Godiva and Peeping Tom that seems to feature voyeurism and exhibitionism alike? And finally: (3) What did Peeping Tom do wrong? Related to HRM, these questions point toward the potential of SNSs and their content for improving HR decisions, the relevance of privacy for designing HRM policies and practices, and the problems that HRM faces from a moral perspective. We will turn to these issues next.

Does Knowledge About Personal SNS Content Improve HR Decisions?

The current literature raises two different types of concerns about using SNSs in HRM decision making. First, scholars question the validity of data gathered from SNS. This data does not reflect how people "really" (?) are but rather how they want to be perceived (see the preceding). Others argue, based on some empirical evidence, that the difference between "real" and "image of real" is crucial. From this point of view, SNSs are valid sources for information about people's characteristics simply because their broadcasted self-picture allows to figure out what they perceive as socially attractive and appropriate (e.g., Davison, Maraist, and Bing 2011). Thus, even if information provided in profiles is not entirely true, it may permit conclusions about the key characteristics and values of users. Second, even if SNSs constitute a valid source, it remains unclear whether this type of information improves HRM decisions, in particular related to selection.

This touches a core problem of personnel selection: What selection criteria support good decisions that also in hindsight turn out to be right? Surprisingly, definite empirical evidence on that is still missing. Studies have been struggling with demonstrating a clear association of individual characteristics of candidates and firm performance (however measured) (Brown and Vaughn 2011; Davison, Maraist, and Bing 2011; Slovensky and Ross 2011).

How Could Concepts of Privacy Guide HRM?

Privacy has become a strong public claim toward companies like Facebook or even the state. Examples include executive compensation of public officials, political decision processes, or protection of individual health care data. But what actually is privacy? The recent literature from different fields such as legal and organizations studies, political theory, or philosophy is vast and, in a quite normative underlying tune, increasingly draws attention to privacy as a "lost right" (e.g., Mills 2008) and addresses the problem of "no place to hide" (e.g., O'Harrow 2006), also in terms of new technological achievements. Despite this strong interest, privacy still appears to be "a concept in disarray" (Solove 2006, 477), and conceptualizations are, if existent, widely "vague and multifaceted" (Spinello 2010, 367). Basically, much of the confusion seems to originate from a conflict between two opposed "iconic towers" (Docherty 2011): privacy on the one hand and transparency on the other. Literature suggests construing those as manifestations of "two different western cultures of privacy"— dignity and liberty (Whitman 2004).

What indeed seems quite obvious is that once foundational ideas on privacy are now heavily challenged. As in the late-19th century discussed by Warren and Brandeis (1890), the term privacy was developed to denote a comprehensive right to maintain control of personal informational integrity—and even back then, disruptive technical advances had been the discussion's driving forces (Nissenbaum 2009). Privacy was mainly developed to push back unwelcome new "Kodak friends" that emerged: "This season there is something at the seaside worse than sharks. It is the amateur photographer" (cited after *The Economist* 2013, 13). The U.S. Supreme Court may still hold privacy as the right of control over personal information (Spinello 2012, 373)—yet, "privacy as the claim of an individual to determine what information about himself or herself should be known to others" (Westin 2003, 431) seems rather put on jeopardy in the online era. But even against the backdrop of people's obvious willingness to share personal details online on SNSs, preventing others from accessing personal information at their discretion seems crucial (Reiman 2004). Recent empirical evidence shows strong direct association of the readiness to disclose personal information on SNSs and the possibility to maintain control over its flow (Christofides, Muise, and Desmarais 2009; Joinson et al. 2010).

The appropriateness of certain information for the task pursued is apparently a central criterion to whether seeking access to it is perceived as legitimate or not. In the beginning of the 20th century, Ford employed people that covertly inspected company workers' bank accounts in order to assess if those spent their money according to the moral standards of the company (Boatright 2003). Such in this case historic, but nevertheless highly illustrative practices turn attention to the contextual integrity aspect of privacy (Nissenbaum 2009) and the "plurality of distinct realms" (Zimmer 2007, 5). What privacy means and what is appropriate strongly depends on the context. Accordingly, the notion of "publicness" and "privateness" (Benn and Gaus 1983) not only were contingent on the conditions under which private information flows, but also on its appropriateness for the respective context at hand, for example, a personnel selection decision (Nissenbaum 2009).

What Do Facebook Voyeurs Do Wrong from a Moral Perspective?

Much of the present discussion on privacy rights carries a distinct moral tone. But even if morality is widely perceived as an essential part of privacy, its "moral foundations" (Moore 2010) remain fuzzy. Nevertheless, scholars who discuss the issue of SNSs in personnel selection vividly agree on the presence of yet unsolved ethical problems. The legend of Lady Godiva also suggests that Peeping Tom was guilty, but his fault was certainly not to get caught: No, the moral of the story rather seems to be the significance of moral itself. But what are related tangible concerns that touch the sphere of moral values? In this respect, scholars have not yet agreed on much more than the mere existence of "ethical problems" when SNSs are used for HRM purposes (Brown and Vaughn 2011; Clark and Roberts 2010; Draeger 2011). Empirical research on SNSs taking a more in-depth view on the intricate interplay between HR managers' moral values and concerns and organizational practices (Martin and Woldring 2001) is still missing. Anecdotal evidence suggests that SNSs are regularly used but managers do not feel very comfortable with it. Still, the whole issue seems to be rather neglected, which may confirm its ethical significance since people are less inclined to talk about their own practices when they hold them morally questionable (Sandel 2012). One major reference to a moral problem seems rather obvious: HR professionals would surely not like to be seen as "undetectable voyeurs" (Clark and Roberts 2010, 518). Voyeurism carries a distinct negative connanation—even despite the promising potential that related practices might have.

So what can the present HR literature contribute to ethical problems like ours? Not very much, it seems: Scholars who notice ethical problems with SNSs mainly relate them to privacy issues, often with an emphasis on the legal dimension and a "right" to privacy (see the aforementioned). On the one hand, there are many voices arguing that ethical problems within HRM can truly be said to "come with the territory of human resources" (Hosmer 1987, 313) and that the nature of the resource is the reason for the need of ethics (Greenwood 2002). Following such a "logical" connection of HRM and ethics, HR-related jobs have been perceived as "guardian[s] of ethics" (Winstanley and Woodall 2000, 7) as well as "a laboratory of ethical scenarios" (Wiley 1998, 148). On the other hand, recent publications have come to the disillusioning conclusion that "[i]ntriguingly, the field of ethics and HRM remains underdeveloped" (Greenwood 2013, 355)—and that HRM "has not inclined to admit an ethical perspective" at all (Winstanley and Woodall 2000, 7; for a notable recent exception see Klikauer 2014). Consequently, this strand of research does not seem ready to provide concrete answers to moral problems that are "complex because harm to some groups is often accompanied by benefits to others" (Miller 1996, 2). Facebook voyeurism is such a phenomenon that potentially results in such contrasting outcomes for firms and individuals that both have legitimate, though divergent interests: And therefore it requires further ethical analysis "in addition to the more common financial, legal, and behavioral forms of reasoning" (Hosmer 1987, 313). This analysis should not only apply normative ethical concepts to problematic situations in order to suggest normative guidance but foremost elaborate a more comprehensive meta-ethical perspective on the overall problem. Such an ethical perspective on Facebook voyeurism may take the problem of seemingly incommensurable values (such as economic values versus more "absolute" moral values) as a starting point for investigation and also account for the distinct negative moral connotation that voyeurism carries (Leixnering and Mayrhofer 2013).

Conclusion

In this chapter, we outline how the integration of different perspectives on the issue from management and legal studies, sociology, psychology, philosophy, and also arts may valuably contribute to a more comprehensive analysis of the problem of Facebook voyeurism. We start with a simple insight regarding the ubiquity of SNSs: The present flow of private information through the Internet, addressed to ever-growing audiences, is enormous. Building on the widely unquestioned assumption that more information about people would lead to better selection decisions and the fact that SNSs usually provide information which cannot be obtained from conventional sources, HRM has discovered SNSs as tools. Empirical evidence shows that SNSs are already heavily used for this matter. Yet, it remains doubtful whether this also improves decision making. We then elaborate the involved "privacy paradox." Even when people are willing to share online details about their intimate lives with broader audiences, they do not give up claims to control the diffusion of such information—which, no surprise, proves rather elusive. So, if control of private information flow is an illusion, the idea of privacy independent of any context appears to be an empty concept. Finally, we turn to the danger of HR managers becoming online peepers by profession, turning into "lurkers" who rather observe than participate in SNSs and, by consuming content but not producing anything in return, violate SNSs' fundamental principle of "presuming."

By those affected, covert lurking of HRM professionals—"Facebook voyeurism"—is undoubtedly perceived as deviant behavior that is morally offensive. Conceptually, the ancient story of Lady Godiva and Peeping Tom, serving as etiology for voyeurism, captures the essence of the problem we discuss in our chapter. The story reminds us that the present problem of using SNSs as HRM tools is a modern version of a rather abstract and old phenomenon: the complex and conflicting interplay between public display and privacy concerns, between personal benefit and moral values. Lady Godiva's desire to broadcast and hide on the one hand and Tom's urge for personal benefit and obligation for respect on the other hand are illustrations of this.

Eventually, we are far from suggesting substantive solutions for the emerging problems in HRM. However, our analysis allows for better informed questions that should be addressed by future research in three areas: theoretical debate, empirical research, and professional HR practice. In particular, future work should focus on whether information on SNSs contributes to better HR decisions, how conceptualizations of privacy may guide HRM, and—probably most central to the issue—how ethical consideration could support a more thorough picture of involved value conflicts.

So, is Facebook voyeurism a problem for HR management? Apparently. Is it also a blind spot? Definitely. Is it becoming a dark side of it? Too early to tell.

References

American Psychiatric Association. 2013. "Voyeuristic Disorder." In *Diagnostic and Statistical Manual of Mental Disorders*. 5th ed. Washington, DC. doi:10.1176/appi.books.9780890425596.744053

Arndt, H.W. 1949. "The Cult of Privacy." *Australian Quarterly* 21, no. 3, pp. 68–71. doi:10.2307/20633180

Barnes, S.B. 2006. "A Privacy Paradox: Social Networking in the United States." *First Monday* 11, no. 9. doi:10.5210/fm.v11i9.1394

Baruh, L. 2010. "Mediated Voyeurism and the Guilty Pleasure of Consuming Reality Television." *Media Psychology* 13, no. 3, pp. 201–21. doi:10.1080/15213269.2010.502871

Belk, R.W. 2013. "Extended Self in a Digital World." *Journal of Consumer Research* 40, no. 3, pp. 477–500. doi:10.1086/671052

Benn, S.I., and G.F. Gaus. 1983. "The Public and the Private: Concepts and Action." *Public and Private in Social Life*, pp. 3–27.

Boatright, J.R. 2003. *Ethics and the Conduct of Business*. 4th ed. Upper Saddle River, NJ: Pearson Education.

Brown, V.R., and E.D. Vaughn. 2011. "The Writing on the (Facebook) Wall: The Use of Social Networking Sites in Hiring Decisions." *Journal of Business and Psychology* 26, no. 2, pp. 219–25. doi:10.1007/s10869-011-9221-x

Calvert, C. 2000. *Voyeur Nation: Media, Privacy, and Peeping in Modern Culture*. Boulder, CO: Westview Press.

Calvert, C., and J. Brown. 2000. "Video Voyeurism, Privacy, and the Internet: Exposing Peeping Toms in Cyberspace." *Cardozo Arts and Entertainment Law Journal* 18, no. 3, pp. 469–566. Retrieved from http://cardozoaelj.com/wp-content/uploads/Journal%20Issues/Volume%2018/Issue%203/Brown.pdf

CareerBuilder. August 19, 2009. "Forty-Five Percent of Employer Use Social Networking Sites to Research Job Candidates, CareerBuilder Study Finds." Retrieved from www.careerbuilder.com/share/aboutus/pressreleasesdetail.aspx?id=pr519&sd=8/19/2009&ed=12/31/2009&siteid=cbpr&sc_cmp1=cb_pr519_&cbRecursionCnt=1&cbsid=8412d5b32ef54ce6854a035cf3a59d12-303995843-x3-6

Carpenter, C.J. 2012. "Narcissism on Facebook: Self-Promotional and Anti-Social Behavior." *Personality and Individual Differences* 52, no. 4, pp. 482–86. doi:10.1016/j.paid.2011.11.011

Chauhan, R.S., M.R. Buckley, and M.G. Harvey. 2013. "Facebook and Personnel Selection: What's the Big Deal?" *Organizational Dynamics* 42, no. 2, pp. 126–34. doi:10.1016/j.orgdyn.2013.03.006

Chen, X., and S. Shi. November 2009. "A Literature Review of Privacy Research on Social Network Sites." *Proceedings of the 2009 International Conference on Multimedia Information Networking and Security*, pp. 93–97. Wuhan, China. doi:10.1109/MINES.2009.268

Chunyan, X., R.P. Bagozzi, and S.V. Troye. 2008. "Trying to Prosume: Toward a Theory of Consumers as Co-Creators of Value." *Journal of the Academy of Marketing Science* 36, no. 1, pp. 109–22. doi:10.1007/s11747-007-0060-2

Christofides, E., A. Muise, and S. Desmarais. 2009. "Information Disclosure and Control on Facebook: Are They Two Sides of the Same Coin or Two Different Processes?" *CyberPsychology & Behavior* 12, no. 3, pp. 341–45. doi:10.1089/cpb.2008.0226

Clark, L.A., and S.J. Roberts. 2010. "Employer's Use of Social Networking Sites: A Socially Irresponsible Practice." *Journal of Business Ethics* 95, no. 4, pp. 507–25. doi:10.1007/s10551-010-0436-y

Collier, J. 1897. Lady Godiva [Painting]. BBC. http://ichef.bbci.co.uk/arts/yourpaintings/images/paintings/herb/large/war_herb_355_large.jpg

Comer, R., N. McKelvey, and K. Curran. 2012. "Privacy and Facebook." *International Journal of Engineering and Technology* 2, no. 9, pp. 1626–30. Retrieved from http://iet-journals.org/archive/2012/sep_vol_2_no_9/33281346857818.pdf

Comscore. December 21, 2011. "It's a Social World: Top 10 Need-to-Knows About Social Networking and Where It's Headed." Retrieved from www.comscore.com/ger/Insights/Presentations-and-Whitepapers/2011/it_is_a_social_world_top_10_need-to-knows_about_social_networking

Davison, H.K., C. Maraist, and M.N. Bing. 2011. "Friend of Foe?: The Promise and Pitfalls of Using Social Network Sites for HR Decisions." *Journal of Business and Psychology* 26, no. 2, pp. 153–59. doi:10.1007/s10869-011-9215-8

Day, S. 2013. "Self-Disclosure on Facebook: How Much Do We Really Reveal?" *Journal of Applied Computing and Information Technology* 17, no. 1, p. 2013. Retrieved from www.citrenz.ac.nz/jacit/JACIT1701/2013Day_Facebook.html

deLaat, P.B. 2008. "Online Diaries: Reflections on Trust, Privacy, and Exhibitionism." *Ethics and Information Technology* 10, no. 1, pp. 57–69. doi:10.1007/s10676-008-9155-9

Docherty, T. November 10, 2011. "The Unseen Academy." *Times Higher Education*. Retrieved from www.timeshighereducation.co.uk/418076.article

Doyle, T. 2009. "Privacy and Perfect Voyeurism." *Ethics and Information Technology* 11, no. 3, pp. 181–9. doi:10.1007/s10676-009-9195-9

Draeger, J. 2011. "What Peeping Tom Did Wrong." *Ethic Theory and Moral Practice* 14, no. 1, pp. 41–9. doi:10.1007/s10677-010-9225-z

Ellison, N.B. 2007. "Social Network Sites: Definition, History, and Scholarship." *Journal of Computer-Mediated Communication* 13, no. 1, pp. 210–30. doi:10.1111/j.1083-6101.2007.00393.x

Ellison, N.B., and D. Boyd. 2013. "Sociality Through Social Network Sites." In *The Oxford Handbook of Internet Studies*, ed. W.H. Dutton, 151–72. Oxford, UK: Oxford University Press.

Ellison, N.B., C. Steinfield, and C. Lampe. 2007. "The Benefits of Facebook 'Friends': Social Capital and College Students' Use of Online Social Network Sites." *Journal of Computer-Mediated Communication* 12, no. 4, pp. 1143–68. doi:10.1111/j.1083-6101.2007.00367.x

Every Step You Take. 2013. *The Economist,* November 16. Retrieved from www.economist.com/news/leaders/21589862-cameras-become-ubiquitous-and-able-identify-people-more-safeguards-privacy-will-be

Foregger, S.K. 2008. *Uses and Gratifications of Facebook.Com* [Doctoral Dissertation]. Retrieved from ProQuest (UMI Microform 3331906).

Greenwood, M. 2013. "Ethical Analyses of HRM: A Review and Research Agenda." *Journal of Business Ethics* 114, no. 2, pp. 355–66. doi:10.1007/s10551-012-1354-y

Greenwood, M.R. 2002. "Ethics and HRM: A Review and Conceptual Analysis." *Journal of Business Ethics* 36, no. 3, pp. 261–78. doi:10.1023/a:1014090411946

Hawthorn, J. 2003. "Morality, Voyeurism, and 'Point of View': Michael Powell's Peeping Tom (1960)." *Nordic Journal of English Studies* 2, no. 2, pp. 303–24.

Herbert, W. 2011. "Workplace Consequences of Electronic Exhibitionism and Voyeurism." *IEEE Technology & Society Magazine* 30, no. 3, pp. 25–33. doi:10.1109/MTS.2011.942310

Hollenbaugh, E.E., and A.L. Ferris. 2014. "Facebook Self-Disclosure: Examining the Role of Traits, Social Cohesion, and Motives." *Computers in Human Behavior* 30, no. 1, pp. 50–8. doi:10.1016/j.chb.2013.07.055

Hosmer, L.T. 1987. "Ethical Analysis and Human Resource Management." *Human Resource Management* 26, no. 3, pp. 313–30. doi:10.1002/hrm.3930260302

Joinson, A.N., U.D. Reips, T. Buchanan, and C.B.P. Schofield. 2010. "Privacy, Trust, and Self-Disclosure Online." *Human-Computer Interaction* 25, no. 1, pp. 1–24. doi:10.1080/07370020903586662

Karl, K., J. Peluchette, and C. Schlaegel. 2010. "Who's Posting Facebook Faux Pas?: A Cross-Cultural Examination of Personality Differences." *International Journal of Selection and Assessment* 18, no. 2, pp. 174–86. doi:10.1111/j.1468-2389.2010.00499.x

Klikauer, T. 2014. *Seven Moralities of Human Resource Management.* Houndmills, United Kingdom, and New York: Palgrave Macmillan.

Lampe, C., N. Ellison, and C. Steinfield. November 2006. "A Face (Book) in the Crowd: Social Searching Versus. Social Browsing." In *CSCW '06 Proceedings of the 2006 20th Anniversary Conference on Computer Supported Cooperative Work*, pp. 167–70. New York: ACM. doi:10.1145/1180875.1180901

Leixnering, S., and W. Mayrhofer. September 2013. "Peeping Tom? Die Nutzung Sozialer Netzwerke bei Personenbezogenen Managemententscheidungen—Eine Ethische Analyse." Paper Presented at the VHB WK Personal Wirtschaft Herbstworkshop, Hamburg, Deutschland.

Liu, H. 2007. "Social Network Profiles as Taste Performances." *Journal of Computer-Mediated Communication* 13, no. 1, pp. 252–75. doi:10.1111/j.1083-6101.2007.00395.x

Madden, K. April 4, 2011. "12 Ways to Get Fired for Facebook." CareerBuilder. Retrieved from http://www.careerbuilder.ca/blog/2010/09/08/cb-12-ways-to-get-fired-for-facebook/

Mäntymäki, M., and A.K.M.N. Islam. June 2014. "Voyeurism and Exhibitionism as Gratifications from Prosuming Social Network Sites." Paper presented at the 28th European Conference on Information Systems, Tel Aviv, Israel. Retrieved from http://ecis2014.eu/E-poster/files/0242-file1.pdf

Martin, G., and K. Woldring. 2001. "Ready for the Mantle?: Australian Human Resource Managers as Stewards of Ethics." *International Journal of Human Resource Management* 12, no. 2, pp. 243–55. doi:10.1080/09585190010014629

Mazer, J.P., R.E. Murphy, and C.J. Simonds. 2007. "I'll See You on 'Facebook': The Effects of Computer Mediated Teacher Self-Disclosure on Student Motivation, Affective Learning, and Classroom Climate." *Communication Education* 56, no. 1, pp. 1–17. doi:10.1080/03634520601009710

McAndrew, F.T., and H.S. Jeong. 2012. "Who Does What on Facebook?: Age, Sex, and Relationship Status as Predictors of Facebook Use." *Computers in Human Behavior* 28, no. 6, pp. 2359–65. doi:10.1016/j.chb.2012.07.007

Metzl, J.M. 2004. "Voyeur Nation?: Changing Definitions of Voyeurism." *Harvard Review of Psychiatry* 12, no. 2, pp. 127–31. doi:10.1080/10673220490447245

Microsoft. January 26, 2010. "Data Privacy Day: Your Online Reputation Is on the Line." Retrieved from http://news.microsoft.com/2010/01/26/data-privacy-day-your-online-reputation-is-on-the-line/

Miller, P. 1996. "Strategy and the Ethical Management of Human Resources." *Human Resource Management Journal* 6, no. 1, pp. 5–18. doi:10.1111/j.1748-8583.1996.tb00393.x

Mills, J.L. 2008. *Privacy: The Lost Right.* New York: Oxford University Press.

Moon, Y. 2000. "Intimate Exchanges: Using Computers to Elicit Self-Disclosure From Consumers." *Journal of Consumer Research* 26, no. 4, pp. 323–39. doi:10.1086/209566

Moore, A.D. 2010. *Privacy Rights: Moral and Legal Foundations.* University Park, PA: Pennsylvania State University Press.

Munar, A.M. 2010. "Digital Exhibitionism: The Age of Exposure." *Culture Unbound* 2, no. 23, pp. 401–22. doi:10.3384/cu.2000.1525.10223401

Nass, C., and Y. Moon. 2000. "Machines and Mindlessness: Social Responses to Computers." *Journal of Social Issues* 56, no. 1, pp. 81–103. doi:10.1111/0022-4537.00153

Nathan, D.O. 1990. "Just Looking: Voyeurism and the Grounds of Privacy." *Public Affairs Quarterly* 4, no. 4, pp. 365–86. Retrieved from www.jstor.org/stable/40435762

Niedzviecki, H. 2009. *The Peep Diaries: How We're Learning to Love Watching Ourselves and Our Neighbors.* San Francisco, CA: City Lights Bookstore.

Nissenbaum, H. 2009. *Privacy in Context: Technology, Policy, and the Integrity of Social Life.* Stanford, CA: Stanford University Press.

O'Harrow, R. 2006. *No Place to Hide.* New York: Free Press.

Panek, E.T., Y. Nardis, and S. Konrath. 2013. "Mirror or Megaphone?: How Relationships Between Narcissism and Social Networking Site Use Differ on Facebook and Twitter." *Computers in Human Behavior* 29, no. 5, pp. 2004–12. doi:10.1016/j.chb.2013.04.012

Reiman, J. 2004. "Driving to the Panopticon: A Philosophical Exploration of the Risk to Privacy Posed by the Information Technology of the Future." In *Privacies: Philosophical Evaluations*, ed. B. Rössler, 194–214. Stanford, CA: Stanford University Press.

Rice, J.D. 1978. "Privacy Legislation: Its Effect on Pre-Employment Reference Checking." *The Personnel Administrator* 23, no. 2, pp. 46–51. Retrieved from https://sciencescape.org/paper/10306451

Sabbadini, A. 2000. "Watching Voyeurs: Michael Powell's Peeping Tom (1960)." *International Journal of Psychoanalysis* 81, no. 4, pp. 809–13. doi:10.1516/0020757001600039

Sandel, M.J. 2012. *What Money Can't Buy: The Moral Limits of Markets.* New York: Farrer, Straus and Giroux.

Slovensky, R., and W.H. Ross. 2011. "Should Human Resource Managers Use Social Media to Screen Job Applicants?: Managerial and Legal Issues in the USA." *Info* 14, no. 1, pp. 55–69. doi:10.1108/14636691211196941

Smith, R.S. 1976. "Voyeurism: A Review of Literature." *Archives of Sexual Behavior* 5, no. 6, pp. 585–608. doi:10.1007/BF01541221

Smith, W.P., and D.L. Kidder. 2010. "You've been Tagged! (Then Again, Maybe Not): Employers and Facebook." *Business Horizons* 53, no. 5, pp. 491–9. doi:10.1016/j.bushor.2010.04.004

Smock, A.D., N.B. Ellison, C. Lampe, and D.Y. Wohn. 2011. "Facebook as a Toolkit: A Uses and Gratification Approach to Unbundling Feature Use." *Computers in Human Behavior* 27, no. 6, pp. 2322–29. doi:10.1016/j.chb.2011.07.011

Solove, D.J. 2006. "A Taxonomy of Privacy." *University of Pennsylvania Law Review* 154, no. 3, pp. 477–564. doi:10.2307/40041279

Spinello, R.A. 2010. "Informational Privacy." In *The Oxford Handbook of Business Ethics*, eds. G.G. Brenkert, and T.L. Beauchamp, 366–87. New York: Oxford University Press.

Su, P.J. 2012. *Mediated Voyeurism on Social Networking Sites: The Possible Social Needs and Potential Motivations of the Voyeurs on Facebook* [Thesis]. RIT Scholar Works. Retrieved from http://scholarworks.rit.edu/cgi/viewcontent.cgi?article=4097&context=theses

Taddicken, M. 2014. "The 'Privacy Paradox' in the Social Web: The Impact of Privacy Concerns, Individual Characteristics, and the Perceived Social Relevance on Different Forms of Self Disclosure." *Journal of Computer Mediated Communication* 19, no. 2, pp. 248–73. doi:10.1111/jcc4.12052

Tennyson, A.L. 1877. "Godiva." In *Poems of Places: An Anthology in 31 Volumes*, ed. H. Wadsworth Longfellow. England: Vol. I, 166–167. London: Macmillan.

Warren, S.D., and L.D. Brandeis. 1890. "The Right to Privacy." *Harvard Law Review* 4, no. 5, pp. 193–220. doi:10.2307/1321160

Westin, A.F. 2003. "Social and Political Dimensions of Privacy." *Journal of Social Issues* 59, no. 2, pp. 431–53. doi:10.1111/1540-4560.00072

Whitman, J.Q. 2004. "The Two Western Cultures of Privacy: Dignity Versus Liberty." *Yale Law Journal* 113, no. 6, pp. 1151–221. doi:10.2307/4135723

Wiley, C. 1998. "Reexamining Perceived Ethics Issues and Ethics Roles Among Employment Managers. *Journal of Business Ethics* 17, no. 2, pp. 147–61. doi:10.1023/a:1005795731002

Wilson, R.E., S.D. Gosling, and L.T. Graham. 2012. "A Review of Facebook Research in the Social Sciences." *Perspectives on Psychological Science* 7, no. 3, pp. 203–20. doi:10.1177/1745691612442904

Winstanley, D., and J. Woodall. 2000. "The Ethical Dimension of Human Resource Management." *Human Resource Management Journal* 10, no. 2, pp. 5–20. doi:10.1111/j.1748-8583.2000.tb00017.x

Zimmer, M. October 2007. "Privacy and Surveillance in Web 2.0: A Study in Contextual Integrity and the Emergence of Netaveillance." Paper Presented at the Society for Social Studies of Science Annual Meeting, Montreal, Canada. Retrieved from http://michaelzimmer.org/files/Zimmer%204S%20 2007%20talk.pdf

Zimmer, M., and A. Hoffman. 2011. "Privacy, Context, and Oversharing: Reputational Challenges in a Web 2.0 World." In *The Reputation Society: How Online Opinions Are Reshaping the Offline World*, eds. H. Masum and M. Tovey, 175–84. Cambridge, MA: MIT Press.

CHAPTER 3

University Student Plagiarism in the Digital Age and the Professors' Role in Detecting and Reporting

Maria del Mar Pàmies Pallisé, Gerard Ryan, Mireia Valverde Aparicio, Gilda María Hernández Maskivker, and Dorina Chicu

Department of Business Management
Universitat Rovira i Virgili

Introduction

Plagiarism in higher education is a serious and persistent problem for universities worldwide (Marcus and Beck 2011; Yazici, Yazici, and Erdem 2011). Although it is not a new phenomenon (Colnerud and Rosander 2009; Ellahi, Mushtaq, and Kahn 2013; Heather 2010), in the last decade plagiarism has become a very common and widespread problem in higher education (Park 2003; Quah, Stewart, and Lee 2012). This chapter reviews the academic literature on plagiarism, considering plagiarism as an element of the dark side of university education. It also reports on a qualitative exploratory study of plagiarism carried out among university professors in a public university in Spain.

One of the reasons for the growth of plagiarism is the large amount of instant-access information provided by the Internet which makes it easy for students to engage in activities considered plagiarism, such as copy-paste information, paraphrasing without citation, or downloading an entire prepared essay from an Internet site (Batane 2010; Brown and Howell 2001; Heather 2010; Pickard 2006). According to Atkinson and Yeoh (2008, 222) "plagiarism is probably as old as the first recorded documents but the rise of the Internet has made it particularly easy for individuals to search, retrieve, and copy and paste from electronic documents."

Plagiarism is a form of academic dishonesty or academic misconduct (de Jager and Brown 2010; Kelley 2007; Youmans 2011) and more specifically, a type of cheating (Bing et al. 2012; Park 2004). McCabe, Butterfield, and Treviño (2006) surveyed almost 50,000 undergraduates across more than 60 campuses in a longitudinal study as a part of CAI's (Center for Academic Integrity) Assessment Project. The results showed that in most university campuses, 70 percent of students admit to some form of cheating.

There are many definitions of plagiarism but all of them coincide in that they include concepts related to the appropriation, whether intentional or unintentional, of others' ideas without a clear reference to the original author (de Jager and Brown 2010). Some of these definitions are:

"Taking the words or ideas of another person and using them without proper acknowledgement" (Culwin and Lancaster 2001, 36).

"Plagiarism involves literary theft, stealing (by copying) the words or ideas of someone else and passing them off as one's own without crediting the source" (Park 2003, 475).

"Plagiarism occurs when a student intentionally or unintentionally uses another person's words or ideas without properly crediting their source" (Youmans 2011, 749).

"Passing off someone else's work, whether intentionally or unintentionally, as your own for your own benefit" (Williams and Carroll 2009, 9).

There is general agreement on the essential words or ideas used to define plagiarism but some confusion and a lack of consensus arises when determining what specific behaviors constitute plagiarism (Bennett 2005; Bennett, Behrendt, and Boothby 2011; Broeckelman-Post 2008; Pickard 2006; Walden and Peacock 2006). According to the literature, plagiarism includes a wide range of activities or behaviors such as including some sentences without reference to the original author, copying verbatim, changing just a few words without including quotation marks, poorly paraphrasing, citing incorrectly, submitting an assignment previously submitted for another course, including references that the author has not ever read, copying and reproducing sentences, writing a paper for another student, submitting another student's work, preparing a piece of course work in a group and then submitting it (separately by various students) as if it were the work of an individual, copying a complete document, and so on (Batane 2010; Bennett, Behrendt, and Boothby 2011; Bennett 2005; Beute, van Aswegen, and Winberg 2008; Comas et al. 2011; Flint, Clegg, and Macdonald 2006; Kidwell, Wozniak, and Laurel 2003; Kwong et al. 2010; Lin and Wen 2007; Martin 1994; Park 2003, 2004; Selwyn 2008; Sheridan, Alany, and Brake 2005; Trost 2009; Underwood and Szabo 2003).

According to a popular website on the topic, some of the most common types of plagiarism, ordered in terms of severity of intent, are clone (submitting another's work, word-for-word, as one's own), CTRL-C (contains significant portions of text from a single source without alterations), find-replace (changing key words and phrases but retaining the essential content of the source), remix (paraphrases from multiple sources, made to fit together), recycle (borrowing generously from the same writer's previous work without citation), hybrid (combines perfectly cited sources with copied passages without citation), mashup (mixes copied material from multiple sources), 404 error (includes citations to nonexistent or inaccurate information about sources), aggregator (includes proper citation to sources but the paper contains almost no original work) and retweet (includes proper citation, but relies too closely on the text's original wording or structure; plagiarism.org 2014).

Therefore, it is important to keep in mind that plagiarism is not simply copying and pasting without reference to the original author. It covers a wide range of behaviors, as explained previously.

Agents Involved in a Plagiarism Situation

Although generally it has been assumed that the main concern in higher education is that plagiarism is a topic related only to students, in reality, professors and universities also play important roles. Indeed, a plagiarism situation in higher education involves three agents: students, faculty, and universities (Flint, Clegg, and Macdonald 2006; Macdonald and Carroll 2006). All of them play an important role in the prevention, detection, and management of a plagiarism situation.

The following sections focus on how students, faculty and universities can influence the prevention, detection, and management of plagiarism in higher education. Finally, the last section presents plagiarism as an element of the dark side of the management of higher education by examining why in some situations professors decide to turn a blind eye to plagiarism among their students.

Students

Students may be considered the central players in plagiarism in the sense that they plagiarize in their coursework. Indisputably the main focus of plagiarism in higher education is on students. However, students also play an integral role in the prevention of plagiarism. Their perceptions regarding the definition (Comas and Sureda 2008; Gullifer and Tyson 2010) and the seriousness of plagiarism (Kwong et al. 2010; McCabe 2005; Rísquez, O'Dwyer, and Ledwith 2013) can influence their propensity to partake in it. Therefore, part of the responsibility falls on the students because they should be concerned about understanding the definition of plagiarism and the importance of avoiding it, including becoming familiar with the academic policy outlined by the university.

Although students are often knowledgeable about the importance and serious nature of plagiarism, they often decide to plagiarize intentionally. In this sense, they have a range of tricks and strategies to avoid detection at their disposal. This includes modifying the document to be submitted through plagiarism detection software (by modifying the character map, by rearranging the glyph in the font itself or converting the text to Bézier curves) (Heather 2010) or by slightly altering sentences in order to avoid detection (Rosenberg 2011). Therefore, students play a role in the detection of plagiarism because they may take steps to evade plagiarism detection software.

Finally, indirectly, students can also play a role in the management of plagiarism. In this sense, faculty tend to react differently to plagiarism according to the course the student is undertaking (Coren 2011;

Keith-Spiegel et al. 1998; Sutherland-Smith 2011). Sutherland-Smith (2011) found that the penalties applied differ among students in their first year who may be unfamiliar with university regulations and students in their final year who are expected to be familiar with university policy and procedures.

Faculty

Students' perceptions of faculty's lack of concern about plagiarism (Broeckelman-Post 2008; Hard, Conway, and Moran 2006; McCabe and Trevino 1996; Yazici, Yazici, and Erdem 2011) can lead them to plagiarize. Hence, professors would be well advised to demonstrate their concern for this problem in order to help in its prevention. In this sense, faculty should be familiar with the definitions of plagiarism (Marcus and Beck 2011) and should design assignments accordingly in order to avoid plagiarism (Batane 2010; Ramzan et al. 2012). They should include plagiarism information in the syllabus (Broeckelman-Post 2008; Lim and Coalter 2006), ask students to sign a declaration against plagiarism (Culwin and Lancaster 2001; Samuels and Bast 2006; Sims 2002), or train students on how to avoid plagiarism (Bennet, Behrendt, and Boorhby 2011; Beute, Van Aswegen, and Winberg 2008; de Jager and Brown 2010).

Faculty have a number of tools or strategies to detect an instance of plagiarism. The most examined in previous research is the use of plagiarism detection software (Batane 2010; Brinkman 2013; Hayes and Introna 2005; Heather 2010; Heckler, Rice, and Bryan 2013; McKeever 2004; Sheridan, Alany, and Brake 2005; Youmans 2011). However, faculty can also develop a number of personal strategies to detect plagiarism, such as searching online (copying and pasting extracts from students' work into a search engine to check if has been copied) (Austin and Brown 1999; Sutherland-Smith 2005) or paying attention to the writing style in order to consider if the student is capable of using such sophisticated terminology (Larkham and Manns 2002).

When faculty detect plagiarism, they have to decide whether or not to act. The decision not to act will be addressed later in this chapter. When faculty decide to act, they may follow university procedures or deal with the situation in their own way (Simon et al. 2003; Bennett, Behrendt, and Boothby 2011). The main reason that leads professors to act in a personal and informal way is a lack of confidence in the university procedures (Sutherland-Smith 2005).

Generally, when a case of plagiarism is detected, a number of actions can be carried out by faculty, such as allowing the student to resubmit the work, failing the part of the assessment that has been plagiarized, failing the complete subject, or expelling the student from the university (Larkham and Manns 2002; Sutherland-Smith 2011). Nevertheless, faculty can only punish plagiarism without hesitation if a clear academic policy exists.

Universities

Universities play a crucial role in the prevention of plagiarism by designing an academic integrity policy (Austin and Brown 1999; Caldwell 2010; Park 2004) and promoting it among faculty and students (Goh 2013; Macdonald and Carroll 2006; McCabe, Treviño, and Butterfield 2002; Park 2004). Moreover, informing faculty and students of the use of plagiarism detection software (Goh 2013; Ledwith and Rísquez 2008; Samuels and Bast 2006), organizing courses on plagiarism, and how to avoid it for both faculty and students (Caldwell 2010; Goh 2013; Macdonald and Carroll 2006) are also effective prevention tools.

As mentioned earlier, universities have a number of plagiarism detection software products at their disposal. This software helps faculty to detect plagiarism. They include Turnitin, EVE, Copycatch, Wordcheck, Ferret, or Plagiserve, among others. Despite the wide range of existing software, the most popular is Turnitin (Heather 2010). According to the software producer:

> Turnitin compares the submission's text with a vast database of 40+ billion pages of digital content (including archived Internet content that is no longer available), over 300 million submissions in the student archive, and 120,000+ professional, academic and commercial journals and publications (turnitin.com).

After submission, an Originality Report with a percentage of coincidences is reported (Batane 2010; Youmans 2011). It should be taken into account that, in some cases, this percentage is magnified when the submitted paper contains citations, quotations, reference pages, or famous names (Youmans 2011). In this way, students can see their own submissions and originality reports (Batane 2010).

To reiterate, in order to help faculty in the management of plagiarism, universities should support them by designing a clear academic policy.

Plagiarism as an Element of the Dark Side of Higher Education Management

Avoiding plagiarism is important for students, professors, and universities. First, if students plagiarize they do not achieve the academic skills and, consequently, their learning process is truncated (Atkinson and Yeoh 2008; Batane 2010; Bennett 2005; Sadler 2007). Second, the professionalism of professors may be damaged when they are involved in a plagiarism situation (Sutherland-Smith 2005). Third, the reputation and the integrity of the university may be affected (Batane 2010; Vardi 2012).

Although everyone is aware of the existence of plagiarism and the need to remove it, not everyone makes an effort to act. In this sense, plagiarism can be considered an element of the dark side of higher education management because we are all aware of its existence and the need to remove it, but acting upon it is an entirely different and challenging matter. Sometimes universities and faculty don't make the necessary efforts to deal with plagiarism. Institutions cannot act individually as they rely on a national university system that does not necessarily strive to tackle plagiarism. For this reason, this section focuses on professors' role in the management of plagiarism.

As explained earlier, faculty may decide not to act when they detect a plagiarism case among their students. According to Coren (2011, 292), based on previous studies, "approximately 40 percent of faculty respondents have reported ignoring cheating on one or more occasions." Considering the importance and the consequences of plagiarism this may be reasonably considered a significant percentage. Therefore, despite the effort of universities to prevent and detect plagiarism, a high percentage of faculty decide not to act for several reasons. These reasons can be classified according to whether they are related to the plagiarism situation, to the students, to the faculty themselves, or to the university. First, regarding the plagiarism situation, some faculty consider that unintentional plagiarism should not be punished (Sutherland-Smith 2005). Moreover, when there is a lack of evidence, professors decide not to act (Coren 2011; Keith-Spiegel et al. 1998). Second, some professors do not act in order to avoid uncomfortable situations when they confront students and because they are concerned about retaliation (Coren 2011; Keith-Spiegel et al. 1998). Third, the main reason for deciding not to act is related to the considerable time required to present the evidence and to verifying plagiarism (Sutherland-Smith 2005). This often makes it difficult and not worthwhile to act (Sutherland-Smith 2005). Moreover, dealing with plagiarism is considered a stressful situation (Coren 2011; Keith-Spiegel et al. 1998) that may affect their image or professionalism (Austin and Brown 1999; Sutherland-Smith 2006; Atkinson and Yeoh 2008). Finally, regarding universities, in some cases faculty decide not to act because they feel that the institution does not support them (Burke 2007; Keith-Spiegel et al. 1998; Lim and Coalter 2006) or because they don't really understand the academic policy (Barrett and Cox 2005; Marcus and Beck 2011).

Considering the important role that faculty play in students' plagiarism in higher education, a study was undertaken that focused, in particular, on professors' perceptions of plagiarism, by examining the role they play and their position and actions taken when faced with this phenomenon, as explained in the next section.

Professors' Perceptions of Plagiarism

This section reports on a study undertaken at a Catalan public university (located in the north east region of Spain) on the views of faculty of plagiarism among university students. The study aims to help fill some of the gaps in the existing literature.

The main focus of research on this issue has traditionally been on students and their attitudes to and perceptions of plagiarism. In contrast, this study focuses on university professors' definitions of plagiarism, perceptions, and attitudes to plagiarism, and their individual strategies for detection and prevention of plagiarism in university coursework.

Unlike much of the existing research, this study takes a qualitative approach with the intention of developing a holistic understanding of this complex problem. Specifically, the data collection was based on in-depth interviews and focus groups with university professors.

In addition, unlike many existing studies undertaken in the context of the "Anglo Saxon" university model, this study was carried out in the Spanish public university education system in a university located in Catalonia. It is important to note that although the strategies adopted in the Anglo-Saxon system to prevent plagiarism are also applicable in the Spanish context, the legal situation regarding student discipline requires a very different approach to responding to plagiarism once it is detected.

The motivations for embarking on a study of plagiarism are based on the personal experiences of the authors, the most senior of whom have worked in academia for almost 20 years and in many different national contexts including the United Kingdom, the Republic of Ireland, Spain, Argentina, Mexico, and the United States. The authors are members of an interuniversity network of professors concerned about the growing problem of plagiarism in university education. Currently, the network includes members from various disciplines such as business studies, economics, and geography, as well as members of the university library services.

Methodology

There is a notable lack of variety in methodological choice in previous research on these issues and an overwhelming emphasis on survey research. As the purpose of the present study was to examine the perceptions of plagiarism from the subjective viewpoint of professors, the decision was taken to adopt an exploratory approach with an emphasis on qualitative data collection. More precisely, the authors decided that a grounded theory approach (Glaser and Strauss 1967) was appropriate given the exploratory and subjective nature of the research (Strauss and Corbin 1998; Silverman 2000). An initial focus group involving both teaching staffs and postgraduate students was carried out in order to identify and discuss aspects of how plagiarism is understood and interpreted. This focus study was followed by 15 in-depth interviews with faculty from a range of specializations within the area of business and economics (marketing, human resources, mathematics, microeconomics, and international economy, among others) in the business school at the same institution.

All the interviews were recorded. The qualitative data was fully transcribed and then analyzed with the aid of the NVivo software.

Results

The results of the study are divided into the interpretations of plagiarism, the variance among professors, and the reactions to plagiarism.

Interpretations of Plagiarism

There is a wide range of interpretations and perceptions on the part of professors of the precise definition of plagiarism. Although there is general agreement on the fact that plagiarism is a significant and growing problem in university education, there is a marked difference of opinion among participants as to how plagiarism should be defined. Indeed, there is agreement among authors on the difficulty and the complexity of defining plagiarism (Leask 2006). There are a large number of varied definitions of plagiarism (Atkinson and Yeoh 2008; Gullifer and Tyson 2010; Park 2003; Youmans 2011). This can lead to confusion among faculty about what really constitutes plagiarism.

In general, the qualitative data suggests that plagiarism is associated with "copy-paste" from the Internet. This behavior is described as "obviously unacceptable," "cheating," and "dishonest." Interestingly, although participants agreed that to "copy-paste" was to plagiarize, there was much emphasis placed on the degree or extent to which students copied from other sources.

While many of the participants related stories of encountering entire essays copied from one source, they felt that copying and pasting a few lines from a source without including the reference was a minor offense in comparison. The following quotation is representative of this category:

> I don't really mind if they copy the basic company information from the company website […] that's standard information. I'm more concerned that they will copy the whole essay from the "Lazy Corner" student website.

Many of the other forms of plagiarism prompted by the interviewer were in general greeted with varying reactions. For example, summarizing or paraphrasing without properly referencing the original source was seen by some as a minor offense that could be easily forgiven. Anything that was not a direct copy-paste was seen as a less serious offense. Self-plagiarism was greeted with indifference and even skepticism.

> I think that there are different degrees of plagiarism. One thing is to copy an entire assignment. I think this is pure plagiarism. Then, another thing is not adequately referencing the original authors in the bibliography. I think that the last one is a result of a lack of formation on our part.

This view could be related to the Sutherland-Smith (2005) contribution that unintentional plagiarism should not be punished.

Therefore, the main discovery about the types and perceptions of plagiarism is that it is not so much the type of plagiarism that concerns professors but the degree to which students plagiarize. Hence, further research needs to move beyond plagiarism and focus more on the degree of plagiarism. Instead of asking what is and what is not plagiarism, there is a need to identify and consider the variables that determine the degree of plagiarism from the viewpoint of professors.

Variance Among Professors

The data analysis shows the age of the professor is one variable that distinguishes among different types of professors according to their ability to detect and willingness to pursue plagiarism.

In this sense, there is a marked difference in junior and senior members of the participants in terms of their formal training in identifying and avoiding plagiarism. While none of the more senior participants had any form of formal "antiplagiarism" training, the younger members of staffs have benefited from attending research seminars as part of their PhD training course, on referencing techniques and referencing software.

Indeed, the analysis of the data suggests that senior faculty are more likely to turn a blind eye to plagiarism, and avoid getting involved in pursuing students who plagiarize. Unlike younger faculty, when a possible case of plagiarism arouses their suspicions, they don't tend to go directly to the Internet to check. This lack of action could be related to different types of searching skills on the part of different members of faculty.

The next quotations reflect the concern of young professors to avoid plagiarism among their students:

> I design very specific assignments in order to make sure that students can't copy from the Internet.

> In order to detect plagiarism I check some sentences from their coursework in a search engine. I especially do so when the sentences are so well written that I suspect that the students are not the original authors.

Reactions to Plagiarism

One of the more surprising outcomes was the emergence of the category "it's their problem, not mine" in which some professors expressed their lack of concern when detecting plagiarism in coursework. In this sense, the professors expressed their opinion that the consequence of plagiarizing would be suffered by the offending student, as they would not benefit from the learning activity. In a way, some of the professors distanced themselves from the consequences of plagiarism. As explained previously, faculty have a number of reasons for not acting when they detect plagiarism, but this one has not been considered in previous studies.

However, when professors decide to do something in response to a case of plagiarism a number of issues arise. There is a general unawareness in terms of the options open to a professor who detects plagiarism. In this sense, professors don't know what they can and cannot do in terms of penalizing plagiarism. This creates a feeling of uncertainty and produces a desire to be supported in their decisions by the institution. Some of them even realized that doing something about it could bring further complications and problems to all parties involved, themselves, the students, and the institution. One of the quotations from the interviews sums this up very well:

If I had known how complicated this would become and how much of my own time I would have to invest in this, and the negative reactions of my colleagues, I would have kept my mouth shut.

In the specific case of the university where we carried out our interviews, there was no formal institutional policy on plagiarism (a policy has since been introduced). An initial search shows that this is the case in many universities in Spain. However, this should not be interpreted as a lack of interest on the part of Spanish universities. Rather, this is an outcome of the current legal framework that governs matters of plagiarism. The relevant laws date from the 1950s and they deal with the limited ability of universities to impose sanctions on students. Indeed, it would only be possible to sanction a student after a complex disciplinary process that is normally reserved for the most serious disciplinary issues. The prevailing law was formulated at a time when the access to information now provided by the Internet was beyond comprehension.

The outcome of this situation is that the most common consequence of plagiarism is that the student fails the specific piece of plagiarized coursework and if this leads to a fail grade on the subject, the student may take the course again at the earliest possible opportunity.

Conclusions

At present, the existence of a number of factors can lead us to think that the end of the widespread plagiarism problem is in sight. First, despite the fact that the expansion of the Internet makes it easier to produce dishonest behaviors (Akbulut et al. 2008; Embleton and Helfer 2007; Heather 2010; Park 2004; Underwood and Szabo 2003; Vanacker 2011), the Internet also facilitates the detection of plagiarism (Heather 2010; Lyon, Barrett, and Malcolm 2006; McKeever 2004; Park 2003). In this sense, technology provides faculty and universities with a number of tools that help to detect plagiarism (Comas and Sureda 2008, Comas-Forgas and Sureda-Negre 2010; McKeever 2004). Second, according to the results of our study, new generations of academic personnel are more aware of plagiarism and better trained to handle it when it arises. Thus, the proportion of new and incoming faculty attuned to this problem should increase over time. Lastly, universities are becoming increasingly aware of the importance of designing and promoting an academic policy that clearly deals with plagiarism.

Despite this favorable context, we cannot expect that the plagiarism problem will be solved and will disappear. A joint effort among students, professors, and universities is necessary to improve the current situation. For the moment, plagiarism is still considered as an element of the dark side of higher education management.

References

Akbulut, Y., S. Sendag, G. Brinici, K. Kilicer, M.C. Sahin, and H.F. Odabasi. 2008. "Exploring the Types and Reasons of Internet-Triggered Academic Dishonesty Among Turkish Undergraduate Students: Development of Internet-Triggered Academic Dishonesty Scale (ITADS)." *Computers and Education* 51, pp. 463–73.

Atkinson, D., and S. Yeoh. 2008. "Student and Staff Perceptions of the Effectiveness of Plagiarism Detection Software." *Australasian Journal of Educational Technology* 24, no. 2, pp. 222–40.

Austin, M.J., and L.D. Brown. October 1999. "Internet Plagiarism: Developing Strategies to Curb Student Academic Dishonesty." *The Internet and Higher Education* 2, no. 1, pp. 21–33.

Barrett, R., and A.L. Cox. 2005. "At Least They're Learning Something: The Hazy Line Between Collaboration and Collusion." *Assessment and Evaluation in Higher Education* 30, no. 2, pp. 107–22.

Batane, T. 2010. "Turning to Turnitin to Fight Plagiarism Among University Students." *Educational Technology and Society* 13, no. 2, pp. 1–12.

Bennett, R. 2005. "Factors Associated with Student Plagiarism in a Post-1992 University." *Assessment and Evaluation in Higher Education* 30, no. 2, pp. 137–62.

Bennett, K.K., L.S. Behrendt, and J.L. Boothby. 2011. "Instructor Perceptions of Plagiarism: Are We FindingCommon Ground?" *Teaching of Psychology* 38, no. 1, pp. 29–35.

Beute, N., E.S. van Aswegen, and C. Winberg. 2008. "Avoiding Plagiarism in Contexts of Development and Change." *Ieee Transactions on Education* 51, no. 2, pp. 201–05.

Bing, M.N., H.K. Davison, S.J. Vitell, A.P. Ammeter, B.L. Garner, and M.M. Novicevic. 2012. "An Experimental Investigation of an Interactive Model of Academic Cheating Among Business School Students." *Academy of Management Learning & Education* 11, no. 1, pp. 28–48.

Broeckelman-Post, M.A. 2008. "Faculty and Student Classroom Influences on Academic Dishonesty." *Ieee Transactions on Education* 51, no. 2, pp. 206–11.

Brown, V.J., and M.E. Howell. 2001. "The Efficacy of Policy Statements on Plagiarism: Do They Change Students' Views?" *Research in Higher Education* 42, no. 1, pp. 103–18.

Brinkman, B. 2013. "An Analysis of Student Privacy Rights in the Use of Plagiarism Detection Systems." *Science and Engineering Ethics* 19, pp. 1255–66.

Burke, J.A. 2007. "Academic Dishonesty: A Crisis on Campus." *The CPA Journal* 77, no. 5, pp. 1–17.

Caldwell, C. 2010. "A Ten-Step Model for Academic Integrity: A Positive Approach for Business Schools." *Journal of Business Ethics* 92, no. 1, pp. 1–13.

Colnerud, G., and M. Rosander. 2009. "Academic Dishonesty, Ethical Norms and Learning." *Assessment and Evaluation in Higher Education* 34, no. 5, pp. 505–17.

Comas, R., and J. Sureda. 2008. "El Ciberplagi Acadèmic: Esbrinant-Ne Les Causes Per Tal D'enllestir Les Solucions." In *El ciberplagi acadèmic* (Dossier En Línea). Digithum, 10. UOC.

Comas-Forgas, R., and J. Sureda-Negre. 2010. "Academic Plagiarism: Explanatory Factors from Students' Perspective." *Journal of Academic Ethics* 8, no. 3, pp. 217–32.

Comas, R., J. Sureda, A. Casero, and M. Morey. 2011. "Academic Integrity Among Spanish University Students." *Estudios Pedagogicos* 37, no. 1, pp. 207–25.

Coren, A. 2011. "Turning a Blind Eye: Faculty Who Ignore Student Cheating." *Journal of Academic Ethics* 9, no. 4, pp. 291–305.

Culwin, F., and T. Lancaster. 2001. "Plagiarism Issues for Higher Education." *Vine* 31, no. 2, pp. 36–41.

De Jager, K., and C. Brown. 2010. "The Tangled Web: Investigating Academics' Views of Plagiarism at the University of Cape Town." *Studies in Higher Education* 35, no. 5, pp. 513–28.

Ellahi, A., R. Mushtaq, and M.B. Khan. 2013. "Multi Campus Investigation of Academic Dishonesty in Higher Education of Pakistan." *International Journal of Educational Management* 27, no. 6, pp. 647–66.

Embleton, K., and D.S. Helfer. 2007. "The Plague of Plagiarism and Academic Dishonesty." *Searcher* 15, no. 6, pp. 23–26.

Flint, A., S. Clegg, and R. Macdonald. 2006. "Exploring Staff Perceptions of Student Plagiarism." *Journal of Further and Higher Education* 30, no. 2, pp. 145–56.

Glaser, B.G., and A.L. Strauss. 1967. *The Discovery of Grounded Theory: Strategies for Qualitative Research.* New York: Aldine de Gruyter.

Goh, E. 2013. "Plagiarism Behavior Among Undergraduate Students in Hospitality and Tourism Education." *Journal of Teaching in Travel and Tourism* 13, no. 4, pp. 307–22.

Gullifer, J., and G.A. Tyson. 2010. "Exploring University Students' Perceptions of Plagiarism: A Focus Group Study." *Studies in Higher Education* 35, no. 4, pp. 463–81.

Hard, S.F., J.M. Conway, and A.C. Moran. 2006. "Faculty and College Student Beliefs About the Frequency of Student Academic Misconduct." *Journal of Higher Education* 77, no. 6, pp. 1058–80.

Hayes, N., and L. Introna. 2005. "Systems for the Production of Plagiarists? The Implications Arising from the Use of Plagiarism Detection Systems in UK Universities for Asian Learners." *Journal of Academic Ethics* 3, no. 1, pp. 55–73.

Heather, J. 2010. "Turnitoff: Identifying and Fixing a Hole in Current Plagiarism Detection Software." *Assessment and Evaluation in Higher Education* 35, no. 6, pp. 647–60.

Heckler, N.C., M. Rice, and H. Bryan. 2013. "Turnitin Systems: A Deterrent to Plagiarism in College Classrooms." *Journal of Research on Technology in Education* 45, no. 3, pp. 229–48.

Keith-Spiegel, P., B.G. Tabachnick, B.E. Whitley, Jr., and J. Washburn. 1998. "Why Professors Ignore Cheating: Opinions of a National Sample of Psychology Instructors." *Ethics and Behavior* 8, no. 3, pp. 215–27.

Kelley, D. 2007. "I Bet You Look Good on the Sales Floor." *Journal of Strategic Marketing* 15, no. 1, pp. 53–63.

Kidwell, L.A., K. Wozniak, and J.P. Laurel. 2003. "Student Reports and Faculty Perceptions of Academic Dishonesty." *Teaching Business Ethics* 7, no. 3, pp. 205–14.

Kwong, T., H.M. Ng, M. Kai-Pan, and E. Wong. 2010. "Students' and Faculty's Perception of Academic Integrity in Hong Kong." *Campus-Wide Information Systems* 27, no. 5, pp. 341–55.

Larkham, P.J., and S. Manns. 2002. "Plagiarism and Its Treatment in Higher Education." *Journal of Further and Higher Education* 26, no. 4, pp. 339–49.

Leask, B. 2006. "Plagiarism, Cultural Diversity and Metaphor-Implications for Academic Staff Development." *Assessment and Evaluation in Higher Education* 31, no. 2, pp. 183–99.

Ledwith, A., and A. Rísquez. 2008. "Using Anti-Plagiarism Software to Promote Academic Honesty in the Context of Peer Reviewed Assignments." *Studies in Higher Education* 33, no. 4, pp. 371–84.

Lim, C.L., and T. Coalter. 2006. "Academic Integrity: An Instructor's Obligation." *International Journal of Teaching and Learning in Higher Education* 17, no. 2, pp. 155–59.

Lin, C.H.S., and L.Y.M. Wen. 2007. "Academic Dishonesty in Higher Education—A Nationwide Study in Taiwan." *Higher Education* 54, no. 1, pp. 85–97.

Lyon, C., R. Barrett, and J. Malcom. 2006. "Plagiarism Is Easy, but Also Easy to Detect." *Plagiary: Cross-Disciplinary Studies in Plagiarism, Fabrication and Falsification* 1, no. 5, pp. 57–65.

Macdonald, R., and J. Carroll. 2006. "Plagiarism-a Complex Issue Requiring a Holistic Institutional Approach." *Assessment and Evaluation in Higher Education* 31, no. 2, pp. 233–45.

Marcus, S., and S. Beck. 2011. "Faculty Perceptions of Plagiarism at Queensborough Community College." *Community and Junior College Libraries* 17, no. 2, pp. 63–73.

Martin, B. 1994. "Plagiarism: A Misplaced Emphasis." *Journal of Information Ethics* 3, no. 2, pp. 36–47.

McCabe, D.L. 2005. "CAI Research." www.waunakee.k12.wi.us/hs/departments/lmtc/Assignments/McConnellScenarios/AcadHonesty_5Article.pdf (accessed May 15, 2015).

McCabe, D.L., K.D. Butterfield, and L.K. Treviño. 2006. "Academic Dishonesty in Graduate Business Programs: Prevalence, Causes, and Proposed Action." *Academy of Management Learning and Education* 5, no. 3, pp. 294–305.

McCabe, D.L., and L.K. Trevino. 1996. What We Know About Cheating in College Longitudinal Trends and Recent Developments. *Change: The Magazine of Higher Learning* 28, no. 1, pp. 28–33.

McCabe, D.L., L.K. Treviño, and K.D. Butterfield. 2002. "Honor Codes and Other Contextual Influences on Academic Integrity: A Replication and Extension to Modified Honor Code Settings." *Research in Higher Education* 43, no. 3, pp. 357–78.

McKeever, L. 2004. "Online Plagiarism Detection Services–Saviour or Scourge?" *Assessment and Evaluation in Higher Education* 31, no. 2, pp. 155–65.

Park, C. 2003. "In Other (People's) Words: Plagiarism by University Students-Literature and Lessons." *Assessment & Evaluation in Higher Education* 28, no. 5, pp. 471–88.

Park, C. 2004. "Rebels Without a Clause: Toward an Institutional Framework for Dealing With Plagiarism by Students." *Journal of Further and Higher Education* 28, no. 3, pp. 291–306.

Pickard, J. 2006. "Staff and Student Attitudes to Plagiarism at University College Northampton." *Assessment & Evaluation in Higher Education* 31, no. 2, pp. 215–32.

Plagiarism.org. 2014. "Types of Plagiarism." www.plagiarism.org/plagiarism-101/types-of-plagiarism (accessed May 15, 2015).

Quah, C.H., N. Stewart, and J.W.C. Lee. 2012. "Attitudes of Business Students' Toward Plagiarism." *Journal of Academic Ethics* 10, no. 3, pp. 185–99.

Ramzan, M., M.A. Munir, N. Siddique, and M. Asif. 2012. "Awareness About Plagiarism Amongst University Students in Pakistan." *Higher Education* 64, no. 1, pp. 73–84.

Rísquez, A., M. O'Dwyer, and A. Ledwith. 2013. "'Thou Shalt No Plagiarise': From Self-Reported Views to Recognition and Avoidance of Plagiarism." *Assessment & Evaluation in Higher Education* 38, no. 1, pp. 34–43.

Rosenberg, M. 2011. "Principled Autonomy and Plagiarism." *Journal of Academic Ethics* 9, no. 1, pp. 61–69.

Sadler, B.J. 2007. "The Wrongs of Plagiarism: Ten Quick Arguments." *Teaching Philosohpy* 30, no. 3, pp. 283–91.

Samuels, L., and C. Bast. 2006. "Strategies to Help Legal Studies Students Avoid Plagiarism." *Journal of Legal Studies Education* 23, no. 2, pp. 151–67.

Selwyn, N. 2008. "'Not Necessarily a Bad Thing …': A Study of Online Plagiarism Amongst Undergraduate Students." *Assessment & Evaluation in Higher Education* 33, no. 5, pp. 465–79.

Sheridan, J., R. Alany, and D.J. Brake. 2005. "Pharmacy Students' Views and Experiences of Turnitin-An Online Tool for Detecting Academic Dishonesty." *Pharmacy Education* 5, nos. 3–4, pp. 241–50.

Silverman, D. 2000. *Doing Qualitative Research.* London: Sage.

Simon, C.A., J.R. Carr, S.M. McCullough, S.J. Morgan, T. Oleson, and M. Ressel. 2003. "The Other Side of Academic Dishonesty: The Relationship Between Faculty Scepticism, Gender and Strategies for Managing Student Academic Dishonesty Cases." *Assessment & Evaluation in Higher Education* 28, no. 2, pp. 193–207.

Sims, R.L. 2002. "The Effectiveness of a Plagiarism Prevention Policy: A Longitudinal Study of Student Views." *Teaching Business Ethics* 6, no. 4, pp. 477–82.

Strauss, A., and J. Corbin. 1998. *Basics of Qualitative Research: Techniques and Procedures for Developing Grounded Theory.* Thousand Oaks, CA: Sage.

Sutherland-Smith, W. 2005. "Pandora's Box: Academic Perceptions of Student Plagiarism in Writing." *Journal of English for Academic Purposes* 4, no. 1, pp. 83–95.

Sutherland-Smith, W. 2011. "Crime and Punishment: An Analysis of University Plagiarism Policies." *Semiotica* 2011, no. 187, pp. 127–39.

Trost, K. 2009. "Psst, Have You EverCheated? A Study of Academic Dishonesty in Sweden." *Assessment & Evaluation in Higher Education* 34, no. 4, pp. 367–76.

Underwood, J., and A. Szabo. 2003. "Academic Offences and e-Learning: Individual Propensities in Cheating." *British Journal of Educational Technology* 34, no. 4, pp. 467–77.

Vanacker, B. 2011. "Returning Students' Right to Access, Choice and Notice: A Proposed Code of Ethics for Instructors Using Turnitin." *Ethics and Information Technology* 13, no. 4, pp. 327–38.

Vardi, I. 2012. "Developing Students' Referencing Skills: A Matter of Plagiarism, Punishment and Morality or of Learning to Write Critically?" *Higher Education Research and Development* 31, no. 6, pp. 921–30.

Walden, K., and A. Peacock. 2006. "The i-Map: A Process-Centered Response to Plagiarism." *Assessment & Evaluation in Higher Education* 31, no. 2, pp. 201–14.

Williams, K., and J. Carroll. 2009. *Referencing and Understanding Plagiarism*. Basingstoke: Palgrave Macmillan.

Yazici, A., S. Yazici, and M.S. Erdem. 2011. "Faculty and Student Perceptions on College Cheating: Evidence from Turkey." *Educational Studies* 37, no. 2, pp. 221–31.

Youmans, R.J. 2011. "Does the Adoption of Plagiarism-Detection Software in Higher Education Reduce Plagiarism?" *Studies in Higher Education* 36, no. 7, pp. 749–61.

CHAPTER 4

Selling Science Through University Entrepreneurship: Debates and Implications for Emerging Economies

Debabrata Chatterjee

Indian Institute of Management, Kozhikode, India

Introduction

Universities have traditionally fulfilled two roles in society—knowledge generation through research and knowledge dissemination through teaching. Their primary contribution to the economy has been through the latter function. However, globally, there is a trend among universities to take on a third role—that of contributing more directly to the economy through entrepreneurial activities of Faculty members. At the core, this role involves commercializing research carried out by Faculty members. It takes several forms—setting up science-based entrepreneurial ventures by academics, joint ventures with industry, supporting new ventures in business incubation centers and setting up science parks in the vicinity, and so on (Hendry and Brown 2006; Miller, Richard, and Arora 2011). Scholars such as Etzkowitz and his colleagues (Etzkowitz and Leydesdorff 2000; Etzkowitz et al. 2000) have described this shift in terms of the "Triple Helix" framework and the "third mission" of universities. In this essay, all these forms of contribution are subsumed under the term "university entrepreneurship."

These changes are accompanied by modifications in the organizational structures, practices, processes, and cultures in order to facilitate commercialization of Faculty research of universities. For example, their internal policies supporting Faculty entrepreneurship might include specifying Faculty roles in this regard, provide leave, access to risk capital, encouraging the development of science parks in their vicinity, and having efficient technology transfer offices (Caldera and Debande 2010).

While this global movement toward universities commercializing scientific research is being facilitated by several forces, its effect is open to question. Some argue that the effect of academic entrepreneurship on the original missions of universities may not always be desirable. The success of such entrepreneurial efforts in impacting the economy substantially may also be questioned. Several confounding factors that are contextual to emerging economies add to this debate.

In this essay, this question on the impact of university entrepreneurship is discussed in depth, and its implications for emerging economies are outlined. The main thrust of the arguments advanced is that there appears to be a sense of inevitability in this movement toward university entrepreneurship, driven by an array of changes taking place in economies around the world. In this context, university entrepreneurship may be seen as an outcome and a mode of adjustment to these changes. Yet, the process is dialectical, in that the particular response to this change may undermine the very ability of universities to sustain this mode of response in the long run.

This argument is developed in three steps. First, in order to set the tone, institutional changes in science, research and technology development, and in higher education are discussed. The purpose of this discussion is to highlight how university entrepreneurship seems to be inevitable in today's context. Next, some research findings are highlighted to suggest that the outcome of university entrepreneurship is not quite straightforward, and indeed debatable. In the process, the contradictions inherent in university entrepreneurship are elaborated. Finally, specific issues in emerging economies are discussed in order to suggest how appreciating this dialectic is especially relevant in their cases.

Institutional Changes Encouraging University Research Commercialization

Fundamental shifts are underway in the field of higher education with regard to institutional preferences for certain modes of science and technology development. These shifts are simultaneously exerting push and pull forces on universities and encouraging them to commercialize their scientific research.

Scientific discoveries have long impacted product development in industries. For example, the field of biotechnology is sometimes traced back to discoveries in genetics and molecular biology (McMillan, Narin, and Deeds 2000; Owen-Smith and Powell 2003). Similarly, entire industries in display devices, energy storage devices, and so on are today dependent on advancements in the basic science behind these technologies. However, these changes have gathered pace over the last three decades or so and the role of scientific advances in technological and product development is increasingly seen as vital across many industries. Part of the reason is the increasing competition in industry, as captured in scholarly and practitioner literature alike, and driven largely by product and technological innovations. An indication of this pace is the rapid increase in patenting across the world.

One outcome of this increasing product and technology-based competition is that the pace at which industrial R&D reaches the limits of technology frontiers has also hastened. For example, as companies try to shrink the size of electronic devices, or make them more "intelligent" by increasing their computing power, the need to increase the number of transistors in integrated circuit chips increases almost exponentially. However, as this happens, the known physics of silicon, which is the basic building material for such chips, starts becoming a limiting factor. Therefore, the role of basic science assumes importance when these frontiers are reached. It influences the process of technological progress by helping innovators to understand the limitations of technologies and product components and their interactions, allowing them to recognize theoretically difficult solutions and open up new possibilities to overcome the limits (Fleming and Sorenson 2004).

This could be a reason why a paradigm shift is evident in the management of industrial R&D as well. Trends suggest that companies are increasingly lifting their self-imposed restrictions on limiting R&D to their internal laboratories, and turning to universities for research and intellectual inputs. This move toward "open innovation" (Chesbrough 2006) involves richer and deeper interactions with universities than more traditional interaction modes such as seeking consulting help in specific projects. Besides seeking technologies off the shelf, such as those that universities wish to license out or sell, companies in many industries are increasingly interested to collaborate with Faculty members on long-term research collaborations through dedicated research centers. These collaborations may or may not have immediate commercial outcomes, but nevertheless may have potential applications in future. On the part of the Faculty, their research productivity, joint papers with industry, and interdisciplinary research are likely to increase during the years they are associated with the centers (Ponomariov and Boardman 2010). In other words, there appears to be increasing convergence between the interests of both universities and industry to collaborate with each other.

Besides these "pull" factors, several other developments are also pushing universities to commercialize their research. Traditionally, governments have played an important role in catalyzing the growth of university education for a variety of reasons. For example, in the late-19th century United States, land grants by state governments acted as incentives in setting up universities. Around the same time, the German government's policies ensured that universities were assured an important role in national development. In India and several other countries under British colonial rule, universities were set up to train local youth in English so that they could act as interlocutors with the local population on behalf of the rulers and occupy the lower ranks of the administration.

Over the last few decades, however, government policies in several countries have shifted in the other direction. The trend is visible at least since the 1980s, when international monetary institutions such as the World Bank began advocating a position in which education is seen as a private rather than a public good (Crespi et al. 2011). One fall out of this has been that governments are reducing their support toward higher education and encouraging universities to explore alternate means to raise revenues. Therefore, with this reorientation of public management, universities are forced to go beyond government support or compete for state funding to sustain themselves (Bolli and Somogyi 2011). Competitive research funding is an important instrument in this context (Auranen and Nieminen 2010) as governments can influence the direction and intensity of research by modifying the rules governing such funding.

Besides such funding policies, encouraging universities to source funds from industry has been a natural consequence that fits the overall philosophy of the reorientation of public management in higher education. This has taken several forms. In the United States, this shift has been recognized through the promulgation of the Bayh-Dole Act that grants universities the right over intellectual property generated in their laboratories. Similar trends are noticeable across the world as other advanced countries and developing countries alike implement or plan to implement similar legislations and policies (Loewenberg 2009).

Another important development evident in recent years is the rising importance of university rankings across the world. The field of higher education is increasingly becoming globalized, with standards for evaluating universities tied to global rankings. The importance accorded to rankings is based on the premise that universities are largely motivated by improvements in their reputation and standing (Porter and Toutkoushian 2006). The implication of this development is that various stakeholders besides governments are interested to scrutinize university performance on a wide range of indices. University rankings are regularly published in media, with important implications, because these rankings act as proxies for the quality of universities, and hence impact on their ability to attract quality students, as well as funding from government and nongovernment sources. The rankings also provide a basis for national policies on higher education, science and technology, across many nations (Saisana, d'Hombres, and Saltelli 2011). As the comparative study of the most popular ranking systems by Rauhvargers (2011) suggests, university research commercialization features as part of several of these ranking systems.

Finally, there are normative pressures on universities to follow practices of some leading U.S. and European universities that have been successful in research commercialization. Very visible examples of the so-called "knowledge clusters" include, beside others, regions such as the

Silicon Valley in the United States, the Cambridge area in the United Kingdom, Ottawa in Canada, and Helsinki in Finland (Huggins 2008). The success of some universities in these regions to spawn science-based industries in their vicinity by supporting science-based entrepreneurship through incubating and consulting for businesses, are taken as exemplars of what university, science and technology policy should aim for in the 21st century. Attempts are being made to replicate similar clusters in other regions of the world.

To summarize, institutional changes in the field of university education are simultaneously pulling and pushing universities to actively pursue entrepreneurial activities. The pull factor includes changes in how companies compete. This basis is shifting from the ability to achieve scale to the ability to innovate, thus motivating them to engage with state-of-art science. Simultaneously, the paradigm of closed-door corporate R&D is changing to "open innovation" in which partnerships with universities form an important feature. The push factors include decreasing public funding, competitive research funding, and global rankings, which are encouraging universities to devote attention to Faculty entrepreneurial ventures and other means of earning from research.

Debating the Effects of Academic Entrepreneurship

The question that is increasingly being researched and debated in this context is the effect of these changes on universities and economies. There are two issues at hand here—the impact of research commercialization activities on pure academic activities, and the impact of "third mission" (Etzkowitz and Leydesdorff 2000; Etzkowitz et al. 2000) activities on the economy at large.

Research Commercialization and Academics

Does research commercialization complement or compete with traditional academic activities such as basic research and teaching? The evidence tends to favor the view that research commercialization impedes pure academic activities at least to some extent. In one study, the investigators (Landry et al. 2010) compared three noncommercial forms of knowledge transfer activities (publications, teaching, and informal knowledge transfer) and three commercial forms of knowledge transfer (patenting, forming spin-off companies, and consulting). The issue was whether these forms of knowledge transfer complemented, substituted, or were independent of each other. They did not find statistical support for any relationship between publications and patenting or spin-off creation. Similarly, they did not observe any statistically significant link between teaching and the three commercial forms of knowledge transfer.

On the other hand, another study (Crespi et al. 2011) found that the relationship between patenting and publishing appeared to follow an inverted parabolic shape. Thus, till a threshold of about 10 patents or so, the two complemented each other, after which patenting substituted publishing, and a crowding out effect was evident. This relationship appeared to be moderated by the type of academic discipline. Crowding out was more in basic scientific disciplines such as physics and chemistry, while a reverse crowding-in, that is, complementary effect, was observed in applied disciplines such as computer science and engineering. Comparisons between patenting, research collaborations with industry, contract research, consulting, jointly supervising PhD programs, and participating in spin-offs through equity exposure revealed similar patterns as well.

The motivation behind research commercialization, in particular the type of beneficiaries, also appears to have an effect on pure academic research. Thus, Czarnitzki, Glänzel, and Hussinger (2009) observed that the number and quality of publications tend to be positively correlated to the number of patents that are assigned to nonprofit entities such as universities, nonprofit research institutes, or the academic inventors themselves. Conversely, this correlation tends to be slightly negative when the assignee is a for-profit entity. A somewhat similar idea comes from another study by Thursby and Thursby (2011). They analyzed an interesting dataset—Faculty invention disclosures—and studied how such disclosures affect the ability of Faculty to attract government and industrial funding for research. Disclosing invention is the first step in the research commercialization process, where Faculty members inform their university technology transfer office details of their inventions so that their commercial implications and likelihood of being granted patents could be estimated. Arguing that government research funds tend to have a bias toward basic and fundamental research, they found that beyond a threshold, such funding tends to taper off as the number of invention disclosures increased. On the other hand, a general positive effect was evident on industry funding. Thus, it is important to distinguish the mere act of research commercialization from the motivation behind it. There is a possibility that patenting with the intent to profit (as would be the case when patents are assigned to for-profit entities such as business organizations) might have an adverse effect on academic research. On the other hand, commercializing research for nonprofit use may not have similar adverse effects.

A fundamental point that arises from this discussion is that the notion of science itself, and role of the scientist who is engaged in the noble pursuit of knowledge for its own sake, is under challenge. Science as a calling is rooted in a certain identity of the scientist that is peculiar to itself, and distinct from that required to be a successful entrepreneur. Pursuing academic entrepreneurship, therefore, is likely to cause an identity conflict among academics who are compelled to commercialize their research due to institutional changes. Some researchers have pointed to this fundamental shift that seems to be occurring in the motivation and identities of researchers as they shift to commercializing their research. Thus, Duberley, Cohen, and Leeson (2007) suggest that the motivation for scientific research has shifted from curiosity of individual scientists to extend the frontiers of science to the application of science into technology through interdisciplinary and collaborative research. Jain, George, and Maltarich (2009) have differentiated between the role identities of academic and entrepreneurial science on their norms, processes, and outputs. University scientists make a distinction between their identities as pure science researchers, and more applied entrepreneurial science researchers, with a hybrid identity as a possible outcome for many scientists (Jain, George, and Maltarich 2009; Lam 2010).

Impact of Academic Entrepreneurship

Flowing from these questions of identity and impact on traditional academic functions are the more instrumental questions of whether academic research commercialization delivers what many believe is its promise, and what are its long-term implications. The question then is, what evidence is there that by commercializing their research, and thereby fulfilling their "third mission" (Etzkowitz and Leydesdorff 2000; Etzkowitz et al. 2000), universities do indeed contribute to regional economic development? Two aspects of this question are considered—the immediate and direct impact on local economic development, and the long-term impact on advancing the cause of science, and hence on future technological developments.

Regarding the first aspect, the growth of "knowledge clusters" in some countries has been introduced earlier as one of the normative pressures acting on universities to commercialize their research and spawn science-based industries. However, the role that universities have actually played in the development of such clusters is open to question (Doutriaux 2003). The evidence, at best, is equivocal and open to interpretation. For example, in their study of Waterloo University in Canada, Bramwell, and Wolfe (2008) noted a significant role in the development of the local knowledge cluster. On the other hand, the evidence provided by Huggins (2008) is less certain. This study compared four areas—the Silicon Valley, Cambridge, Ottawa, and Helsinki and found different levels of influence on the part of universities. A more substantial role was evident in Cambridge and Helsinki than in the Silicon Valley and Ottawa. In the last two locations, government and corporate R&D laboratories played an important role.

On the second aspect, an important observation from studies on technological innovations is that firms usually tend to operate within certain "technological paradigms" (Dosi 1982, 152). Therefore, the focus of this stream of research is to understand the circumstances in which new technologies and products arise or don't arise. Two key concepts are knowledge exploration, which refers to seeking out or discovering new knowledge, and knowledge exploitation, which is about referring to an existing knowledge base to solve problems (March 1991).

Considerable research effort has gone into understanding the implications for organizations relying on knowledge exploration or exploitation in their efforts at technology or product innovation. The findings suggest some interesting conclusions. Thus, the usefulness of knowledge for an organization tends to decrease as the same knowledge is reused repeatedly (Fleming 2001). More specifically, it has been seen that the ability of an organization to impact the development of a technology in future is adversely impacted if it continues to exploit the same knowledge (Rosenkopf and Nerkar 2001). Similar observations have also been reported with respect to the number of new products (Katila 2002; Katila and Ahuja 2002). The converse is true when organizations explore new knowledge. It enables organizations to increase new product offerings (Katila 2002; Katila and Ahuja 2002), and impact the development of technologies (Rosenkopf and Nerkar 2001).

Although this research stream is focused largely on technological innovation by firms, it nevertheless has important pointers for our understanding of the long-term implications for university research commercialization. As pointed out earlier, the evidence regarding the impact of academic research commercialization on basic research suggests the possibility that the latter might be adversely impacted if Faculty members actively pursue commercialization-related activities. The importance of basic science and new knowledge in developing new technologies, and extending the functionality of existing ones (Fleming and Sorenson 2004) is well established since such basic research is the prime route to extend the frontiers of science and explore new knowledge.

Although this discussion was evidently not supposed to be an extensive review of the relevant literature, its purpose is served if it provides the material to trigger a debate on the role that research commercialization plays in economies. To summarize, there is a need to appreciate the implications of university research commercialization even as it acquires institutional legitimacy. One of the points noted was that research commercialization activities might impede the ability of Faculty members to continue advancing science beyond the immediate time frame. Apart from the practical aspects of balancing pure academic and commercialization activities, Faculty members are also likely to confront the more fundamental issue of their identity. Thus, beyond this reference period, commercialization activities are likely to increasingly depend on existing discoveries and inventions. In the long term then, without access to cutting-edge science, the very ability to invent science-based products is compromised. In other words, in the long run, the act of research commercialization is likely to contradict itself and come up against its own promise.

This discussion highlights the salient aspects of the debate, and tentative conclusions, on the question raised in the introductory section, namely, what is the impact of academic research commercialization. Given these conclusions, the question is what are the implications of academic research commercialization on emerging economies? As discussed in the following section, further confounding factors contributed by historical issues are encountered while considering the context of higher education in emerging economies.

The Context of University Education in Emerging Economies

The argument developed thus far has been that the raison d'être for commercializing academic science, namely that it contributes to economic development, may be problematic for several reasons. The evidence for this was largely drawn from studies in developed economies, namely the North American continent and Western Europe. It is argued in this section that these are not the only reasons why emerging economies need to be cautious. Rather, at least three important contextual factors confound the issue in their case. First, considering the historical legacy, traditional roles, and contemporary economic context, the roles expected from universities in emerging economies are vastly different. Research is the second area. As elaborated next, universities in many of these countries have traditionally not taken an interest in research. Some of these countries are already making rapid strides in this regard. Yet, the question remains, what should be researched, and how should university Faculty define their areas for research? Third, while discussing academic science, it is often assumed that all science (and the technology derived from it) should necessarily be evaluated by Western standards. The fact that modern Western science is a relatively recent development and a product of a particular historical process is often ignored. Hence, the role of universities vis-à-vis traditional knowledge also requires examination. Each of these contextual factors are discussed next.

Special University Roles in Emerging Economies

At least some non-Western economies, including China, Japan, and India have had universities of global repute in ancient and medieval times. However, modern universities in many Asian and African economies are of more recent origin and stem from their colonization by Western nations. Often the sole purpose was to create a cadre among the indigenous population with necessary skills to act as intermediaries on behalf of colonial rulers, and run the lower echelons of their administration. Given their background, teaching has traditionally been an important mission in most universities in emerging economies.

In Latin America, the history was slightly different. In many of these countries, some of the earliest universities were founded by religious orders as part of the original colonial set up. However, most of these countries were able to become independent of Europe by the 19th century; hence, they started the quest to reform these universities, or establish new ones with the objective of nation building and to usher in modernity and rationality (Schwartzman 2007).

Although the origins of modern universities in Asia, Africa, and Latin America stemmed from different motivations, nevertheless they largely share one common trait—historically, they have stressed largely on teaching, in many instances even at the expense of research. Of course, there have been isolated instances of brilliant researchers working in these universities. For example, in India, Prof. C.V. Raman won the 1930 Nobel Prize in physics for discovering the "Raman" effect, and Prof. S.N. Bose, whose collaboration with Albert Einstein led to the idea of the so-called "boson" subatomic particle, worked at the University of Calcutta during the 1930s. However, these were largely exceptions.

Some of the newly industrialized economies of Asia have made great strides in product and technological innovations. However, the role of universities seems to be rather limited, and by and large, universities in many of these countries have focused mostly on teaching, and not on research. They have been forced to become more and more teaching oriented to cater to the aspirations of their post-Independence generations for higher qualifications (Altbach 2009). With regard to Indian universities, Datta and Saad (2011) point out that modern universities in India started off basically as examination bodies during the British colonial era. Their role in teaching was limited initially but picked up gradually later. All this has led to the separation of teaching and research. A similar conclusion is drawn by empirical studies carried out in the so-called "knowledge clusters" in the Indian cities of Mumbai, Pune, Bangalore, and Delhi. Higher education institutions in these regions are largely involved in teaching, less in research, and even less in entrepreneurial or knowledge transfer activities to local industries (Basant and Chandra 2007; Basant and Mukhopadhyay 2009; Vang and Chaminade 2006; Vang, Chaminade, and Coenen 2007). Even the Indian Institutes of Technology, otherwise known through their alumni presence in high-technology companies and start-ups across the world, are known more for their teaching than research or commercialization (Sen 2010). Malaysian universities appear to play a limited role in reaching out to industries through research and entrepreneurship although government policies in this regard are clearly encouraging toward these activities (Abdrazak and Saad 2007). Almost similar is the case of Thailand, where most of the knowledge inputs required for high-technology industries are brought in by multinational corporations rather than universities (Liefner and Schiller 2008).

But apart from the historical legacy that is invoked to explain the importance attached to teaching, some authors even suggest that normatively, universities should not abandon their mission to teach. Thus, Liefner and Schiller (2008, 281) suggest that universities should play an important role in sharpening their academic capabilities, which they define "as an act of functional skills and organizational ability of the country's higher education institutions to carry out their extended role in the process of technological upgrading and learning." Through an extensive study of Thailand's higher education system, they suggest that the role of universities in this regard should be properly acknowledged. Their conclusion is that far from deviating into academic entrepreneurship, universities in that country should, therefore, concentrate on improving their academic capabilities.

As mentioned previously, the evolution of universities in Latin America has followed a slightly different trajectory than universities in many Asian and African countries. Given this context, it has been argued that the universities have traditionally played, and should continue to play, certain unique roles. For example, Ordorika and Pusser (2007) suggest that universities may have a central role in nation building. Such "nation-building" universities embody certain distinctive characteristics—they symbolize the hopes and dreams of the nations under transformation, and link various social groups and social movements by providing their intellectual base and support. Schwartzman (2007) takes a similar line while arguing that in addition to the emphasis on research, societies also require universities to educate and develop students to take up multifarious roles such as politicians, lawyers, diplomats, civil servants, and historians.

The Context of Research in Emerging Economies

It can be argued that while there is widespread optimism about the role that science can play in improving the human condition, it is also true that much of this optimism arises from science as it is practiced in developed economies. Therefore, the kind of problems that are taken up for investigation, the technologies that arise out of science, and solutions that are proposed are often relevant in the context of these economies. In fact, as Drori et al. (2003) argue, Western scientific developments often lead to the discovery of problems that arise from scientific developments themselves. For example, studies on environmental pollution, global warming, and so on are possible using modern science, but at the same time, these problems are also the result of scientific and technological developments themselves. With greater awareness of these problems it is likely that economic activities that trigger them will also invite policy interventions aimed at limiting them. Consistent with this line of thinking, Drori et al. (2003) found support for the hypothesis that science aimed at addressing social concerns may actually adversely affect economic development in the short term. Indeed, for underdeveloped economies, economic efficiency resulting from engaging local issues may diverge from national development when measured from Western points of view so that the correlation between Western science and national development remains relevant only for Western economies (Shenhav and Kamens 1991).

The point here is that science that is commercially relevant may not always be interested in being socially relevant. Conversely, socially relevant science, especially when measured from the point of view of emerging economies, may not always be commercially relevant. For example, the amount of research funding by global pharmaceutical companies that is devoted to research on Western lifestyle diseases far outweighs the amount that is spent on diseases that are prevalent in emerging economies (Sterckx 2004).

In the discussion on university entrepreneurship, the stress invariably is on linkages with industry. Very little, if at all, is discussed about the link between universities and local communities. Yet, improving standards of living of local communities, including small-scale industry and farmers, is equally important in emerging economies. For example, finding out novel farming methods or providing technical solutions to marginal farmers would be highly relevant for some of these economies yet may not merit attention within the rubric of university entrepreneurship. Indeed, it is seen that measuring research productivity of universities based only on scientific publications may hide significant contributions when evaluated from the point of view of new recommendations made by agricultural scientists and new techniques developed by them (Rivera-Huerta et al. 2011).

Science and Traditional Knowledge

The third issue is deeper and questions the entire enterprise of Western science itself. Western science arose out of a unique historical process. European societies developed the norms of modern science post the rediscovery of their ancient philosophical and scientific heritage, and the explosion of intellectual inquiry during and after their renaissance. Its epistemology, for example, incorporating rationalism and empiricism of Western philosophy, emerged during this renaissance (Russell 1961). The science as we know today emerged by the 19th century through this historical process. In conjunction with the rising economic and military power of Western nation states, Western science has become institutionalized and globalized such that other forms of knowledge are regarded as unscientific.

Several decades back, Basalla (1967) proposed a three-phase model of the spread of Western science in many of the countries classified as "emerging economies" today. In his view, this spread is characterized by three phases—"prescientific," spread of colonial science, and struggle and establishment of independent but indigenous scientific culture (1967, 611). He qualified that using the term "prescientific" did not imply that the concerned societies were without any science or technology before the arrival of Western colonizers, but rather that at least some of these societies had different indigenous traditions for scientific advancement. China, India, and Japan were some of the examples he mentioned in this context.

These "prescientific" traditions include traditional knowledge, philosophy, mathematics, astronomy, medicine, environmental knowledge, and so on that mankind has always needed to survive in often harsh conditions. This knowledge has been gained over generations and millennia, captured, stored, and transmitted through language and practices of communities. In certain instances, some of this knowledge has been investigated very systematically by groups of scholar communities that have thrived specifically to develop and systematize this knowledge. The examples of China, India, and Japan that Basalla (1967) mentions would fall under this category. Yet he errs by mentioning only these societies to illustrate the term "prescientific." In fact, all traditional communities and societies had their own bases of knowledge to solve various problems related to surviving in natural environments.

However, the norms to generate useful knowledge prevalent in ancient civilizations in Asia were different from Western conceptualizations (Northrop 1946). The same has also been noted by researchers studying aboriginal communities such as those in the Americas (Aikenhead 2002; Tsuji and Ho 2002). Given the unique contexts in which traditional science has developed, it has always had a deep and sustainable relationship with the environment, living in harmony with it, and making life possible within the constraints imposed by local resources and challenges. This unique body of knowledge may be at risk of disappearing unless they are given the same legitimacy and institutional backing as Western science. Indeed, as Walsh and Shapiro (2006) suggested in the context of meditative traditions and modern psychology, Western science may ignore traditional knowledge, or contest it, or maybe even assimilate it. The use of aboriginal knowledge in scientific projects may be contested by scientists themselves (Tsuji and Ho 2002), while traditional medicinal methods may be diluted to make them more acceptable to clinicians trained in Western medicine (Frank and Stollberg 2004). Even in the best case scenario, where traditional knowledge is assimilated within Western science, there is a possibility that the former may be decontextualized and thereby rendered ineffective (Walsh and Shapiro 2006).

With economic development, many traditional communities are being uprooted from their ecosystems. Even in ancient civilizations such as China and India, which have had written scripts for several thousand years, the governance of traditional knowledge systems is falling apart in the absence of nurturance from seats of higher learning such as universities. With the disappearance of these repositories of knowledge, the world is likely to lose knowledge that has served communities for millennia without creating environmental imbalance.

It is important, therefore, for universities in emerging economies to recognize their important role to serve as the repositories of traditional knowledge. The discourse on university research commercialization misses this point completely. It is likely that with increasing institutional pressures on universities in emerging economies to become entrepreneurial, they shall be alienated further from the traditional bases of knowledge in their countries.

University Entrepreneurship in Emerging Economies: Is a Synthesis of Roles Possible?

It is undeniable that emerging economies need capabilities to efficiently commercialize scientific discoveries and inventions. Without some form of encouragement for science commercialization, these economies may be kept out of advances in product and technological advancements in cutting-edge industries. It is also beyond doubt that modern technology—medicines, biomedical devices, space technology, mobile telephony, information and communication technology, and so on— are changing societies for the better. They are impacting individual lives by improving health care, agriculture, improving connectivity, access to information, and in a host of other ways. Without some form of entrepreneurship, universities in emerging economies are likely to deprive their indigenous industries from enjoying the fruits of basic scientific research. The question rather is how can a balance be achieved in contexts discussed at length in the preceding? The larger question, therefore, is what role should universities in emerging countries play in their national innovation systems?

There are basically two choices before emerging economies with regard to their higher education policies—should they focus on building the capabilities of their universities to impart state-of-art knowledge and skills, or should they encourage at least a few universities to become entrepreneurial success stories (Hershberg, Nabeshima, and Yusuf 2007). The choice is not easy. The previous arguments suggest that university science has increasingly become intertwined with nations' abilities to compete economically, commercially, politically, and militarily because the link between science and technology has become stronger and more direct over time. Hence the importance of efficiently converting science into innovations increases with each passing decade. It is, therefore, undeniable that nations cannot afford either to fall behind in science, or in the application of science for technological advancement, especially as science and technology are inseparable from development. The trend of universities getting involved in technology development and commercialization then needs to be understood in this context.

For emerging economies, this is an opportunity, since with the right investments in universities and similar science and technology institutions, they may hope to catch-up with developed nations in the foreseeable future. Yet, it is also a challenge. The trends and pressures that are facilitating the commercial applications of science, may also contradict the very reasons that made science relevant to technological development in the first place—namely the rapid pace of technological changes. Science, when seen purely from a utilitarian point of view, is about appropriating rent from scientific discoveries, and hence it is about limiting access to the common pool of knowledge. The advancement of science itself may be compromised when it becomes tied up with such utilitarian considerations. Science, when seen as the quest to discover new knowledge, advances when it is treated as a community resource, which is open to all, and where scientists contribute and grow the common pool of knowledge. In other words, technology commercialization is about closing research advancement, replacing the openness of science (Jain, George, and Maltarich 2009). Therefore, one distinct possibility is that in the long run, commercially oriented science is likely to render incumbents more and more technologically deprived.

While this is a general argument that applies whenever the application of science is encouraged more than science itself, the special context of universities in emerging economies complicates the issue further. Undeniably, teaching continues to be an important function. This is especially true for many of the Asian and African countries with high rates of population growth. Providing high-quality instruction, therefore, is likely to be an important contribution on the part of universities in these countries in the foreseeable future. In fact, while many of these countries have set up, and continue to set up, universities at a rapid rate, the quality of these institutions is often a matter of concern (Altbach 2009). Thus, a primary task should be to enhance the quality of Faculty and innovate on curricula and pedagogy so as to impart knowledge that is relevant to making the young generations capable of enhancing the quality of life in their societies. Without quality human-resource development, the sustainability of cutting-edge science-driven entrepreneurship is open to question.

Quality of human resources, capable of engaging with cutting-edge science is important for two reasons. First, a prerequisite is that the quality of scientific personnel, including Faculty, researchers, and scientists needs to be attended to if science in emerging economies comes up to the standards in developed economies. Academic entrepreneurship without adequate investments and infrastructure to do basic research may lead to suboptimal solutions such as engaging in low-end consulting for technologically deficient entrepreneurial ventures. More importantly, underinvestment in basic science may imply long-term dependence on advanced economies for cutting-edge scientific discoveries and inventions. Second, the quality of industrial manpower needs to go up in order for industry to be capable of absorbing research inputs from the frontiers of science and engineering. One of the crucial inputs to enhancing this absorptive capacity (Cohen and Levinthal 1990) is investments in high-quality education. Thus, either way, developing a sustainable ecosystem for science-based industries requires that teaching and basic research missions cannot be compromised by universities in emerging economies.

Given the normative expectations of global science, it is important that universities in emerging economies do not shy away from undertaking research on subjects that are important to them, but are nevertheless not "prestigious" in terms of impact factors, citation counts, prizes, and awards. It requires courage on the part of universities and encouragement on the part of stakeholders to reorient their research agenda to carry out cutting-edge science on topics that are not at the forefront of attention of global scientific communities. Nevertheless, this is undeniably an important part of these universities that is beyond the interest in commercializing research, because clearly, much of the output of this research may not be commercially viable. In other words, policies to limit support to universities and supplement their income from research commercialization may need to be reconsidered.

As discussed in the preceding, indigenous knowledge passed on through tradition or held by communities form an important but ignored aspect of "science" in many emerging economies. Universities have a role to play in rediscovering, documenting, and building a research and academic tradition to investigate and pass on this knowledge to future generations systematically. They have a role to institutionalize this process and build an ecosystem to make it self-sustaining and prevent the loss of this traditional knowledge. Recognizing that this knowledge belongs to a common human heritage is important. As public institutions, universities are best placed to take up this role. In their absence, it is quite possible, and indeed highly probable, that at least some of this knowledge with potential for immediate commercial application may be appropriated by industry for profit, with copyright claims and restrictions.

Connected to this point, the importance of intellectually rejuvenating the intelligentsia of emerging economies cannot be overestimated. Many of these countries have been under colonial rule, and exposed to alien thought processes and ideologies for centuries. In the process, they are largely cut-off from their own value systems, indigenous epistemologies, and avenues for intellectual inquiry that are independent from globalized Western scientific and philosophical traditions. At the same time, these economies also need Western traditions of rationality and the rationalization of their social architecture. Not all emerging societies are equally adept or welcoming of this change, or have the wherewithal for making the transition.

Therefore, universities in emerging economies need to play difficult balancing roles. They need to recognize that their teaching role extends to developing intellectual capabilities in three areas—developing cadres of highly trained researchers and scientists capable of doing cutting-edge science; producing engineers and industry personnel capable of engaging with this research and seeing its commercial applications; and intellectuals who are simultaneously proud of their tradition and confident of modern science. Second, universities need to appreciate that their research roles are also extended: in addition to developing capabilities to contribute to global science, they must also set the research agenda by looking at issues and problems that are contextually important in their societies, but ignored by mainstream global science. Simultaneously, they are required to rediscover, document, research, apply, and disseminate traditional indigenous knowledge. Finally, with regard to research commercialization, their role definition should include an agenda to connect science and technology to products that are useful and affordable in their societies. As public institutions, they are probably better placed to bring the fruits of academic research to benefit economically weaker sections in emerging economies through low cost innovations.

It is also necessary to think of different mechanisms in which additional university roles in emerging economies can be appropriately balanced with the admittedly important research commercialization role. It is probably important to adhere to the earlier strict role definition of universities, intermediary actors such as public laboratories and R&D of large organizations acting as brokers to translate university science into engineering and technology. It will be important for policy makers and university administrators to formulate policy to encourage extensive and thick networking between these institutions, while encouraging them to remain true to their respective roles. Further, it will also be important to put in place policies to encourage science-based innovations (not necessarily from a commercial angle) that address problems in emerging economies.

The purpose of this essay is limited to bringing to the forefront issues of practical and ethical interest related to academic research commercialization and their relevance to emerging economies. Hence, going into a discussion on alternatives is perhaps beyond its scope. It will be sufficient to conclude by saying that academic research commercialization may have captured the imagination of the global academic community, giving it a kind of institutional legitimacy. Yet, research into its efficacy, impact, and relevance, especially in the context of emerging economies, suggests caution. Therefore, governments, policy makers, and university administrators in emerging economies need to recognize the need for alternative formulations that may be more useful to their societies.

References

Abdrazak, A., and M. Saad. 2007. "The Role of Universities in the Evolution of the Triple Helix Culture of Innovation Network: The Case of Malaysia." *International Journal of Technology Management & Sustainable Development* 6, no. 3, pp. 211–25.

Aikenhead, G. 2002. "Whose Scientific Knowledge? The Colonizer and the Colonized." *Science Education as/for Sociopolitical Action* 210, pp. 151–166.

Altbach, P.G. 2009. "One—Third of the Globe: The Future of Higher Education in China and India." *Prospects* 39, no. 1, pp. 11–31. doi:10.1007/s11125-009-9106-1

Auranen, O., and M. Nieminen. 2010. "University Research Funding and Publication performance—An International Comparison." *Research Policy* 39, no. 6, pp. 822–34. doi:10.1016/j.respol.2010.03.003

Basalla, G. 1967. "The Spread of Western Science." *Science* 156, no. 3775, pp. 611–22.

Basant, R., and P. Chandra. 2007. "Role of Educational and R&D Institutions in City Clusters: An Exploratory Study of Bangalore and Pune Regions in India." *World Development* 35, no. 6, pp. 1037–55. doi:10.1016/j.worlddev.2006.05.010

Basant, R., and P. Mukhopadhyay. 2009. *"An Arrested Virtuous Circle? Higher Education and High—Tech Industries in India."* Indian Institute of Management. www.iimahd.ernet.in/assets/snippets/workingpaperpdf/2009-05-01Basant.pdf

Bolli, T., and F. Somogyi. 2011. "Do Competitively Acquired Funds Induce Universities to Increase Productivity?" *Research Policy* 40, no. 1, pp. 136–47. doi:10.1016/j.respol.2010.10.001

Bramwell, A., and D.A. Wolfe. 2008. "Universities and Regional Economic Development: The Entrepreneurial University of Waterloo." *Research Policy* 37, no. 8, pp. 1175–87. doi:10.1016/j.respol.2008.04.016

Caldera, A., and O. Debande. 2010. "Performance of Spanish Universities in Technology Transfer: An Empirical Analysis." *Research Policy* 39, no. 9, pp. 1160–73. doi:10.1016/j.respol.2010.05.016

Chesbrough, H.W. 2006. *Open Innovation: The New Imperative for Creating and Profiting from Technology.* Boston, MA: Harvard Business School Press.

Cohen, W.M., and D.A. Levinthal. 1990. "Absorptive Capacity: A New Perspective on Learning and Innovation." *Administrative Science Quarterly* 35, no. 1, p. 128. doi:10.2307/2393553

Crespi, G., P. D'Este, R. Fontana, and A. Geuna. 2011. "The Impact of Academic Patenting on University Research and Its Transfer." *Research Policy* 40, no. 1, pp. 55–68. doi:10.1016/j.respol.2010.09.010

Czarnitzki, D., W. Glänzel, and K. Hussinger. 2009. "Heterogeneity of Patenting Activity and Its Implications for Scientific Research." *Research Policy* 38, no. 1, pp. 26–34. doi:10.1016/j.respol.2008.10.001

Datta, S., and M. Saad. 2011. "University and Innovation Systems: The Case of India." *Science and Public Policy* 38, no. 1, pp. 7–17.

Dosi, G. 1982. "Dosi—Technological Paradigms and Technological Trajectories. pdf." *Research Policy* 11, pp. 147–62.

Doutriaux, J. 2003. "University—Industry Linkages and the Development of Knowledge Clusters in Canada." *Local Economy* 18, no. 1, pp. 63–79. doi:10.1080/0269094032000073843

Drori, G.S., J.W. Meyer, F.O. Ramirez, and E. Schofer. 2003. "Science and National Economic Development." In *Science in the Modern World Policy: Institutionalization and Globalization*, eds. G.S. Drori, J.W. Meyer, F.O. Ramirez, and E. Schofer, 221–48. Stanford, CA: Stanford University Press.

Duberley, J., Cohen, L., and Leeson, E. 2007. "Entrepreneurial Academics: Developing Scientific University Settings." *Higher Education Quarterly* 61, no. 4, pp. 479–97.

Etzkowitz, H., and L. Leydesdorff. 2000. "The Dynamics of Innovation: From National Systems and 'Mode 2' to a Triple Helix of University–Industry–Government Relations." *Research Policy* 29, no. 2, pp. 109–23.

Etzkowitz, H., A. Webster, C. Gebhardt, and B.R.C. Terra. 2000. "The Future of the University and the University of the Future: Evolution of Ivory Tower to Entrepreneurial Paradigm." *Research Policy* 29, no. 2, pp. 313–30.

Fleming, L. 2001. "Recombinant Uncertainty in Technological Search." *Management Science* 47, no. 1, pp. 117–32.

Fleming, L., and O. Sorenson. 2004. "Science as a Map in Technological Search." *Strategic Management Journal* 25, no. 89, pp. 909–28. doi:10.1002/smj.384

Frank, R., and G. Stollberg. 2004. "Conceptualizing Hybridization on the Diffusion of Asian Medical Knowledge to Germany." *International Sociology* 19, no. 1, pp. 71–88.

Hendry, C., and J. Brown. 2006. "Organizational Networking in UK Biotechnology Clusters." *British Journal of Management* 17, no. 1, pp. 55–73. doi:10.1111/j.1467-8551.2005.00464.x

Hershberg, E., K. Nabeshima, and S. Yusuf. 2007. "Opening the Ivory Tower to Business: University–Industry Linkages and the Development of Knowledge—Intensive Clusters in Asian Cities." *World Development* 35, no. 6, pp. 931–40. doi:10.1016/j.worlddev.2006.05.006

Huggins, R. 2008. "The Evolution of Knowledge Clusters: Progress and Policy." *Economic Development Quarterly* 22, no. 4, pp. 277–89. doi:10.1177/0891242408323196

Jain, S., G. George, and M. Maltarich. 2009. "Academics or Entrepreneurs? Investigating Role Identity Modification of University Scientists Involved in Commercialization Activity." *Research Policy* 38, no. 6, pp. 922–35. doi:10.1016/j.respol.2009.02.007

Katila, R. 2002. "Katila—New Product Search over Time—Past Ideas in Their Prime.pdf." *Academy of Management Journal* 45, no. 5, pp. 995–1010.

Katila, R., and G. Ahuja. 2002. "Something Old, Something New: A Longitudinal Study of Search Behavior and New Product Introduction." *Academy of Management Journal* 45, no. 6, pp. 1183–94.

Lam, A. 2010. "From 'Ivory Tower Traditionalists' to 'Entrepreneurial Scientists'?: Academic Scientists in Fuzzy University—Industry Boundaries." *Social Studies of Science* 40, no. 2, pp. 307–40. doi:10.1177/0306312709349963

Landry, R., M. Saïhi, N. Amara, and M. Ouimet. 2010. "Evidence on How Academics Manage Their Portfolio of Knowledge Transfer Activities." *Research Policy* 39, no. 10, pp. 1387–403. doi:10.1016/j.respol.2010.08.003

Liefner, I., and D. Schiller. 2008. "Academic Capabilities in Developing Countries—A Conceptual Framework with Empirical Illustrations from Thailand." *Research Policy* 37, no. 2, pp. 276–93. doi:10.1016/j.respol.2007.08.007

Loewenberg, S. 2009. "The Bayh–Dole Act: A Model for Promoting Research Translation?" *Molecular Oncology* 3, no. 2, pp. 91–93. doi:10.1016/j.molonc.2008.12.004

March, J.G. 1991. "Exploration and Exploitation in Organizational Learning." *Organization Science* 2, no. 1, pp. 71–87.

McMillan, G.S., F. Narin, and D.L. Deeds. 2000. "An Analysis of the Critical Role of Public Science in Innovation: The Case of Biotechnology." *Research Policy* 29, no. 1, pp. 1–8.

Miller, C.R., B. Richard, and S. Arora. 2011. "Alternate Signs of Life: The Growth of Biotechnology Industries in Shanghai and Bangalore." *Technological Forecasting and Social Change* 78, no. 4, pp. 565–74. doi:10.1016/j.techfore.2010.11.002

Northrop, F.S.C. 1946. *The Meeting of East and West: An Inquiry Concerning World Understanding*. New York: The Macmillan Company.

Ordorika, I., and B. Pusser. 2007. "La Maxima Casa de Estudios: Univesidad Nacional Autonoma de Mexico as a State—Building University." In *World Class Worldwide: Transforming Research Universities in Asia and Latin America*, eds. P.G. Altbach and J. Balan, 189–215. Baltimore: The John Hopkins University Press.

Owen-Smith, J., and W.W. Powell. 2003. "The Expanding Role of University Patenting in the Life Sciences: Assessing the Importance of Experience and Connectivity." *Research Policy* 32, no. 9, pp. 1695–711. doi:10.1016/S0048-7333(03)00045-3

Ponomariov, B.L., and P.C. Boardman. 2010. "Influencing Scientists' Collaboration and Productivity Patterns Through New Institutions: University Research Centers and Scientific and Technical Human Capital." *Research Policy* 39, no. 5, pp. 613–24. doi:10.1016/j.respol.2010.02.013

Porter, S.R., and R.K. Toutkoushian. 2006. "Institutional Research Productivity and the Connection to Average Student Quality and Overall Reputation." *Economics of Education Review* 25, no. 6, pp. 605–17. doi:10.1016/j.econedurev.2005.06.003

Rauhvargers, A. 2011. *Global University Rankings and Their Impact*. Brussels, Belgium: European University Association. www.eua.be/pubs/global_university_rankings_and_their_impact.pdf

Rivera-Huerta, R., G. Dutrénit, J.M. Ekboir, J.L. Sampedro, and A.O. Vera-Cruz. 2011. "Do Linkages Between Farmers and Academic Researchers Influence Researcher Productivity? The Mexican Case." *Research Policy* 40, no. 7, pp. 932–42. doi:10.1016/j.respol.2011.05.001

Rosenkopf, L., and A. Nerkar. 2001. "Beyond Local Search: Boundary—Spanning, Exploration, and Impact in the Optical Disk Industry." *Strategic Management Journal* 22, no. 4, pp. 287–306.

Russell, B. 1961. *History of Western Philosophy and Its Connections with Political and Social Circumstances from Earliest Times to the Present Day*. London: George Allen & Unwin Limited.

Saisana, M., B. d'Hombres, and A. Saltelli. 2011. "Rickety Numbers: Volatility of University Rankings and Policy Implications." *Research Policy* 40, no. 1, pp. 165–77. doi:10.1016/j.respol.2010.09.003

Schwartzman, S. 2007. "Brazil's Leading University: Original Ideals and Contemporary Goals." In *World Class Worldwide: Transforming Research Universities in Asia and Latin America*, eds. P.G. Altbach and J. Balan, 146–88. Baltimore: The John Hopkins University Press.

Sen, N. 2010. "Performance Based Funding of IITs." *Current Science* 86, no. 3, pp. 369–71.

Shenhav, Y.A., and D.H. Kamens. 1991. "The Costs of Institutional Isomorphism: Science in Non-Western Countries." *Social Studies of Science* 21, no. 3, pp. 527–45.

Sterckx, S. 2004. "Patents and Access to Drugs in Developing Countries: An Ethical Analysis." *Developing World Bioethics* 4, no. 1, pp. 58–75.

Thursby, J.G., and M.C. Thursby. 2011. "Faculty Participation in Licensing: Implications for Research." *Research Policy* 40, no. 1, pp. 20–29. doi:10.1016/j.respol.2010.09.014

Tsuji, L.J.S., and E. Ho. 2002. "Traditional Environmental Knowledge and Western Science: In Search of Common Ground." *Canadian Journal of Native Studies* 22, no. 2, pp. 327–60.

Vang, J., and C. Chaminade. 2006. "Building RIS in Developing Countries: Policy Lessons from Bangalore, India." *Globelic India 2006*. http://wp.circle.lu.se/upload/CIRCLE/workingpapers/200602_Vang_Chaminade.pdf

Vang, J., C. Chaminade, and L. Coenen. 2007. "Learning from the Bangalore Experience: The Role of Universities in an Emerging Regional Innovation System." New Asian Dynamics in Science, Technology and Innovation. http://wp.circle.lu.se/upload/CIRCLE/workingpapers/200704_Jan_et_al.pdf

Walsh, R., and S.L. Shapiro. 2006. "The Meeting of Meditative Disciplines and Western Psychology: A Mutually Enriching Dialogue." *American Psychologist* 61, no. 3, pp. 227–39. doi:10.1037/0003-066X.61.3.227

PART III

Individuals: Behaviors and Perceptions

CHAPTER 5

Whistling Past the Graveyard of Our Own Demise

How Neoliberalism, Corruption, Status Hierarchies, and The Imperium Threaten Higher Education

Duncan Waite

Texas State University

Introduction

We professors are, in Bourdieu's (1991a, 655) terms, the dominated dominants. We are caught in webs of power relations, dynamics and changes. These changes threaten our cherished autonomy and our academic freedom, as they sweep over us and the world at large.

In this chapter, I shall discuss the social, political, economic, and cultural changes affecting the academy, at least as it has historically been constituted. Universities and other institutions of higher education, especially in the United States and in other "developed countries," are or are soon to become bent and broken vestiges of their former selves. Though others will no doubt focus their analyses of higher education on many of the other, critical features of schools, universities, colleges, and institutes, my analysis here will deal particularly with the themes of corruption, our organizational forms, and their inherent hierarchies, neoliberalism, corporativism, and The Imperium.

The Professoriate as We Know It

For Bourdieu (1991a), to be considered an intellectual the "cultural producer" (i.e., professor) must "belong to an autonomous intellectual world (a field), ... independent from religious, political, and economic powers ... [and] must invest the competence and authority ... acquired ... in political action, ... carried out outside the intellectual field proper" (656). One of the main objectives of this political action is "the capture or recapture of the means of guaranteeing or defending autonomy" (665). Though threats to the intellectual's autonomy are numerous and insistent (as we shall see), one which particularly concerned Bourdieu was that of "technocrats and their organic intellectuals" (667). These technocrats and their organic intellectuals monopolize "the public debate to the prejudice of professional politicians and intellectuals. And this often occurs with *the complicity of intellectuals* who ... increasingly refuse the total 'positions' of the total intellectual" (667, emphasis added). Bourdieu suggested inventing forms of organization, a network of intellectuals to "mobilize resistance to encroachments on the autonomy of the intellectual world, and especially to all forms of *cultural imperialism*" (667, emphasis in original). Professors, Bourdieu noted, "while declaring themselves routinely progressive," themselves "contribute in many ways to the perpetuation of the social order, notably, through their strategies of reproduction or their pedagogical strategies, which unconsciously endorse the dominant values, or through their 'esprit de corps' (ranking, discipline, and so on), which has led them ... vigorously to resist any attempt whatsoever to change the contents of education or the forms of pedagogical organization" (668).

The Compromises We Make, or Our Devil's Bargain

What's it going to be: *¿Plata o plomo?* Silver or lead? A bribe or a bullet? Carrot or stick? Resist, compromise, or acquiesce? Resistance is difficult work. Societal forces—group norms and processes, what Nietzsche referred to as the herd instinct, especially, can domesticate us, if we let them, if we offer no resistance.

Lingis (2007) observed how:

> Michel Foucault showed that the procedures of surveillance, control, and discipline of the modern institutional archipelago were invented piecemeal. Once mechanisms of social power are invented, they can be used in diverse ways, one of which is dominance. The cues and watchwords that order these uses also are invented piecemeal. What makes language powerful, a language of power, is not the consistency and coherence of an overall theory of domination—which the social critique in fact does not unearth but constructs—but the peculiar force of fragmentary, discontinuous, order words in local power couplings.

> Collective work and common defense [i.e., resistance] require language that formulates truly the way things are and what has to be done. (86)

So what is to be done? First comes the social critique. How are we then to think of education today, of society at large, and the relation between the two? Why do so few, professors and university administrators among them, seem concerned with emancipation, with freedom, both for themselves and for others? Is it simply a herd mentality? Or is it that we've been compromised, have compromised ourselves and fitted ourselves to the yoke? Bourdieu (1991b) observed how universities and their professors participate in the reproduction of social hierarchies, social inequalities, especially in the functioning and legitimization of the state nobility, who in turn form a part of what I call The Imperium. The Imperium, similar in many ways to what Rancière (2004, 2010) referred to as the police order, oppresses all those who are not among the elite. Indeed, and in many subtle and veiled ways, it may even oppress *them*. But times change, and the nature of that which threatens us has grown both more complex and more immediate than Bourdieu or others were able to foresee.

Hierarchies, the systems that control and direct us, are spread across each and every field and domain in society. The puppeteers—those pulling the strings within each of these hierarchies—are members of an elite group I refer to as The Imperium. Membership in this elite group often is inherited, passed from generation to generation, as societal rank, status and the resultant inequalities are reproduced generation upon generation. Still, there is an element of accident, happenstance, and even chaos in the formation of this elite group. It is not necessarily formed consciously. The Imperium is more of a patchwork of the elites of numerous hierarchies who share common interests—though they may not even know one another or be a part of the other's social network. Terms such as oligarchy and plutocracy—even Jean Tirole's notion of the oligopolies (Zarroli 2014)—fail to capture the complexity of The Imperium, its reach, and the effect(s) it has on us.

Still, as a (social) hierarchy, it *is* socially constructed. That is, *we*—most of anyway—are complicit in its construction and maintenance. To the extent that we do so (contribute to the formation and maintenance of The Imperium, that is) we also contribute to our own oppression, our hastening demise.

Lingis (2007) observed how:

It is "the most superficial and worst part" of ourselves, Nietzsche said, that is formulated in the language of self-consciousness .... Self-consciousness formulated our life for ourselves as needy and dependent. Expressing ourselves in the commonplaces of language is debilitating and capitulating.

When we engage in this language, we end by making our words true. Expressing ourselves as a bundle of needs and cravings, we make ourselves common and dependent, parasitic .... Others do understand and want to hear about our needs and lacks. Our needs are apprehended by them as appeals, expressions of dependence on them, declarations of subservience, invitations to subjugation .... Through our needs and lacks we appeal to the will in the others—the will to power in others, the will to dominate. (94–95)

The herd and our stance toward it may at first seem irrelevant or tangential to a discussion of what is wrong with today's university, the evils both operant within it, and those to which it contributes, to which we all contribute. They are not. Our groups, our communities, our organizations condone, call forth, and enlist us or otherwise make us complicit in institutional dysfunction, misbehavior, malfeasance, and evil (Adams and Balfour 2009; Zimbardo 2007).[1]

Hierarchies, Organizations and Corruption

Consider this brief example illustrating just a few of the problems within a representative U.S. organization: the U.S. Department of Veterans Affairs. This organization came under fire recently for the way its personnel callously manipulated military veterans' medical appointments to game the government's accountability system. Administrators and operatives lied and cheated, and put veterans at risk, in order that they might avoid sanctions, score higher on the government accountability rankings, and win bigger cash bonuses for themselves. (Note the similarity to so-called cheating scandals in U.S. schools, whether in Atlanta, El Paso, or elsewhere.)

One aspect of the deep-seated systemic problems in the U.S. Department of Veterans Affairs (Daly 2014), recently revealed, involved the retaliation by supervisors and other administrators against whistle-blowers—those who call attention to the problems or illegalities in an organization. Such retaliation is itself against the law. But documents show that at least one person who raised concerns was threatened with suspension "for sending e-mails 'that contained disrespectful and inappropriate statements about your service chief'" (A2). Such level-conscious presumption of the rights or entitlements by the supervisor or administrator and the obligations imposed upon the other—the subordinate or lower-level employee, is an example of *lèse majesté*—offending the dignity of a sovereign; an offense which in many places yet today is punishable by imprisonment or death.[2] The presumption that subordinates or those of a

---

[1] The herd is one model, a tool to think with about human behavior, especially group and organizational behavior; another is the hive, which may be more appropriately-suited for complex, more postmodern "organizations," groups, networks and affiliations (see Waite 2010).

[2] Lest you think that *lèse majesté* is simply some quaint anachronism from a bygone age, today's *New York Times* (November 5, 2014, A6) reported that a university student in Thailand was sentenced to two-and-a-half years in prison for a posting on Facebook that Thai authorities felt insulted the Thai king.

"lower class" owe deference to a "superior" simply because of their status or rank is but one characteristic of what I call imperial hubris (Waite 2014)—something which, to some degree, affects or infects leaders in all types of organizations worldwide. Imperial hubris is antithetical to egalitarianism, a critical component of democracy and social justice.

Systems and Other Dynamics

Some of the problems associated with higher education—whether college, university, or institute—are due to the systems, structures, policies, and processes of these institutions. (Here we are using Habermas' notion of system, as apart from life world [Bohman and Rheg 2014].) Some of these systems are external to the institution, but influence it. Other problems are caused or aggravated by systems within the university or college. Still other problems and the concomitant dark sides of universities result from more personal or interpersonal and immediate dynamics. Some grow out of the personalities and psychoses of the people involved and their inter-relationships or interactions (Adams and Balfour 2009; Kets de Vries 2011; Lipman-Blumen 2005).

Then, of course, there are those problems or dark sides occasioned by the interplay of the global and the local. These various systems and structures, whether global or local, may be at the root of dysfunctional local adaptations or responses to the demands of said systems, always keeping in mind that it is the people who inhabit our institutions who are ultimately responsible.[3]

Freedom Versus Security, Courage Versus Cowardice

We are left wondering why people turn away from freedom. How is it that people in such diverse contexts as Eastern Ukraine and Russia, Hong Kong, Syria, Egypt, Iraq, and various enclaves in the United States and elsewhere give themselves over to reactionary and authoritarian leaders?

---

[3] Elsewhere (Waite 2010, 2011), I have discussed some of these organizational and systemic impediments to educational change, school improvement and personal actualization, emancipation, and liberation more generally.

Put another way, how is that people are willing to surrender their freedom for some modicum of security or simply the promise of it?[4] To bring the point home: Why do (some) university professors acquiesce in the face of threats to our freedom and autonomy?

Mencken ([1926] 2009), the iconoclastic journalist cum public intellectual, touched upon this in his discussion of security, freedom, and courage. Ever the cynic, Mencken noted how:

> All the revolutions in history have been started by hungry city mobs ... I can think of no city revolution that actually had liberty for its object, in any rational sense ... When the city mob fights it is not for liberty, but for ham and cabbage. When it wins, its first act is to destroy every form of freedom that is not directed wholly to that end. And its second is to butcher all professional libertarians. (53)

Ever a product of his day, though also apart from it (and heavily influenced by the writings of Friedrich Nietzsche, especially his notions of the herd and the superman), Mencken wrote derogatorily of the inferior man. "The fact is that liberty," he wrote:

> In any true sense is a concept that lies quite beyond the reach of the inferior man's mind. He can imagine, even esteem, ... certain false forms of liberty—for example the right to choose between two political mountebanks ... but the reality [of true liberty] is incomprehensible to him. And no wonder, for genuine liberty demands of its votaries a quality he lacks completely, and that is courage. The man who loves it must be willing to fight for it; blood, said [Thomas] Jefferson, is its natural manure. More, he must be able to *endure* it—an even more arduous business. Liberty means self-reliance, it means resolution, it means enterprise, it

---

[4] Benjamin Franklin, that great American revolutionary, printer, scientist, statesman, and kite enthusiast felt that "those who would give up essential liberty, to purchase a little temporary safety, deserve neither liberty nor safety" (http://en.wikiquote.org/wiki/Talk:List_of_misquotations).

means the capacity for doing without. The free man is one who has won a small and precarious territory from the great mob …, and is prepared to defend it and make it support him. All around him are enemies, and where he stands there is no friend. He can hope for little help from other men of his own kind, for they have battles of their own to fight. (53–54, emphasis in original)

Lipman-Blumen (2005) discussed this self-same issue, the tensions between freedom and security. She explained the phenomenon in psychological terms, describing how it is that we transfer our dependency on our parents to leaders, some of whom are autocratic or toxic or both:

When our freedom unnerves us, we tend to gravitate toward any leader who will make us feel safe, protected and good about ourselves. Toxic leaders, who promise security and assure us that we are special or "chosen," become particularly powerful magnets for our unmoored egos. We may find them so compelling that we willingly relinquish some, if not all, of our newly found freedom. (35)

When independence produces feelings of loneliness in an individual, a "sense of isolation and smallness" (35), people may join groups to

huddle in one another's warmth. There, we can also find comfort via submission to someone we perceive as stronger than ourselves, a powerful, broad-shouldered leader.

Another alternative … is to pledge allegiance to something—an organization, a religion, a political ideology, a social movement, or the state. Those, too, can offer safety and comfort in times of fear and loneliness. (35)

This group or community attachment is what Nietzsche (1967) referred to as the herd instinct: "one would rather obey an existing law than create a law oneself—better to submit than to react" (159).

Fear may cause someone to capitulate, to surrender his freedom, or liberty in exchange for the security of the herd. A lack of ontological security (Giddens 1990) may precipitate such fear. Cowardice or complicity or both in groups, at the individual and collective levels, allows toxic leaders (Lipman-Blumen 2005) to emerge and flourish. Cowardice is one of a medley of dispositions that cause middle managers, administrators, or leaders to go along with the unethical, corrupt (and corrupting), even vile and evil schemes of higher-ups. Deference to authority (Lipman-Blumen 2005; Milgram 1974) is another such disposition that props up authoritarian, oppressive regimes—in the board room or the university president's office. Avarice and self-interest are others.

Of cowardice, Lingis (2007) noted how it "husbands our forces, holds back, intensifying the sense of our needs and wants, produces an inward sense of importance and misery. Every misery we feel over ourselves is the result of some cowardice" (43).

Courage, on the other hand, is, according to Aristotle, the first of all virtues (Lingis 1994):

> It is not simply the first on the list of equivalent virtues; it is the transcendental virtue, the condition for the possibility of all the virtues. For no one can be truthful, or magnanimous, or a friend, or even congenial in conversation, without courage. And every courage is an act done in risk: of one's reputation, of one's job, of one's possessions, of one's life. (107–108)

Maintaining The Imperium

At the time that some of the world's great early universities came into being, there were two major, though largely tacit, understandings of what universities were, and by implication, what the work of those associated with them entailed. This distinction has epistemological implications. Briefly, universities and their faculty were considered to be either largely concerned with discovering new knowledge or transmitting what was already known (Burke 2000). Burke informs us that during the founding of the early great universities (i.e., from the later Middle Ages through the founding of the university in Glasgow in 1451), "it was assumed rather than argued that universities ought to concentrate on transmitting knowledge as opposed to discovering (or creating) it" (33). What is more, those involved vested epistemological authority in "the great scholars and philosophers of the past," as their "opinions and interpretations … could not be equaled or refuted by posterity, so that the task of the teacher was to expound the views of authorities" (33).

Whatever else they are, or aspire to be, universities are corporations. This shouldn't surprise us. Indeed, Bourdieu (1991a) observed how even "families are *corporate bodies*" (643, emphasis in original). As Burke (2000) pointed out, "these [early] universities were corporations. They had legal privileges, including independence and monopoly of higher education in their region, and they recognized one another's degrees" (33).

Burke (2000) also recalled Francis Bacon's pithy assessment of universities and their faculty as "merchants of light" (quoted in Burke, 46). This epithet expresses early universities' association with mercantile exchanges—such as "'India House' in Lisbon (A Casa da India). In Seville, the 'House of Trade' (La Casa de Contratación), founded in 1503" (36). Bacon's characterization of faculty as merchants of light reminds us of the dualisms (and more) inherent in academies, historically, and in universities and other centers of knowledge and learning. These historical dynamisms are still felt in today's university—as seen, for example, in the difference between the itinerant scholar and the more sedentary one; or in the rush to be more entrepreneurial. Bacon's characterization calls to mind the often conflicting epistemologies circulating within academies (and, by extension, the general public) privileging the creation of new knowledge and the propagation of authoritative, existent knowledge. Bacon's phrase evokes the itinerant scholar, the commercial or economic side of knowledge and its creation, and the entrepreneurial nature of the university. Recognition of these aspects of the university acknowledges its corporatization and its role in the commodification of knowledge.

Viewing universities as corporations, in whole or in part, helps us understand the mission of the university, its goals, motives, strategies, processes and policies, its historical antecedents, and its possibilities. Recognizing that universities are also corporations allows us to demythologize the university, to disabuse us of our romantic notions about them. These myths and romantic images of universities—as ivy-covered halls of learning, for instance—have shielded and protected universities, allowing them to, on the whole, remain relatively unchanged and unchallenged.

These idealized visions of universities permit many of us to ignore or avoid the political aspect, while all the time imagining ourselves working in the pure pursuit of objective, neutral knowledge, where knowledge is equated with The Good. These idealized or mythologized versions of universities and the work of the professorate permit many of us to be in denial of the fact that we are, again in Bourdieu's (1991a) terms, dominated dominants, that we are both oppressed and oppressor. We, many of us, also refuse to acknowledge that we enable and are otherwise complicit in the very systems, policies, bureaus, offices, and departments which oppress us. We are complicit in legitimizing the state nobility (Bourdieu 1991b).

When we look at universities as corporations, we begin to ask questions about such things as profit (not only profit, but productivity is implicated here as well). For example, in doing so, we might ask to what extent does profit-seeking drive curricular and pedagogical decisions? We might ask what academic freedom means within a corporation?

Arendt ([1958] 1998) developed her ideas on freedom and work using Aristotle's differentiation between freedom and slavery as a starting point. She recalled how:

> Aristotle distinguished three ways of life (*bioi*) which men might choose in freedom, that is, in full independence of the necessities of life and the relationships they originated. This prerequisite of freedom ruled out all ways of life chiefly devoted to keeping one's self alive—not only labor, which was the way of life of the slave, who was coerced by the necessity to stay alive and by the rule of his master, but also the working life of the craftsman and the acquisitive life of the merchant. In short, it excluded everybody who involuntarily or voluntarily, for his whole life or temporarily, had lost the free disposition of his movements and activities. (12)

In the attendant footnote, Arendt elaborated how:

> Westermann ... holds that the "statement of Aristotle ... [ellipsis in the original] that craftsmen live in a condition of limited slavery meant that the artisan, when he made a work contract, disposed

of two of the four elements of his free status [viz., of freedom of economic activity and right of unrestricted movement], but by his own volition and for a temporary period"; ... Westermann shows that freedom was then understood to consist of "status, personal inviolability, freedom of economic activity, right of unrestricted movement," and slavery consequently "was the lack of these four attributes." [Aristotle] ... mentions ... "the life of money-making" and rejects it because it too is "undertaken under compulsion." (fn. 4, 12–13)

Thinking of universities as corporations allows us to theorizing them differently. Of course, we must resist essentializing the university, refusing to think of it as only a corporation. And, of course, there are many different types of corporations, just as there are many different kinds of universities. The picture becomes even more complicated when we admit that, as complex modern organizations, different aspects of different universities may be more or less corporativist, in all the senses of the term (e.g., colonized by outside corporate interests, or with units organized and functioning corporativistically).

Corporativism (Waite 2014) is distinct from corporatism in that, to my mind, corporatism is simply a sociological observation having to do with the presence of corporations and their interests. For example, we might note how Coca-Cola sponsors the Olympics or how that corporation and its monies (and influence) are present in high school athletics. We might note how the Coca-Cola logo is on not just billboards, but on polo shirts and more and wonder how and why people affiliate with a brand. What role does the corporation and its brand play in one's identity and identity formation? We might note, in passing, how the Coca-Cola company operates in more countries than the United Nations has members.[5] It is not surprising, then, that Coca-Cola is one of the most recognizable brands worldwide (having only recently been supplanted from the top spot in international recognizablity by Apple and Google).

---

[5] According to its own website, the Coca-Cola company operates in over 200 countries (http://www.coca-colacompany.com/history/the-chronicle-of-coca-cola-a-global-business).

Coca-Cola is also one of the most valuable brands; the brand alone being worth approximately $79 billion (Elliot 2013). Universities, too, have their brands, and many, if not most, of these brands have been reworked recently (i.e., universities and their images have been rebranded) to fit with more modern sensibilities (Waite 2011). But brands, as mental images, can be constraining, even oppressive or hegemonic, when individuals—self and others—use the brand as the ideal or the standard against which others are judged. Using brands in this way, as normative ideals, can oppress, especially, employees such as professors and others, when administrators and others invoke the brand, its image(s), and standards to discipline and norm. The social constructs of status and rank and the image or perceptions of a university in the public mind are major factors in its brand(ing) and, as such, can be tools for the oppression of those who work there, just as they are (or can be) tools of oppression for those on whom the university works. Universities are imperialistic in this sense, and, in other ways aid the imperialism of their host country.

The Corporate: Corporatism Versus Corporativism

Corporativism, as I've come to think of it (Waite 2014), is the *ontological* manifestation of the corporate—that is, the corporate form, corporate ways of thinking and organizing become hegemonic at a deep, taken-for-granted level. In the process, the corporate is internalized and normalized. It is hegemonic in that it permits consideration of no alternative; in fact, under conditions of corporativism, the corporate model is so totalizing as to permit no awareness or consideration of other forms, other ways of organizing ourselves, and other ways of being in association: the corporation and corporate form (and ways of thinking) are all there is, all there is thought to be. This is evidenced in our language, as when superintendents of schools are referred to (and refer to themselves) as CEOs. The depth and breadth of this colonization of our culture and our language by the corporate is evident in other arenas besides schools, widespread cultural fields such as sports. For example, a recent *New York Times*' article, "On Sidelines, Researchers See C.E.O.s" (Eder 2014), discussed how head coaches of (American) football teams are best thought of as business, corporate leaders. The fact that the corporate has colonized the field of

Figure 5.1 The corporate office of the Education Management Corporation, Pittsburgh, Pennsylvania, United States

Source: Own elaboration.

even *public* education is illustrated by, for example, companies such as the Education Management Corporation (Figure 5.1) and for-profit charter school management companies (in the United States)—such as K-12— the largest online charter school provider in the United States (Saul 2011). The field of higher education has been colonized by the corporate as well.

Universities evolved, as Burke (2000) noted, from trade houses, mercantile exchanges, and other types of centers. This evolution saw a greater exactitude and precision, a fine-tuning of the policies and procedures for managing and administering these ever-growing institutions. Mercantile exchanges and houses of trade were part of the genetic material that went into the creation of universities, as were coffee houses, publishing houses, libraries, and more. Universities aided imperialist nations in their efforts to colonize other territories—not just geographically and physically, but ideationally as well. That is, these "merchants of light" traded in knowledge, sought it out through emissaries and informants. These exchanges were always two-way—universities and their emissaries took information to the colonized people and these "merchants of light" took indigenous knowledge, sanitized and domesticated it, and repackaged the "discoveries" for popular consumption, both by the lay public and by the intelligentsia. Though information and knowledge flow was bidirectional, the exchange heavily favored the imperialistic country's university.

Just as the nature of the corporation continues to evolve, to change, so too does the corporate nature of the university. In the United States, owing to continually decreasing state financial support, universities look for other sources of revenue. As the capitalist and corporatist model is premised on continual growth (i.e., profit), university administrators and other "leaders" seek out new areas to colonize and to "monetize." Recently, Internet-based instruction has seemed attractive, for, as Shirky (2008) and others (e.g., Saul 2011) point out, the production costs or efficiencies of the Internet—which effectively reduces production costs to near zero—make it a very seductive delivery vehicle for goods and services; in this case, the delivery of curriculum packages. This helps explain the explosion of web-based "universities," programs, and other offerings in the education field (e.g., Western Governors' University, University of Phoenix, Kaplan and others [Waite, Rodríguez, and Wadende 2015]), with the attendant fraud, and fraudulent self-appointed educational reformers seeking to break up historically established monopolies of power, influence and territory, and to establish for themselves a foothold in such extremely lucrative markets.

But just as the "discovery" and opening up of "new" territories in the colonial-imperialist period attracted adventurers, profiteers, outlaws, and swindlers, so too has the rapid growth of the Internet and web-based delivery of so-called educational services (Waite 2014; Waite, Rodríguez, and Wadende 2015). In far too many cases, this unmitigated and wholesale use of the Internet by for-profit educational management companies—at all levels of educational "provision" (i.e., primary through tertiary, including institutes and certificate programs)—makes serfs of us all (Carr 2011; de Rosa 2011), especially us teachers and professors (Waite 2014). Such a degradation in the nature of faculty work is wrought by a radical neoliberalism where faculty work the land owned by someone else, where we have no control over our working conditions, and where wages fall to near subsistence levels, especially for part-time and adjunct faculty. Recall Arendt's ([1958] 1998) discussion of slave-hood mentioned previously.

Managerialism Ascendant

In a Foucaultian sense, management and administration have continued to perfect their control over teachers and teaching. Frederick Taylor and his disciples, with their scientific management fervor, contributed might-ily to the managerial control over workers (Saval 2014), including teach-ers and faculty. Taylor and other so-called scientific management experts were highly influential in affecting: how managers perceived themselves and their mission; the practices imposed on the worker (the stopwatch became a loathed and ubiquitous sign of Taylorist managers); and even how the general public viewed not only management and administration, but the very nature of work itself (Saval 2014).

Early in the history of administration and management, administra-tors (so-called office boys) sought to distinguish themselves from other workers, mainly those we think of today as "manual laborers" (Saval 2014). In the early days of factories and workshops, everyone worked together in the same locale—the owner, the "laborer," and the office boy (Saval 2014).[6] Office boys became managers and physically removed themselves from the other workers in an effort to gain more prestige for themselves and their work, adding to the bureaucratic hierarchy of the workplace.

Early sociologists recognized that bureaucracies tend toward self-preservation (Weber 1958). This contributes to the conservative nature of institutions, such as colleges and universities, manifested in risk aversion and in other conservatisms. Our concern here is that these institutions, our employing institutions, are becoming even more conservative and repressive. Said another way, how is anyone able to, in the first case, sur-vive and thrive in an increasingly corporativist university? How does this

---

[6] Not to offend, but use of the masculine noun here is intentional, as it was marked at the time (Saval 2014) and, as we shall see, had and still has substan-tial social implications and far-reaching consequences such as in gender roles in public and private life, the division of labor, compensation, and even the nature of our educational institutions, including universities, institutes, and colleges.

increasing conservatism, abetted by corporativism, affect our work, our lives? What about the students we serve? How are we to encourage their emancipation, or even their self-actualization, in increasingly corporativist institutions?

Universities tend to be conservative (Burke 2000) and have been for most of their history. Part of the reason for this was that, according to Burke:

> In medieval Europe university teachers were almost all clerics. The relatively new institution of the university, which developed in the 12th century, was embedded in a much older institution, the Church. No wonder that it is common to describe the medieval Church as having exercised a monopoly of knowledge. (34)[7]

This conservatizing inclination of organizations and institutions, bureaucracies, and corporations took hold in universities. Burke commented how:

> The universities may have continued to perform their traditional function of teaching effectively, but they were not, generally speaking, the locales in which new ideas developed. They suffered from ... "institutional inertia," maintaining their corporate traditions at the price of isolation from new trends. (48)

What is more, "the creative, marginal and informal groups of one period regularly turn into the formal, mainstream and conservative organizations of the next generation or the next-but-one. This is not to say that the reform or renewal of traditional organizations is impossible" (49).

---

[7] Burke acknowledged the plurality of knowledges then and now. Though early universities were staffed by clergy (one reason why today's professors and faculty are thought of as clerisy) and solidly wedded to the Church, there were other voices, others with different knowledge, some of whom were the "heretics, who multiplied at about the same time ... 'textual communities' held together by their discussions of ideas written down in books." (34)

The complex countenance of the university reflects the paradoxical nature of its authority, autonomy, power, and power relations. That is, universities' monopoly on knowledge (or better said, certain kinds of knowledge) earn it power, or a certain kind of power, especially sanctioning and gatekeeping privileges over certain ranks of certain professions or fields.

Universities are corporations, or seen another way, they have corporate facets and dimensions. This presents us with several problems, especially for those of us who still believe in the emancipatory potential of education. The corporate university (or the corporativization of certain aspects of the university) makes our work all the more difficult. It may be that this corporativization of the university will be the death of the professoriate as we know it.

Besides the faculty, what about the other players? For instance: What role do university and college administrators play in the corporativization of the university and in the deterioration of the faculty role and why? How are administrators affected by these trends? How are students?

Administrators' Role Enactment: Some Theories About Their Motivation(s)

Three of the likely motivations administrators have for the stance they take toward faculty have negative effects for us as knowledge workers: Administrators may enact their role unconsciously and unreflectively; or they may seek to control and manage faculty; or they may be disinterested, distanced and aloof, utterly unconcerned, and unconnected with faculty and their interests.[8] In the first of these scenarios, administrators, managers, and policy makers are not perceived to be actively malicious evil agents, not consciously setting out to disenfranchise university workers—the faculty, staff, support staff, student workers, nonacademic personnel

---

[8] A fourth motivation, the most felicitous as far as faculty are concerned, is one wherein administrators work to sincerely advance faculty and their interests. This stance is not unproblematic, but we shall not deal with it here, given our limited space and the focus of this volume on the dark sides of higher education.

such as janitors, painters, printers, plumbers, electricians, landscapers, computer programmers and instructional technologists, and more.

The second possible motivation in the preceding would set administrators against faculty and their interests, as they seek to manage and control them. In the worst case, professors and other so-called "knowledge workers" toil in serf-like conditions under dominions that do not operate with their best interests at heart, to say the least. That is, such corporate universities—as organizations, institutions, or cultures—either work contrary to the faculty's individual and collective goals and ideals or create, reproduce, or condone toxic work environments (Lipman-Blumen 2005), which can be lethal, spiritually and physically.

The third possibility, aloofness, though seemingly innocuous, is actually a much more injurious disposition. Those administrators who are aloof become disconnected, uninterested in the work and work lives of faculty so that they are no longer in relationship with them.

Aloofness, according to Arendt (1950), is insidious because:

Aloofness … was a more dangerous form of governing than despotism and arbitrariness [as with the bureaucrat] because it did not even tolerate that last link between the despot and his subjects which is formed by bribery and gifts. The very integrity of the British administrators made the despotic government more inhuman and inaccessible … Integrity and aloofness were symbols of an absolute division of interests to the point where they are not even any longer permitted to conflict. In comparison, exploitation, oppression, or corruption look like safeguards of human dignity, because exploiter and exploited, oppressor and oppressed, corrupter and corrupted live in the same world, still share the same goals, fight each other for the possession of the same things; and it is this *tertium comparationis* [point of comparison, commonality] which aloofness destroyed. Worst of all was the fact that the aloof administrator was hardly aware that he had invented a new form of government but actually believed that his attitude was conditioned by "the forcible contact with a people living on a lower plane." So, instead of believing in his individual superiority with some degree of essentially human vanity, he felt that he belonged to "a nation which had reached a comparatively high plane of civilization" and therefore held his position by right of birth, regardless of personal achievements. (309–10, emphasis in original)

Arendt discussed aloofness as an imperialist characteristic. Borrowing from Arendt, I consider aloofness as one of the personal or political aspects of imperial hubris; where imperial hubris is the arrogance of those who assume privileges based on positions of power, rank, or status (Waite 2014)—in this case, the privilege of being detached. Imperial hubris is common to administrators.

The Work of Administrators Versus the Work of Teachers, Supervisors, and Coaches

At the risk of essentializing the qualities, characteristics, and work roles or tasks of administrators, and most certainly not wishing to minimize the (good) work they do, I'd distinguish (as they do) the work of administrators from that of teaching faculty and, in U.S. public schools (K-12), that of teachers, instructional supervisors, and instructional coaches. One place to begin the discussion of the distinctions between administrators and teachers (together with instructional supervisors) is with the historical antecedents or roots of the differences.

Hazony (2012) saw the farmer as the precursor to the administrator. According to Hazony's reading of the Hebrew Scriptures, Cain was the first farmer. His brother, Abel, was a shepherd: "In the History, the shepherd and the farmer are taken as representing contrasting ways of life, and two different kinds of ethics, which come into sharp conflict time and again" (104).

The farmer, according to Hazony (2012), submits to the decrees of the Gods (and God-kings), exhibits pious sacrifice and self-sacrifice, and honors the customs of past generations. The virtues of "obedience, piety, stability, productivity … belong principally to the farmer" (139). The farmer built settlements, a certain type of civilization and the nation state. The farmer was the backbone of the state. And:

in the ethics of the ancient Near East, all action was ultimately directed toward the maintenance of the state since all goodness was seen as flowing from it. Indeed, whatever served to maintain the closed circle of farmer, tax collector, king, soldier, and priest was on its face for the good. (129)

For Hazony (2012), shepherds and farmers complement one another: The farmer builds great cities and maintains the social order, the shepherd troubles that order through innovation, creativity, and dissent. Today, the inheritors of the farmer's legacy have gained control of our schools, their mission, and objectives. This is especially true in higher education in the United States, where administrators and their staff were on track to constitute more than 50 percent of all higher education personnel by 2014 (Greene, Kisida, and Mills 2010; Lewin 2009; Waite and Waite 2010).

This state of affairs is the result of increased managerialization: the rise of the manager and his or her systems, ontology or way of seeing the world (i.e., seeing issues as "manageable").

This occurs within and across numerous domains or fields. Business and industry, indeed the world of work more generally, have come to be dominated by the bookkeeper, and the manager or administrator and the CEO, in turn; but larger domains with global reach (and here I'm thinking of the Church and the state, not just business) have come under the control of the administrator, the farmer. For the Church, it's the clergy or cleric, and their conquest (erasure) of the mystic; for the state, it's the bureaucrat. In universities, not only administrators but also the clerisies (that is, us) do some of this same work.

The managerialization of the university is not that much different from the change which occurred in business in the late 19th and early 20th centuries, when the workforce in offices mushroomed and "the work environment reflected a change in the work itself. Administration and bureaucracy had taken over the world of business" (Saval 2014, 34). Managers have bent schooling to serve statist ends, with the state itself having been corrupted and used by business and market interests, in part, through promotion and acceptance of neoliberal ideologies and their attendant processes and policies. The farmer or administrator props up and otherwise supports what I have come to think of as The Imperium. This is occurring globally.

The Imperium is an amalgamation of the elites in any given society, globally, and the systems they rule over. This is not to say that this has come about consciously. It evolved through what Nietzsche (1967) termed the will to power, where "leaders" emerge in different fields (Bourdieu 1991a), inclusive of their subfields (e.g., industry and manufacturing, the media, the military, telecommunications, knowledge work, art, and popular culture, etc.). As an example, Jean Tirole's work, for which he was awarded the 2014 Nobel Prize in economics, looks at, among other things, oligopolies—"markets that are controlled by a handful of powerful, interdependent companies" (Zarroli 2014, para. 1). Each of these different companies is headed by a "leader" or power elite—all members of The Imperium. The academy is such a subfield, with its status hierarchies, its sovereign states and monopolies of knowledge and power (Burke 2000).

And though universities on the whole are integral parts of The Imperium, like any organization, institution, or other socially constituted entity, there are dominant discourses that course through them, and counterdiscourses. The dominant discourses are the forces of the *status quo*, what Rancière (2004, 2010) referred to as the police and the police order. There are those outside that order who, through politics, seek to subvert that order.

The Shepherd

In Hazony's (2012) philosophical exegesis of the Hebrew Scriptures, the shepherd, being a nomad, is outside the system. (And recall, as an allegory, that Cain, the farmer, killed Abel, the shepherd.) The shepherd:

> Is *outside* the political state and free of any prior commitment to it. From this shepherd's perspective, ethics cannot begin with the state … Ethics must therefore begin with a view of the human being … as being independent of the state … If the state can play a role in assisting the individual to fulfill his responsibilities and

obligations, which are prior to the state and entirely independent of it, then the machinery of the state and its laws can be seen as having a purpose and a reason to exist. But when the state cannot or does not serve this end, the state and its laws cease to have a claim on the individual. So far as he is concerned, they no longer have any reason to exist at all. (133, emphasis in original)

The shepherd resists:

The creeping advance of justified fears and unjustified commitments to human beings and their institutions—which together work to deprive the individual of his freedom to discern what is right and to act in its name. A vigilant maintenance of one's ability to resist these justified fears and unjustified commitments is thus basic to the ethics of the shepherd. (135)

Hazony noted how the shepherd's ethics evolved to include "generosity and bravery in assisting those in distress; avoidance of needlessly harming others; insistence on establishing and observing property boundaries and marital boundaries; piety; loyalty; a willingness to admit errors in judgment; and so on" (134). The ethics of the shepherd, as outsider, are more likely to be found within the teacher and the professor than in the administrator or manager—though certainly not in all faculty.

Many faculty have given themselves over to The Imperium as its managers, administrators, purveyors, or enablers. Some faculty have surrendered themselves, towing the line and working to discipline, normalize other faculty and otherwise keep them in check, domesticating them, policing the police order.

Many take positions at university and readily accept their place in its social/power/dominance hierarchies, hierarchies which make up and contribute to The Imperium. These positions come with their perquisites and privileges. Some take up their positions and attendant role expectations more reluctantly. Some are more aggressive in using their positions to their own benefit. These are the corrupt and the corruptors (Waite and Allen 2003).

Enemies

Corrupt administrators know how to work the system. School and university technocrats and administrators who game accountability systems for personal financial gain or who otherwise take advantage of children (or students) and the trust of parents and the general public are akin to the corrupt bureaucrats who impeded Afghanistan's movement toward a society based on the rule of law. Such societies—those that practice a rule of law, where there is transparency and accountability, and where bureaucrats do not exercise unlimited discretion—are less prone to corruption. Corruption is, as an Indian Supreme Court judge recently ruled, a violation of human rights (Barry 2014) and an evil, venal, malignant process that is emblematic of the worst of human nature and of our organizational forms and their constitutive features. The negative aspects of the common, the communal, or the herd—the herd instinct, tribalism, identity and affiliation, the primal craving for safety and security and the will to power—all corrupt organizations and groups, repressing all but the elite, who are the beneficiaries of corrupt systems. These are our enemies. General Abdul Jamil, who headed the police crime branch in Kabul, referred to these corrupt technocrats and bureaucrats as "the snake in the sleeve" (Watson 2005, A20): "These are the most dangerous enemies," said Jamil, "because they look like friends. (…) But in reality they are our enemies, and these are the people who work alongside us in the government." These are the dangers in our midst. The dysfunctional, repressive systems, and the technocrats or bureaucrats who perpetuate and benefit from such systems are our enemies. Toward them we should be agential and transgressive, not passive and acquiescent. Lingis (2007) observed how:

> There are times when we have to speak up, with our own voice. There are dangers to forestall. There are people we have to avoid lest they poison our lives with their authority or their cynicism. There are people we have to drive off or strike down. (116)

We must beware the herd's tendency to attach itself to such corrupt bureaucrats and to orient to them as "leaders." We must be aware of our own complicity in this.

As professors, as privileged public intellectuals, as Bourdieu's (1991a) dominated dominants, we must act, and act before it is too late to do so. Honor, professionalism, and our ability to do good work are at stake. For, as Lingis (2007) remarked:

> Conflict between betraying our sense of honor as an artist, a healer, or an educator and dishonoring the institution is an eventuality inherent in every institution, as conflict between betraying our sense of honor as a parent or a caretaker of part of the land and work and dishonoring the community is a possibility in every community.

> The established discourse of a collective can accord an attributed honor to someone who occupies a position in the collective without fulfilling or being able to fulfill his or her tasks. He or she can use the attributed honor to attain venal or cynical ends. The honor attributed to the position and established in discourse makes corruption possible. (123–124)

The ethics of the shepherd, the outsider, serve as a counterbalance to the excesses of autocratic, soul-stealing organizations. The collective, the herd in Nietzsche's terms, seduces us, entices us to abandon the I (Lingis 2007) in favor of the we. The shepherd in us, in each of us, and the shepherds among us, surrender to the herd. The balance, the dynamic, between our twin urges—toward security (characteristic of the farmer), on the one hand, and that of freedom (the ethics of the shepherd[9]), on the other, tilts in favor of security.

Within clans, tribes, and our many other organizational forms (Waite 2010), the will to power drives some to become administrators, giving themselves over to protecting the state and the state's interests. This involves domesticating the shepherd, the nomad and the free spirit and bringing creative teachers and free thinkers into line. This is the police order Rancière (2004, 2010) wrote of, that which establishes, reinforces

---

[9] The freedom impulse is what Bourdieu (1991a) labeled the "intent toward autonomy" (659).

and monitors the boundaries of the sensible and its distribution. According to Rancière, we are all a part of that order. Keep in mind, though, that there are better and worse police and police orders.

The police and policing are simply the "administration or 'management' of society … and in particular … what is presupposed in all types of administration: '*the symbolic constitution of the social*'" (Rancière 1998, as cited in Simons and Masschelein 2010, 591, emphasis added). Simons and Masschelein noted how:

> The domain/object of administration does not exist as such, and it is not a natural, pre-existing domain waiting for managerial concern. The domain or object of administration is symbolically constituted although … administration acts "as if" it is a natural or given domain (out there) … For the police there is no outside … [for] what is not "part" of the division of parts and what is not identifiable (as different from other identities) is assumed not to exist … The administration … presents itself as the actualisation of what is the common of a community and … transforms the rules for managing into the so-called natural rules of society. (592)

This failure to recognize, this ignoring of that which is outside, is an act of ignorance (Smithson 1989, 2008). As such, it is similar to the aloofness of the aforementioned imperialist (Arendt [1958] 1998). The worst type of leader is what Lipman-Blumen (2005) described as the toxic leader. One among many of the toxic leaders' characteristic behaviors is that of ignoring or promoting incompetence, cronyism, and corruption. Toxic leaders, administrators, often "set out to dominate even eliminate, their own followers, as well as people and groups beyond their own constituencies" (20). We must beware of this snake in the sleeve, the enemy among us. We must identify and name those actions of ours, the alliances and agreements, which prop up The Imperium, that contribute to our own subjugation. Lingis (2007) reminds us of how "every kind of social organization for the production and distribution of goods and services, power and prestige, and knowledge is maintained by the consent of individuals to fulfill their assigned roles and by coercion—by rewards and sanctions" (77).

But what are we to do?

On Our Responsibility

Responsibility is fundamental to what we do, to who we are; in fact, there are those who believe that responsibility is the essential characteristic of being (Emmanuel Levinas, as cited in Lingis 1998). That is, responsibility is fundamental to existence. If, as is suggested by Levinas, we are responsible for our world, relationships imply responsibility: "responsibility is a bond" (xix).

> Responsibility is in fact a relationship with the other, in his very alterity ... Responsibility is a form of recognition—acknowledgement of a claim, an order, which is constitutive of subjectivity—a summons to arise to be and to present oneself (xix). Let us acknowledge and accept our responsibilities.

Arendt (1961) also discussed responsibility, especially the responsibility of the teacher. The teacher, to Arendt, is responsible for a world he or she didn't make:

> Anyone who refuses to assume joint responsibility for the world should not have children and must not be allowed to take part in educating them ... The teacher's qualification consists in knowing the world and being able to instruct others about it, but his authority rests on his assumption of responsibility for that world. (189)

We must not shirk our responsibilities. Due to our privileged positions at universities—though we be dominated dominants (Bourdieu 1991a), we have responsibilities at all levels. We have unique responsibilities at the personal individual level. We have responsibilities at the communal, organizational level. And we have responsibilities at the global level.

At the personal individual level we ought to be reflexive and to act with integrity. At the organizational level we should refuse complicity in corrupt and corrupting schemes and systems, whether these are the brainchild of a toxic leader or are culturally embedded.

Our responsibility for the world, for our world, must include critique, reflection, and analysis.

But what is more, our responsibility demands action on our part. We must name those systems and those people that oppress us and others, and we must, in Lingis' (2007) terms, avoid them, drive them off, or strike them down.

References

Adams, G.B., and D.L. Balfour. 2009. *Unmasking Administrative Evil*. 3rd ed. Armonk, NY: M.E. Sharpe.

Arendt, H. 1950. "The Imperialist Character." *The Review of Politics* 12, no. 3, pp. 303–20.

Arendt, H. (1958) 1998. *The Human Condition*. Chicago: University of Chicago Press.

Arendt, H. 1961. "The Crisis in Education." In *Between Past and Future*, 173–96. New York: Viking.

Barry, E. 2014. "Indian Official Appealing Corruption Case Is Denied Bail." *New York Times*, October 8, A5.

Bohman, J., and W. Rehg. 2014. "Jürgen Habermas." In *Stanford Encyclopedia of Philosophy* (Fall 2014 Edition), ed. E.N. Zalta. http://plato.stanford.edu/entries/habermas/

Bourdieu, P. 1991a. "Fourth Lecture. Universal Corporatism: The Role of Intellectuals in the Modern World." *Poetics Today* 12, no. 4, pp. 655–69.

Bourdieu, P. 1991b. "Second Lecture. The New Capital: Introduction to a Japanese Reading of State Nobility." *Poetics Today* 12, no. 4, pp. 643–53.

Burke, P. 2000. *A Social History of Knowledge: From Gutenberg to Diderot*. Cambridge, UK: Polity Press.

Carr, D. 2011. "At Media Companies, a Nation of Serfs." *New York Times*, February 12. www.nytimes.com/2011/02/14/business/media/14carr.html

Daly, M. 2014. "Report: Retaliation by Supervisors Widespread at VA." *Austin American-Statesman*, July 22, A2.

de Rosa, A. 2011. "The Death of Platforms." *Soup*, January 17. http://soupsoup.tumblr.com/post/2800255638/the-death-of-platforms

Eder, S. 2014. "On Sidelines, Researchers See C.E.O.s." *New York Times*, September 1.

Elliot, S. 2013. "Apple Passes Coca-Cola as Most Valuable Brand." *New York Times*, September 29. www.nytimes.com/2013/09/30/business/media/apple-passes-coca-cola-as-most-valuable-brand.html?_r=0

Giddens, A. 1990. *The Consequences of Modernity*. Stanford, CA: Stanford University Press.

Greene, J.P., B. Kisida, and J. Mills. 2010. "The Higher Price for Higher Ed." *Austin American-Statesman*, September 7, A6.

Hazony, Y. 2012. *The Philosophy of Hebrew Scripture: An Introduction*. Cambridge, UK: Cambridge University Press.

Kets de Vries, M.F.R. 2011. *Reflections on Groups and Organizations*. San Francisco: Jossey-Bass.

Lewin, T. 2009. "Staff Jobs on Campus Outpace Enrollment." *New York Times*, April 21, A12.

Lingis, A. 1994. *The Community of Those Who Have Nothing in Common*. Bloomington, IN: Indiana University Press.

Lingis, A. 1998. "Translator's Introduction." In Emmanuel Levinas, *Otherwise than Being*, xvii–xlviii. Translated by A. Lingis. Pittsburg, PA: Duquesne University Press.

Lingis, A. 2007. *The First Person Singular*. Evanston, IL: Northwestern University Press.

Lipman-Blumen, J. 2005. *The Allure of Toxic Leaders: Why We Follow Destructive Bosses and Corrupt Politicians—and How We Can Survive Them*. New York: Oxford University Press.

Mencken, H.L. (1926) 2009. *Notes on Democracy*. New York: Alfred A. Knopf. Reprint, New York: Dissident Books. Citations refer to the Dissident edition.

Milgram, S. 1974. *Obedience to Authority: An Experimental View*. New York: Harper Row.

Nietzsche, F. 1967. *The Will to Power*. Translated by W. Kaufman and R.J. Hollingdale. New York: Vintage Books.

Rancière, J. 2004. *The Politics of Aesthetics*. Translated by G. Rockhill. London: Continuum.

Rancière, J. 2010. *Dissensus: On Politics and Aesthetics*. Translated by S. Corcoran. London: Continuum.

Saul, S. 2011. "Profits and Questions at Online Charter Schools." *New York Times*, December 13, A1, A18–19.

Saval, N. 2014. *Cubed: A Secret History of the Workplace*. New York: Doubleday.

Shirky, C. 2008. *Here Comes Everybody: The Power of Organizing Without Organizations*. New York: Penguin Press.

Simons, M., and J. Masschelein. 2010. "Governmental, Political and Pedagogic Subjectivation: Foucault with Rancière." *Educational Philosophy and Theory* 42, nos. 5/6, pp. 588–605.

Smithson, M. 1989. *Ignorance and Uncertainty: Emerging Paradigms*. New York: Springer-Verlag.

Smithson, M. 2008. "Social Theories of Ignorance." In *Agnotology: The Making & Unmaking of Ignorance*, eds. R.N. Proctor and L. Schiebinger, 209–29. Stanford, CA: Stanford University Press.

Waite, D. 2010. "On the Shortcomings of Our Organizational Forms: With Implications for Educational Change and School Improvement." *School Leadership and Management* 30, no. 3, pp. 225–48.

Waite, D. 2011. "Universities and Their Faculties as 'Merchants of Light': Contemplation on Today's University." *Education and Society* 29, nos. 2/3, pp. 5–19.

Waite, D. 2014. "Imperial Hubris: The Dark Heart of Leadership." *Journal of School Leadership* 24, no. 6, pp. 1202–32.

Waite, D., and D. Allen. 2003. "Corruption and Abuse of Power in Educational Administration." *The Urban Review* 35, no. 4, pp. 281–96.

Waite, D., G. Rodríguez, and A. Wadende. 2015. "The Business of Educational Reform." In *Second International Handbook of Globalisation, Education and Policy Research*, ed. J. Zajda, 353–74. The Netherlands: Springer.

Waite, D., and S.F. Waite. 2010. "Corporatism and Its Corruption of Democracy and Education." *Journal of Education and Humanities* 1, no. 2, pp. 86–106.

Watson, P. 2005. "Afghanistan's New Crime Problem." *Austin American-Statesman*, May 29, A20.

Weber, M. 1958. *The Protestant Ethic and the Spirit of Capitalism*. Translated by T. Parsons. New York: Scribner.

Zarroli, J. 2014. "Economics Nobel Awarded for Work on Regulating Big Business." National Public Radio's All Things Considered, October 13. www.npr.org/2014/10/13/355903972/economics-nobel-awarded-for-work-on-regulating-big-businesses

Zimbardo, P. 2007. *The Lucifer Effect: Understanding How Good People Turn Evil*. New York: Random House.

CHAPTER 6

Inside the Dark Sides: A Clinical Experience

Sandro Mameli, Maria Gisa Masia, Francesco Cannia, and Giorgia Cioccetti

Italian National School of Administration—SNA

Introduction

The so-called "dark sides" in business and higher education management have drawn the attention of various scholars in the last decade. From the consequences of economic theories on business ethics (Ghoshal 2005) to the same idea of management (Mintzberg 1973, 2005, 2009; Mowles 2011), we observe a growing critique of the dominant models underpinning training in business administration and management, opening-up new possibilities to understand both managerial and training practices starting from how these dark sides come to life within a management training setting.

To do so, we propose to start from an ongoing clinical experience in training public managers on what we call a managerial competence in the public administration. This chapter draws on a cumulated training experience of more than 1,500 hours over a 48-month period involving 29 different training settings in the context of the Italian National School of Administration, the public organization dedicated to select, recruit, and train public managers of the Italian Central Administration under the umbrella of the Prime Minister's Office.

A preliminary step in this endeavor is to ask ourselves what does "dark sides" mean, and since it is put at the plural, what do they mean in the context of training and managerial competence.

Originally the idea of dark side is a part of the moon that is not visible from our planet, a place of mystery subject to many narratives across civilizations, at least until the 1960s right after pictures were taken by a soviet spacecraft in 1959 of what is now called the far side of the moon. The dark side being inaccessible, it remains at the same time object of curiosity and fear. The dark side of the moon has also been used to interpret the human nature: "Every man is a moon and has a side which he turns toward nobody: you have to slip around behind if you want to see it."[1] This first understanding of the dark side, when looked at from our professional and organizational contexts, is associated with the "scientific" project behind managerial theories and models, where the inaccessible (the organization as a phenomenon or the human being as an agent) becomes a place of "discoveries" and subsequently a "variable" to control. This critique is perhaps the most widespread in the critical management literature since it refers to substantial ontological and epistemological discussions on the nature of reality and on the human nature. (For an extensive discussion, see Alvessona and Deetz 2001; Alvesson and Willmott 1996, 2003; Burrell and Morgan 1979.) Following the evolution of Science Fiction (Sci-Fi) literature, we can develop a more complex understanding of the dark side, bringing in the "plural" to a concept that otherwise would remain indeed only a matter of critique.

Sci-Fi literature evolution will be used as a fil rouge to discuss our training experience at Scuola Nazionale dell'Amministrazione (SNA)—understood as a comprehensive experience that takes into account the training setting and the regulatory and cultural environment—and to develop a reflection on the concept of dark sides in a context of critical analysis of management training practices. The chapter will develop three stages of the Sci-Fi literature revolving around a different understanding of the dark side as a way to interpret our training experience, bringing us to consider not only the shortcomings of mainstream managerial and training models but also a possible interaction, or even integration with those dark sides. Each section will explore how the specific representations of the dark side in the Sci-Fi literature interact with the training

---

[1] Mark Twain, The Refuge of the Derelicts, in "Fables of Man," 1905.

experience (and in particular the participants' training demand), the relationship with the trainers, the evaluation process, and the organizational context of SNA. Before that, we provide a brief outline of the method, that is, a clinical approach in training, and of the context in which this experience takes place.

Clinical Approach: Theoretical Foundations

Adopting a clinical approach in training means essentially redefining the premises of intervention. Clinical social scientists (mainly psychologists and sociologists) aim at intervention in the context (Giust-Desprairies 2013) starting from the organizational demand (in this case the participants perception of it) (Carli 1987, 1993; Carlia and Paniccia 2003). This redefinition entails a series of relationships, in particular the relationship between the individual and its context, and the relationship between rationality and emotions. The relationships among individuals and contexts are considered here as indivisible; organizational practices and social actors are bonded to the context in which they occur and operate.

From this point of view, trying to isolate the meaning of a single action, a behavior, or an artifact outside of its context (i.e., as it is being understood, represented, and symbolized in that specific context) is misleading, if not impossible. From a clinical point of view, the relationship with the context does not imply a diagnosis at a given time and an intervention a T+1. Knowing is already intervening and the act of knowing is more related to the schemata's of the trainers than to the "real" characteristics of reality. In that perspective, a double hermeneutics (Gergen 1973; Giddens 1984) seems to take place; social theories have the capacity to "become" part of reality itself. Rather than theory being caused objectively by reality, social reality is caused by theory. The subject-object relationship departs from a Cartesian definition to embrace a more complex and iterative relationship between the individual and the context and a different view of the Self (Dachler and Hosking 1995; Hosking 2006), considered primarily as a relational Self. Being a practice-led research, its epistemological foundation is the interpretive paradigm (Sandberg 2005, Sandberg and Targama 2007) that sees organization as the enactments determined both by intentionality inspired—by the organization itself—and by values, sentiments, and emotions (Enriquez 1987; Pagès et al. 1979; Ruvolo, De Blasi, and Neri 1995). This theoretical framework implies that the field of investigation is situated within the affective symbolizations that organize the life of productive systems and life within those systems. Central to this is the notion of the unconscious way of being of the mind (Matte Blanco 1975), which entails emotions and their foundational function of social reality. The unconscious is defined as a differentiating emotionality that finds its first categories of differentiation in the relationship with the context (Salvatore and Zitoun 2011).

The parallel proposed here with Sci-Fi literature is based on such premises. The metaphors developed by the Sci-Fi literature provide a "map of the unconscious" (Carotenuto 2001, 21), through which archetypes of the modern psyche emerge. Even though it refers to a future, as Cartenuto proposes, Sci-Fi refers to a less visible present and even to age-old symbolic motives.

This privilege access of Sci-Fi to the unconscious is also its burden. Being in contact with the unconscious contents of the reader means accessing the remote fantasies but also fearful representations, in the same way that what is "other" belongs to us at the same time. What we have chosen not to look at or listen to becomes now concrete, perceivable, and manifested. The dark sides of managerial roles and organization, following the same dynamic outlined earlier, become, in a clinical setting, the object of analysis and reflection from a relational perspective. The relationship between participants (managers or future managers) and these dark sides is what we will focus on.

Managerial Training at the National School of Administration, Italy

This section will outline briefly key information on the organizational context. As explained previously, a clinical approach considers the situated interpretation of both researches and actors as part of the research or intervention process; therefore, no single "objective" account of the organizational context can be given by the researchers. However, a brief outline can be useful for the reader in order to get acquainted with the details of the analysis that will be presented in the following sections. The

Italian National School of Administration (SNA) is a public organization under the umbrella of the Presidency of the Council (Office of the Prime Minister) whose mission is to select, recruit, and train civil servants and public managers. The internal organization of the SNA is, not different from any other higher education organization, composed of an administrative staff and a training staff (about 60 full- or part-time professors).

The managerial training, as we refer to in this chapter, is part of the training offer of SNA that is performed under three main forms:

1. Self-standing laboratories on managerial practice open to public managers;
2. As part of a selective training program for the recruitment of new public managers operated directly by the school; and
3. As part of an induction training program dedicated to newly appointed managers after a competition organized by single central administrations.

During the Academic Year 2013–2014 a master's degree on managerial practice has been designed by SNA in cooperation with University Federico II, Naples. This expands the training approach in various modules and in the final project work.

Inside the Dark Sides, Some Preliminary Elements on Science Fiction Literature

It can be useful before starting this journey to provide a perimeter to what we refer to as Sci-Fi in the context of this chapter. Todorov (1975) identifies three genres of fantastic literature, namely, the marvelous, the strange, and the fantastic. Those genres differentiate themselves on the behavior of protagonists vis-à-vis the supranatural element. The fantastic literature is a synthesis of the previous two, in the sense that is switches constantly between what is explainable and what is not.

Acknowledging the remote origins of Sci-Fi literature, from Homer's Odyssey to More's Utopia, to Swift's Gulliver Travels, and closer to us to Shelley's Frankenstein or Stevenson's Doctor Jekyll and Mister Hyde, all pertaining to what might be called protoscience-fiction, we will focus our attention to the developments occurred from the 20th century onwards, where Sci-Fi becomes a literary pendant of the positivist ideal, bearing unlimited trust in the scientific method and in the impact of science on society. In that perspective, the works of Jules Verne, that himself called roman de la science, represent the fundamental source of inspiration for a new, more popular, and large-scale wave of Sci-Fi that has been then developed around the 1920s.

From this point on, Sci-Fi literature can be divided into three main periods characterized by a different relationship with science, and a differ-ent relationship between Sci-Fi and the real[2] world. We can propose here to develop a typology of Sci-Fi that links the mythology of the dark side (understood here as alien, other, unknown, different than me, irrational, chaotic, complex) to the Sci-Fi genre itself, starting from a psychological Kleinian perspective (Klein 1952), into three modes of functioning—maniacal, schizo-paranoid, and depressive—that can be traced in the training demand as it evolves in the training setting. Of course we are not referring to these concepts in their pathological acceptation—(in our per-spective they represent positions) what will be highlighted further on, is how certain dominant organizational and management theories provide a fertile ground in which such ways to interpret the managerial role and organizational realities (i.e., modes of functioning) are manifested both at conscious and at unconscious level by the participants. In that perspec-tive, the Kleinian categorizations provide an essential bridge between the metaphorical suggestions of Sci-Fi literature and the clinical experience we refer to in this chapter.

Shortly, we can refer to a maniacal position when the narrative is entrenched in a sentiment of triumph and omnipotence. The schizo-paranoid

---

[2] Although we cannot develop fully our argument here, we ask ourselves what is *real*. The boundaries between real and unreal (*fantastic*) are in our view mainly cultural. Replacing real by "concrete" or "factual" does not resolve the issue if we believe, like Schopenauer, that materiality exists only through our look at it, or like Pirandello, that a univocal image is impossible due to the infinite points of view. Sci-Fi embraces this question by revolving the rationale: Do not start from the pre-supposition that there is a unique reality, from which we could only extract ideas or worlds that would be less real. Realities become unlimited in the Sci-Fi realm.

position is related to a sentiment of fear and angst that generates mechanisms of introjection and projection related to an initial understanding of objects and realities as either good or evil. The depressive narrative is diametrically opposed to the maniacal, as the Self is here depicted as evil, and all that pertains to the other is associated with the good.

The dark sides as represented in these categories come across our training experience; we will try, in the next sections, to outline how this parallel come into play in our classrooms, and how they relate to the evaluation process and to the organizational context of SNA.

The First Period: Of Maniacs and Double Bind

The first period, starting allegedly around 1926 till mid-1930s is characterized by the ideal and idealized relationship with science. Trust in scientific discoveries led to believe in a wealthy future for all. Nature, and by extension the whole universe, was the frontier to conquer and colonize with few foreseeable difficulties. The narratives of this period are therefore centered on extraordinary inventions and endless adventures. Although the literary quality of such narratives was highly variable, the imagery produced revealed fascinating space battles and spacecrafts faster than light. This narrative, called with some sarcasm by Isaac Asimov Space Opera, is settled in a creative and innovative (for the time) context; however, it uses a classic structure, where the good—often a young scientist—will certainly defeat evil, that very often operates under irrational rules.

The unconditioned faith in humanity and the supremacy of man *versus* nature provide the ground for defining period as "maniac." There is no trace of anxiety or fear in this narrative. Aliens, when they are depicted, are "humanized," they do not behave as Alien. The Robot sagas, Foundation, or even Notturno are in this sense good examples of such narratives.

Drawing a parallel between this narrative and organizational theories, we could argue that the manager is indeed the young—lonely—scientist fighting the forces of evil, understood here as the forces of chaos contrasting the ideal organization. The power over all decisions, the idea to be in control of all organizational variables, the creation of a managerial profession, and the focus on the manager as the sole determinant of organizational fate are all traits of organizational theories rooted in the positivist tradition that we connect to this first definition of dark side. To this tradition, we can also connect the ideal of a heroic, charismatic manager or leader. The isolation, from the mid-1970s onwards of the leadership model from the managerial models (Kotter 1987; Zaleznik 1977) is a partial novelty that does not put into question the idea of a "just for few only" set of qualities or competences that ought to be possessed in order to perform this role. Let it be the cold, calculating mind of the manager, or the warm, transcending figure of the leader, both are to be attained through the use of science.

Which traces of this maniacal interpretation of the dark side do we encounter in our training experience? First, the persistent idea of a recipe, some kind of protocol that can fix any given situation, appears as a recurrent training demand from the participants. This demand entails a view of the manager or leader as a model of scientific precision. What is requested here, and more often than not proposed in other training settings, is the magical transformation into an ideal-type of manager or leader (Trentini 1997) that finds a corresponding, institutionalized proposal in academia. Second, the idea of a man or woman that is able to capture the interest and fantasy of workers or followers and to guide them to an "unknown" (i.e., the organizational performance rhetoric referring to "the extra mile"). This recurrent demand was not born in a cultural and institutional void. Indeed management and organizational science have being portraying this imagery for over a century and it has influenced the narratives of common men, feeding in that sense the expectations of the persons called upon to perform this managerial role in an organization. Readily available lists of functional and dysfunctional behaviors (Burns 1978; Boyatzis, Goleman, and Rhee 2000), functions (Fayol 1916), roles (Quinn and Rohrbaugh 1983; Quinn 1991) are there to be taken as a consumption product, enabling the manager or leader to bring order into the organization and pursue challenging objectives in a timely and efficient manner. Paradoxically, while such approach is seen as "obvious" by most participants, they acknowledge the practical difficulty in applying such rules and norms. However this reckoning remains within the same paradigm, reinforcing in that sense the idea of a privileged, gifted person capable to make such things happen. As in the Sci-Fi maniacal metaphor, the relationship between individuals and their context remains unexplored, since the solution is to be found in the (scientific) perfection of man itself. As anticipated, there are evolutions of this idea the strong assertive, result-oriented character of the "U.S. style manager" coexists with the image of the "democratic leader,"[3] putting empathy and collaboration as undisputed values. Both models coexist insofar as the latter is a response to the former: The normative realm of public administration reforms has brought forward a strong managerial role, based on a management by objectives model, to which managers tend to respond either by espousing the model, mobilizing the same rhetoric that the legislator used in the decision-making process, or by espousing a counter-role, the democratic leader. Both roles are subject of a similar training demand that is, technical and instrumental ("scientific") to pursue the realization of the preferred role.

In this phase what emerges from the discussions is the modality through which participants want to exercise their role. Starting from a generic definition of leadership as a process of influencing (Antonakis, Cianciolo, and Stemberg 2004), this process is interpreted solely from the side of the leader or manager being portrayed as someone having a hierarchical superiority, and is reduced to qualities and skills that reifies what is proposed as a process. Communication skills, charisma, and empowerment, are all tools to display in order to manipulate organizational and group relationships.

If we consider leadership as a symbolic function within organizations, we realize that adhering to an ideal type, even unconsciously, contributes to developing a particular type of organizational culture. Since such symbols can be criticized within the context acknowledging their relational nature (Hosking 2004), the ideal type of a charismatic or "scientific" leader does not give this opportunity: The only thing that the Other (let it be individual or generalized) can do is adhere to the vision of this leader and assume the passive position of a follower. In this conception of the managerial role, any group or organizational relationship that does not correspond to this logic is portrayed as problematic, resistant, or unwilling.

---

[3] Expressions extracted from conversations in the training setting.

The technicality of the training demand appears to hide a given-for-granted conception of the organizational roles that is reflected also in the training process. The trainer is depicted as an expert able to provide the necessary knowledge in order to perform the role efficiently. This knowledge should be transferred in the same way that vision and objectives should be transferred to followers. Within these premises the clinical approach is seen as "weak" since it does not provide the expected answer. The other is either a void to fill with our own knowledge or is a full container to be emptied in order to fill our own voids. To this reaction toward the method follows a reaction against the professional background of the trainers. Psychology, also given for granted as a discipline in this context, should provide insights on the human psyche that the manager or leader needs in order to perform its manipulative role. Instead, the demander is faced with questions aimed at reinstated the possibility of a relational perspective of both his or her role and the organization, where roles, tools, and skills are constructed through relationships rather than pre-existing them (Dachler and Hosking 1995). The often noted passage from omnipotence to impotence in this phase is related to a leitmotiv, the loneliness of the manager or leader. The dependence expected in the relationship leader or follower is transposed in the relationship trainer or participant. If it remains unspoken, such dependence leaves the participant in a state of solitude. In the same way, the discourse on the solitude of the manager or leader reflects the sense of impossibility of dialogue with the organizational context that this entitative (Dachler and Hosking 1995; Hosking 2006) perspective imposes. Without a context to which we can relate, the development expected from the training process is reified as a value, that is, a-temporal and a-contextual, transforming the demand of development in its opposite: a demand of conformism to undiscussed models.

As we have discussed in the preceding, the training experience is seen as a process of magical transformation into an ideal. The evaluation process after the training is completed reflects to a large extent this conception. The value-laden nature of any evaluation process of training activities will entail a vision of man, and in this context, of the nature of its knowledge (Delplancke 1975). The "happy sheets" delivered at the end of any training at the school reflects the vision of a managerial role to be acquired through notions that the trainer should transfer competently, clearly and in an agreeable manner. This of course leaves very little space to problematize the learning process occurring in a laboratory dedicated to developing the reflection around the managerial role.

The clinical approach brings us to consider also the context in which training takes place. Can this demand, metaphorically represented as maniacal, find a fertile ground in the way training is conceived within the organizational context (The National School of Administration—SNA, and by extension, the Italian public administration)? We have developed elsewhere (Chimienti et al. in press) the complex and permanently negotiated nature of this conception within SNA, along with the consequent sociomaterial practices. The logic of separateness (inside or outside the school), along with an ontological or epistemological reference to the organization that remains unquestionable (organization as a "given") that characterizes one of the discourses structuring SNA activities does certainly find a "match" with this metaphorical proposition of the dark side. This specific discourse enacts a managerial model that is very similar to the one portrayed by the participants' demand at the start of the laboratories. In such discourse, we can argue that the dark side is actually what happens in the classroom, that is, the training experience itself.

The experience we relate here takes its root in the preliminary phase of training, when objectives and method are discussed and shared with the participants. However, this demand does not necessarily disappear after this phase, rather it permeates the discussions and training activities throughout the laboratories. Far from us to expect that a training session will erase such cultural background, our proposal is indeed to create turbulence into the participants' ways of thinking about their managerial role. The presence or absence of such maniacal relationship vis-à-vis the managerial role is not an indicator of success of training. Linking this specific stage of the training process to other contextual elements such as the relationship with the trainers, the evaluation process and the organizational context of SNA, we can see how this demand is rooted, and finds its legitimacy, in organizational practices that have already internalized this specific conception of the managerial role.

The Golden Age: Of Schizo's and Control

From 1939 till 1950, we assist to the development of a more mature relationship with technology. This is the era of Asimov, Van Vogt, Heinlein, and Sturgeon, but the real protagonist is the editor John W. Campbell, then director of the review Astounding Stories.[4] Campbell's directives to the writers were very precise: You must insist so that exceptions become the rule and that a true science is united to a true narrative.

Using true science gave the stories a sense of plausible. Rockets, nuclear weapons, and computers came out of the frenetic imagination of such writers, 10 years before they actually were realized. However, the unconditioned faith in science came to an abrupt end with the explosion of the first atomic bomb. It was also a sign of maturity for this literary genre, since it showed it predictory power.

As Asimov wrote (Asimov 1978), the times where sensible and normal people laugh when reading the stupid stories of rockets, missiles, and bombs were over when the atomic bomb displayed a horrible splendor of rationalism on these same stupid stories.

Nonetheless, from the golden age of Sci-Fi literature emerged other narratives that bring us to consider a different kind of dark side. In the likes of Ted Sturgeon or Ray Bradbury, the genre not only develops an attention to real science, but it starts to consider the possible changes in the social sphere due to the scientific discoveries. The idea that in 1880 it was quite simple to foresee the creation of the automobile, but less simple to foresee the impact of this on traffic, or on the courtship practices of young people, becomes the new challenge for the Sci-Fi genre.

Besides true science appears the alien, this time in a different, more threatening and terrifying role to inhabit what we have earlier defined as a schizo-paranoid turn in Sci-Fi literature. The roots of this turn can be traced to H.G. Wells' *The War of the Worlds* (1898) and to John W. Campbell Jr.'s *Who Goes There?* (1938), where the plot sees the discovery by an American expedition of a spacecraft with an hibernated alien buried under the Antarctic ice. The plot is explicit: Since the alien is different

---

[4] Known today as Analog Science Fiction and Fact (or Analog), the review is the longest standing one in Sci-Fi.

from us, he represents a danger and we need to destroy the spacecraft and kill the alien. The difficulty resides, as we discover in the novel, in the fact that the alien has the capacity to imitate any kind of living being, and therefore rendering its identification impossible. Stuck in the linear thought of We versus the Other, where the Other represents a danger while We are the good ones. Mastering science has had the effect of transforming the nonlinear, unexplainable, into a terrible threat.

The parallel with organizational theories that comes to mind is the relationship between the logic of control underpinning organizational designs such as the Tayloristic model, or the bureaucratic Weberian model, studied in the French context by Crozier, in particular the tobacco monopoly (Crozier 1963) and reality as a complex, unpredictable, and iterative process. As it happened to Campbell's Alien, the Other (different than us) must be eliminated in order for the manager to operate in a control-obsessed organization. This projection of the manager's own ambition of control over reality, passes through emotional states that echoes the Kleinian definition of schizo-paranoid in the sense that these same ambitions, felt as morally condemnable, are expelled through a process of projection that paradoxically increase, instead of putting into discussion, the levels of control in the organizational reality. The dark side here has a name and a face, and represents a clear threat to the established understanding of reality.

The training experience is permeated by this representation of the Other in various occasions. We will try to summarize here the most salient ones.

The first parallel with the metaphorical representation outlined earlier is the critical incident, the "Atomic Bomb" represented by the introduction of a comprehensive performance management system (2009 Reform, see aforementioned) with tight control over managerial decisions and a disciplinary regime that puts managers into a "punish or be punished" situation. This new legal framework is pictured, in the representations of the classroom, as the "death" of managerial autonomy, in sharp contrast with the objectives of the legal framework that propagates the adoption of managerial autonomy and techniques inherited from the private sector experience. This representation is of course the fruit of a reflection under the previous organizational paradigm that enabled managers to cope with the paradoxes of a linear, bureaucratic organization that had already introduced bonus and incentives based on managerial objectives. Almost every manager succeeded in reaching his or her objectives and received the bonus with little or no control over the actual results. This Bomb signifies the end of an era that was characterized by the collusive culture between politics, labor unions, and managers. A "scientific" method enabled everyone to gain from the current set of rules.

The reaction of managers participating to the laboratories to this Bomb resembles the sadistic research of a culprit, an Alien that becomes the source of fear and threat concerning the established order. The holy alliance that characterized the period preceding the entry into force of the 2009 reform (since the early 1990s with the so called privatization of public employment) is put under severe pressure by this new legal framework. The new powers granted to managers, along with a severe disciplinary code, become the pretext to both a technical demand to be able to cope with the new rules, and to a mystification of the role of politics, unions, and civil servants.

The first demand is related to the pre-existing organizational culture: a culture of means rather than ends, where the norm represents the sole vector of communication inside and outside the administration. The aim of the reform, the reflection on the role of the manager and the difficulties that arise from it are set aside in the discussions in order to focus on what can be done, what must be done, and most of all what must not be done as a manager. In this aspect the collusion remains vivid: The scarce trust in the manager's capacity to interpret autonomously this new role brought the legislator to develop an intricate nest of rules and norms that will constrain and guide the manager into complying with the reform design (Borgogelli 2011). In this sense, the training function should indeed be interpreted as the locus where these rules and norms become more evident to managers.

The second demand is related to the development of an ability to cope with the other players around the table—politics, labor unions, and civil servants. The Others are first depicted as a threat to what seems indeed the pursue of the same game as before (a new "holy alliance" to be established). The impossibility to play their own part if the others do not comply is a recurrent manifestation of this paranoid part. What is striking is that, especially in the laboratories dedicated to newly appointed managers, almost all of them where civil servants until the day before training started, and some of them were actively involved in labor unions' activities. The denial of the Other as a part of us (leading in the metaphorical example outlined earlier to a paranoid projection) leads the reflection in the laboratories to expressing the wish to cancel the powers of the other players by increasing their own organizational power, in particular through the acquisition of a technical expertise in managing rules and relationships. What is being fought in this pursue is the possibility to interpret the dependency into an interdependency inside the organization. The specific intermediary role of managers is seen as an unsustainable position that needs to be cancelled. Being both bosses and under the rule of other bosses is seen as "being like a piece of meat between two slices of bread, ready to be eaten."[5] From that perspective, we can consider as almost inevitable the response of managers vis-à-vis the other players, an aggressive response of cancellation.

In particular, the human resource management under the responsibility of the managers highlights how this dark side differs from the first one. While in the first metaphor, the dark side exists only in relation to the fact that the organization coincides totally with the role of the manager, and therefore does not need to be explored since its significance collapses with the acquisition of the right instruments by the manager, in this metaphor, the dark side becomes a tangible threat as the rules of the game have changed and require to conceive new relationships in the organizational context. The legal framework clearly differentiates the roles between managers and civil servants but attributes the responsibility to cope with this differentiation on the heads of the managers only. This implicit recognition that the organization needs roles to cope with uncertainty and dynamic interpretation on the roles brings managers into a state of crisis to which follows the same kind of demand as expressed in the previous metaphor.

The sensation represented by the participants is that the norm provides instruments that rely on the hierarchical status to be enforced, but

---

[5] Extracted from conversations in the training setting.

that there is a need for further instruments that are being categorized as "soft," because they rely on the relational dimension rather than the technical dimension. The hierarchical power is perceived as a power without competence (Carli and Paniccia 2003) to which the participants respond with a training demand that conceives the Other as a threat.

What occurs in this demand is that the given for granted scission between hard and soft skills (artificial and arbitrary as the difference between a manager and a leader) overlaps a scission between rational and irrational behaviors. The demand here has to do with the capability to either remove the irrational (how to control one's emotion) or bring back the irrational (the human being) into the rational, linear design of the organization. The paradoxical nature of organization is looked at with fear and angst, reinforcing the sense of loneliness expressed in the previous metaphor. Here loneliness is not the fate of any successful individual (let us remember that being a manager is also a social status), but the acknowledgement, how narrow and superficial it may be at this stage, that the training demand is indeed a vain pursue of a state of perfection that in fact is unattainable.

This fear and angst is subsumed in the training. We have explored in the previous metaphor the evaluation process of training and trainers; here, we focus instead on the process of evaluation to which the participants are subject. From the guidelines of evaluation dedicated to the training received as a newly appointed manager to the rules defined in the process of recruitment of new managers operated directly by the SNA, we find the same difficulty to integrate a conception of training as a critical experience that puts into question one's own role within an organization and the conception of training as the transmission of knowledge and tools to cope with a managerial role. The criteria are indeed revolved around the possibility to measure how much the participants have assimilated the models and tools promoted during the training experience. The frequent exchanges between participants and the trainers in this context aim at clarifying what is expected from the participants in order to correspond to the idealized models that the participants attribute to the members of the evaluation committee. In this perspective, the evaluation process is reduced to a conformity assessment that reinforces both the previous collusive culture of the participants and the idea that the managerial autonomy stands in the possibility to adhere as much as possible to a predetermined model.

Inside SNA, the decision-making process underpinning the definition of the evaluation rules highlights the same tension between a possibility to conceive what is Other as a resource rather than as a threat, and the need to adhere to the normative model of evaluation that sees the assessment of acquired notions and tools as the only objective, rational way to evaluate the participants. The motivation is centered on the risk that the Other (the participant) might launch a legal complaint against the results if the criteria are not as much objective as possible. The Other is eliminated by eliminating the learning potential that a process of evaluation might provide, both from the participant's and the institution's point of view.

Social Science Fiction and the New Wave: Of Depression, Androids, and Integration

Some of the themes emerged in the conclusive part of the Golden Age are premises to what will later develop into a specific stream: the social Sci-Fi. The roots of such narratives can be traced to Wells of Jonathan Swift, but we can also find in the works of Frederick Pohl, Cyril Kornbluth, and Robert Sheckley the anticipation, in a rather extreme and grotesque fashion, of the social themes that are nowadays recurrent in the Sci-Fi literature. The narrative forms are certainly more sophisticated and the irony with which crucial themes are being treated such as the role of new medias, the invasion of advertisement into our daily lives, the obscure power games played over the heads of millions of people, the power of multinationals, and the dangers of science, gives way to what can be consider a proper social critic. Here again the role played by a review, Morock's New Worlds, the bedrock of this new turn in the Sci-Fi literature. We are in the year 1964, where the experimental tendency in Sci-Fi is more vivid. The reciprocal contaminations between avant-gardes and Sci-Fi enable the development of various subgenres: fantapolitics, apocalyptic Sci-Fi, comic and satiric, alternate history, utopian and dystopian Sci-Fi, and xenofiction are some of the genres emerging from that context besides the dissemination of Sci-Fi into mainstream literature. This dissemination gave birth to new representations of reality with the analysis of new codes of communication, the destructuration of the "real" and, due also to the events of 1968, the introduction of more political content. Norman Spinrad, Roger Zelanzy, Samuel R. Delany, and Ursula K. Le Guin are amongst the protagonists of this movement, where strictly technological aspects are set aside in favor of the contributions of sociology, political science, and anthropology. The exploration of these new territories is the fertile ground on which the Sci-Fi literature of the 1970s will build its identity. The contribution of psychology, with the analysis of the "profound" and the modifications of the unconscious will displace the realm of the Alien invasion. The internal space is the new outer space. The works of Philip K. Dick and James G. Ballard are in this period the most representative of such change:

> The major progress in the immediate future will not take place on the Moon or on Mars, but on Earth: it is the internal space, not the external one, that we must explore. The real Alien planet is the planet Earth. (Ballard 1962)

We assist from the mid-1960s onwards to the progressive decay of the alien invasion as a Sci-Fi representation, in favor of a more reflective literature centered on the human condition. The field of investigation widens considerably to include the analysis of contemporary occidental societies. The stage is not the intergalactic space or idealized futuristic organizations as occurred in the previous stages of Sci-Fi literature, but it is set in equivalent contexts on planet Earth, that is, organizational or social settings that are similar to the ones we know and live in, that provide the context in which this new type of Sci-Fi literature develops what we have named a depressive narrative. The Alien, and by extension what constitutes the Otherness, goes through a process of rehabilitation that is similar to the synthesis between a sentiment of love and a destructive impulse toward the Other that is at the origin of the depressive angst. Its diversity is viewed now as a sign of dissent and opposition to the human universe that is perceived as more and more unsustainable. The depressive angst and its rehabilitation process were already available in novels such as *The Man who Fell to Earth* (Tevis 1963), but we find in Philip K. Dick's *Do Androids Dream of Electric Sheep?* (1968) the most representative work of this era, thanks also to its popular cinematographic adaptation, Blade Runner. The story chasing and disposing of androids coming from colonized planets and mimetizing among humans. The life of this hunter is lived between two kinds (the human and the android), where the subtle difference between the two is of a subtle psychological nature and slowly but surely disappears in front of the technological sophistication. In the time frame where this novel takes place, animals have almost disappear from our planet, to the point that humankind develops a morbid nostalgia leading to an unconditional affection toward any form of living being, be it a fly, a rat, or a spider. The differentiation test between Androids and Humans is based on this particular affectivity that humans now possess and Androids do not.

Probably Rick Deckard, the hero of the novel, would continue endlessly his hunt if it were for the fact that he feels sympathy toward Androids, or if we take into account the cinematographic version, love. This possibility of integration is subsumed by the situation where an Android on the verge of being disposed claims to love life and any living form, provoking a sense of estrangement in the reader that cannot clearly differentiate the difference between humans and androids anymore.

This integrative stage that characterizes this trend in the Sci-Fi literature can be transposed also in the development of organizational theories toward a practice-led (Knorr Cetina, Schatzki, and Von Savigny 2001; Jarzabkowski and Spee 2009; Balogun et al. 2014), chaotic (i.e., with no clear boundaries—Cziarnawska 2009—or always on the verge of change—Stacey 1992). The locus of investigation and intervention is the lived experience of organizations where structures, relationships, and individualities come together into an entangled, sociomaterial experience (Orlikowski and Scott 2008; Orlikowski 2010) that can be experienced by managers as calculated chaos or controlled disorder (Andrews 1976 in Mintzberg 2009). The dark side as portrayed in this metaphor has more to do with the human capacity to emancipate from the arbitrary boundaries set by dominant theories of social science (me or you, inside or outside) to integrate the Other's perspective into his or her own, acknowledging the part of dark side (the theories that inform his or her worldview) that he or she carries when looking at his or her experience.

In such frame of understanding realities, the construction of a managerial role in the training setting lies in the contextual and operational reply that translates the institutional mandate provided by the legal framework of the reform. This translation is never free of values and emotions that become, in the training setting, the object of reflection. The use of case studies brought by the participants themselves or designed on former participants' cases enables to remain in this entangled experience and explore the dark sides that participants carry in the enactment of their roles. The development of such training experience enables to acknowledge, rather than ignore, the differences that inevitably lie in the various organizational contexts in which the participants work. This possibility is given also by the ability to see the working group formed by the participants as a metaphor of their organizational context. The group develops along dynamic of convergences (same selection process, same legal framework) and differentiations (type of managerial role, context of reference). Instead of being seen as obstacles in an individualistic, consumption-oriented training demand (see first metaphor) or a nuisance in a technical-oriented demand to manipulate and control the Other (see second metaphor), convergences and differentiations are used as pretexts to explore the organizational competence that managers develops when they exercise their role. In this perspective, we believe that the organizational competence is a capacity to link one's role to the organizational context in which it takes place (Sandberg 2005), that will necessarily require a questioning of the premises of one's own view of the organization. Reflective training, as Salvatore and Scotto di Carlo (2005) propose, has not the vocation to fill gaps, rather it starts from the current way of thinking one's professional role with the aim of disturbing it and opening up new possibilities to interact with the organizational context. This experience does not have the power, nor is it its intent, to eradicate fear or angst from the participants; rather it provides an opportunity to look at it from a more competent point of view, with the perspective to develop organizational strategies and activities that will enable to hold together the necessity to reach objectives with the necessity to respect the legal framework. A sense of loss and disorientation is regularly felt and recognized among participants, as one of them illustrated, "we have been deprived of our candid ignorance." The return of a demand for instruments, some kind of orthopedic remedy to this feeling, can also be manifested in such situations.

This training experience fails however to find a corresponding evaluation process in the current organizational context of SNA. However, a "forced coexistence" has been made possible through the development of a "learning and evaluation grid" that proposes the same reflective methodology in the evaluation process of training for participants. Although this practice is still under development as we write this chapter, we can already draw some hints from the use of such tool. First, what emerges from the evaluation and learning grids is that the participants view themselves as part of a process recognizing that they were not mere receptacle of an external, preconceived science. In this sense, we depart from the conception of the participant as a customer, acknowledging his role of what is understood in psychological literature (Carli and Paniccia 2003) as a client, that is, holder of a competent training demand. The idea that some of them "have the impression to have not fully grasp the opportunity at hand," or "did not commit fully to the proposal," along with the evaluation of the trainers as "helpers in a process of self-reflection," or as "facilitators, provocateurs, and interpreters," provides a useful insight in the process that the participants have undergone in viewing the training context as a construction and constant redefinition of one's understanding of the managerial role. The critical part of the evaluations is also referred to the process as such rather than to the performance of the trainers as holders of a specific knowledge. In this case, critics are a valuable tool to redefine, rethink, or redesign some settings and activities foreseen in the laboratories as they engage with the way the role of trainer can be more effectively carried. Yet, the—limited—presence in critics that reflects the approach to training as developed in the first two metaphors ("the trainers did not always agree on the same things," "too cryptical") provide valuable information on the learning process of participants.

In the context of training subject to a selective procedure, given the legal constraints and the jurisprudence on public competitions, this approach can only be considered as a "service" rendered to the participants that still need to undergo an examination procedure. However, the possibilities remain open in the future to find an integration between the two necessities, that is, the respect of the rules and the efficacy of such procedures vis-à-vis the objective. Select the most competent managers to serve in public administration.

Conclusions and Possible Developments

The clinical experience related here has been the occasion for the authors to reflect on a 4-year endeavor to bring a different perspective in the institutional context of a National School of Administration training, selecting, and recruiting public managers. The metaphoric parallel between the Sci-Fi literature and the training process may still appear bold to some readers. Certainly there are other narratives in the Sci-Fi literature and other ways to interpret the various eras of Sci-Fi history. If we may still refer to Carotenuto's conception of Sci-Fi as a representation of the unconscious, we certainly must admit that we do not possess the capacity to fulfill the infinite realm of the unconscious with this chapter. Hopefully, what we have provided here is an understanding of what occurs in a training setting when managers are confronted with a training proposal that does not foresee the transfer of knowledge but only the possibility to reflect upon the theories that inform already our ways of being in the (organizational) world. This does not mean that the training is free of content. It is not, as could be misinterpreted, a reproposition of Training Groups (T-groups) in a specific institutional setting.[6] The laboratories have a perimeter, the organizational context of the school, and the specific contexts of the participants' organizations. The training revolves around the managerial role, which can be interpreted as a leadership, communication, negotiation, and conflict management laboratory. Yet it does not depart from a pregiven definition of any of these constructs, rather it puts into place a training context that makes it possible for the participants to explore their own understanding of such constructs. In this exploration, the recurrence of some interpretations figures of speech, slogans, training demands throughout the dozens of laboratories has brought us to consider a possible parallel with the exploration of the concept of dark side in the realm of Sci-Fi as a representation of the Other. From the Other

---

[6] T-groups as a methodology does not foresee any agenda, structure or explicit objective.

as a nonentity, whose void is filled with the enthusiastic expectation of the triumph of science, to the Other as an enemy, both to our own life and to the established order,[7] to (finally?) the Other as a resource in the meaning making processes of our organizational realities (requiring therefore a questioning of our own "dark sides"), we have explored different conceptions of the dark sides that relate to different conceptions and theories of organization, management, and managers. While the maniacal representation gives little space to a clinical analysis whose function is to disturb the (ontological and epistemological) premises on which such conception is made, the schizo-paranoid and the depressive metaphors in Sci-Fi enable us to explore the reactions of participants to a context that can either be seen as a threat or as a possibility. This possibility is what we consider as the main objective of managerial training, that is, the possibility to develop a competence to pass from a faithful repetition of the original cultural matrix and professional backgrounds to a capacity to negotiate one's profession and role within the context (Venza 2007).

Through this account, we have also experienced how the limitations of theoretical frameworks that, to this day, inform public decisions regarding the machinery of government, are lived and interpreted by a specific category of actors involved in the process, that is, the managers. The triad denial-fear-integration is only but one of the possible dynamics of the relationship between managers and their contexts, yet we observe that throughout our training experience this can be understood as a recurrent representation of this relationship.

Nonetheless, we do not conclude that the last stage, the new wave if we refer to the Sci-Fi metaphor, or the integration dynamics occurring in the training setting, represent the final product of such experience. Our own representations of the experience and our journey of research is in constant evolution as we acquired at the same time a deeper understanding of the texture (Gherardi 2006) of managerial work, and a deeper understanding of how our own schemata's might influence what we experience as trainers. To further expand on this thought, we refer, once again,

---

[7] Although we have not exploited this possibility in the Golden Age section, let us remember here that the representation of the Alien as an enemy is a particular feature of the Sci-Fi literature and cinema of the Cold War era.

to a Sci-Fi literature movement, the cyberpunk, that flourished in the 1980s of the last century. This movement is quite characteristic of post-modernism as it rejects a distinction between hard science (as exploited in the first period and the Golden age of Sci-Fi) and soft science (as exploited in the new wave). The rejection of this distinction comes to light in the representation of actors that are neither solely human nor solely machines, namely cyborgs, where humanity and technology are contemporaneous, entangled phenomena. This obviously is not a new theme in literature and history, a parallel can be drawn between cyborgs and Shelley's Frankenstein, or even the mythological character Medusa, an antelitteram expression of the cyborgs depicted by cyberpunk authors such as Gibson, Sterling, or Rucker. This contemporaneity, that goes beyond the concept of integration as expressed in the *new wave* metaphor, puts into discussion both the role of training and the concept of dark side. Moreover, this would not be a virgin territory as far as organizational theory is concerned if we consider theoretical frameworks such as sociomateriality (Orlikowski 2008; Barad 2003) or Actor-Network Theory (Latour 2005) when applied to organizational settings. Furthermore, cyberpunk has a political resonance that can be assimilated to post-Marxist evolutions of critical management studies (Grey and Willmott 2005), bearing in its representations a strong critique of dominant theories without using accepted categorizations such as capital or workers, or elite or mass. This critique however encompasses the possibility to rethink established roles in society, and consequently established categorizations that appear in organizational settings, such as the division between management and workers, or even training and work as sequential activities. In particular, what we, as trainers, might live as our own dark side, is the fact that we contribute in our practice to maintain an artificial distinction between the manager and the rest of the organization by providing training only to them, and we might also contribute to maintain an artificial distinction between hard and soft aspects of management. Could this be the "minimal level of collusion" (Carli 1993) with the context that any clinical endeavor bears as an "original sin," or can this be the start of a different, contemporaneous way of conceiving training? It is too early to attempt to answer to this question, yet we feel that by recognizing this possible contemporaneity in the accounts made by the participants, we do leave the door open for new and more realistic interpretations of the training experience. It would also open the door to acknowledge more clearly, even in a highly institutionalized context such as the SNA, the emancipatory values embedded in the clinical approach.

References

Alvesson, M., and S. Deetz. 2000. *Doing Critical Management Research*. London: Sage.

Alvesson, M., and H. Willmott. 1996. *Making Sense of Management: A Critical Introduction*. London: Sage.

Alvesson, M., and H. Willmott. 2003. *Studying Management Critically*. London: Sage.

Antonakis, J., A. Cianciolo, and R.J. Stemberg. eds. 2004. *The Nature of Leadership*. Thousand Oaks: Sage Publications.

Asimov, I. 1978. "Presentazione ai premi Hugo 1955 to 1975." Milano: Nord.

Ballard, J.G., 1962. "Which Way to Inner Space?" *New Worlds Science Fiction*, May.

Balogun, J., C. Jacobs, P. Jarzabkowski, S. Mantere, and E. Vaara. 2014. "Placing Strategy Discourse in Context: Sociomateriality, Sensemaking and Power." *Journal of Management Studies* 51, no. 2, pp. 175–201.

Barad, K. 2003. "Posthumanist Performativity: Toward an Understanding of How Matter Comes to Matter." *Signs* 28, no. 3, pp. 801–31.

Borgogelli, F. 2011. "I poteri della dirigenza pubblica nella disciplina dei rapporti di lavoro: le novità e i problemi." In *La riforma dell'impiego nelle pubbliche amministrazioni*, eds. S. Borelli and M. Magri. L.15/2009 e D.Lgs. 150/2009, Jovene editore.

Boyatzis, R.E., D. Goleman, and K. Rhee. 2000. "Clustering Competence in Emotional Intelligence: Insights From the Emotional Competence Inventory (ECI)s." In *Handbook of Emotional Intelligence*, eds. R. Bar-On and J.D.A. Parker, 343–62. San Francisco: Jossey-Bass.

Burns, J.M. 1978. *Leadership*. New York: Harper & Row.

Burrell, G., and G. Morgan. 1979. *Sociological Paradigms and Organizational Analysis*. London: Heinemann.

Carli, R., and R.M. Paniccia. 2003. *Analisi della domanda. Teoria e tecnica dell'intervento in psicologia clinica*. Bologna: Il Mulino.

Carli, R. 1987. "L'analisi della domanda." *Rivista di Psicologia Clinica* 1, no. 1, pp. 38–53.

Carli, R. ed. 1993. *L'analisi Della Domanda In Psicologia Clinica*. Milano: Giuffrè.

Carotenuto, A. 2001. *L'ultima medusa. Psicologia della fantascienza*. Milano: Bompiani.

Chimienti, A., G. Cioccetti, S. Mameli, M. Masia. (in press). *Rules, Norms and Materiality, a Clinical Approach, in Organization.* Artefacts and Practice: Palgrave.

Crozier, M. 1963. *Le Phénomène Bureaucratique.* Paris: Editions du Seuil.

Cziarnawska, B. 2009. *A Theory of Organizing.* Cheltenham: Edward Elgar.

Dachler, H.P., D.M. Hosking. 1995. "The Primacy of Relations in Socially constructed Realities." In *Management and Organization: Relational Alternatives to Individualism*, eds. D.M. Hosking, H.P. Dachler, and K.J. Gergen. Norway: Taos Institute Publications.

Delplancke, J.F. ed. 1975. *La Formation permanente.* Paris, CEPL, Centre d'Etude et de Promotion de la Lecture, Les Encyclopédies du Savoir Moderne, p. 254.

Enriquez, E. 1987. *Personalità e Organizzazione.* Rivista di Psicologia Clinica, 2.

Fayol, H. 1916. *Administration industrielle et generale.* Paris: Dunod.

Gergen, K.J. 1973. "Social Psychology as History." *Journal of Personality and Social Psychology* 26, no. 2, pp. 309–20.

Gherardi, S. 2006. *Organizational Knowledge, The Texture of Workplace Learning.* Malden, MA: Wiley-Blackwell.

Ghoshal, S. 2005. "Bad Management Theories Are Destroying Good Management Practices." *Academy of Management Learning & Education* 4, no. 1, pp. 75–91.

Giddens, A. 1984. *The Constitution of Society: Outline of the Theory of Structuration.* Oxford: Polity Press.

Giust-Desprairies, F. 2013. "La clinique, une epistemologie pour les sciences de l'homme." In *La recherche clinique en sciences sociales*, eds. de Gaulejac, Giust-Desprairies, and Massa. Paris: Erés.

Grey, C., and H. Willmott, eds. 2005. *Critical Management Studies—A reader.* UK: Oxford Press.

Hosking, D.M. 2004. "Change Works: A Critical Construction." In *Dynamics of Organizational Change and Learning,* ed. J. Boonstra. Chichester: Wiley.

Hosking, D.M. 2006. "Discourses of Relations and Relational Processes." In *Relational Perspectives in Organizational Studies: A Research Companion*, eds. O. Kyriakidou and M. Özbilgin. Cheltenham, UK: Edward Elgar.

Jarzabkowski, P., and A.P. Spee. 2009. "Strategy as Practice: A Review and Future Directions for the Field." *International Journal of Management Reviews* 11, no. 1, pp. 69–95.

Klein, M. 1952. "Some Theoretical Conclusions Regarding the Emotional: Life of the Infant." In *Developments in Psycho-Analysis*, ed. J. Riviere, 198–236. London: Hogarth Press.

Knorr Cetina, K., T. Shatzki, and E. Von Savigny. 2001. *The Practice Turn in Contemporary Theory.* New York: Routledge.

Kotter, J.P. 1987. *The Leadership Factor.* New York: Free Press.

Latour, B. 2005. *Reassembling the Social: An Introduction to Actor–Network Theory.* New York: Oxford University Press.

Matte Blanco, I. 1975. *The Unconscious as Infinite Sets*. Duckworth: London.

Mintzberg, H. 1973. *The Nature of Managerial Work*. New York: Harper & Row.

Mintzberg, H. 2005. *Managers Not MBA's: A Hard Look at the Soft Practice of Managing and Management Development*. San Francisco: Berrett-Koehler Publishers.

Mintzberg, H. 2009. *Managing*. San Francisco: Berret-Koehler Publishers.

Mowles, C. 2011. *Re-Thinking Management*. London: Gower.

Orlikowski, W.J. 2010. "The Socio Materiality of Organizational Life: Considering Technology in Management Research." *Cambridge Journal of Economics* 34, pp. 125–41.

Orlikowski, W.J., and S.V. Scott. 2008. "Sociomateriality: Challenging the Separation of Technology, Work and Organization." *Annals of the Academy of Management* 2, no. 1, pp. 433–74.

Pagès, M., V. de Gaulejac, M. Bonetti, and D. Descendre. 1979. *L'emprise de L'organization*. Desclee De Brouwer.

Quinn, R.E. 1991. *Beyond Rational Management: Mastering the Paradoxes of Competing Demands of High Performance*. San Francisco: Jossey-Bass.

Quinn, R.E., and J. Rohrbaugh. 1983. "A Spatial Model of Effectiveness Criteria: Toward a Competing Values Approach to Organizational Analysis." *Management Science* 29, pp. 363–77.

Ruvolo, G., M. Di Blasi, E. Neri. 1995. "Il gruppo come strumento psicosociale." In *La psicodinamica dei gruppi*, eds. F. Di Maria and G. Lo Verso, 87–138. Milano: Raffaello Cortina.

Salvatore, S., and M. Scotto di Carlo. 2005. *L'intervento psicologico per la scuola— modelli, metodi, strumenti*. Roma: Carlo Amore.

Salvatore, S., and T. Zitoun. 2011. *Cultural Psychology and Psychoanalysis: Pathways to Synthesis*. Charlotte: Information Age Publishing.

Sandberg, J. 2005. "How Do We Justify Knowledge Produced Under Interpretive Approaches." *Organizational Research Methods* 8, no. 1, pp. 41–68.

Sandberg, J., and A. Targama. 2007. *Managing Understanding in Organizations*. London: Sage Publications.

Stacey, R.D. 1992. *Managing Chaos*. London: Kogan Page.

Tevis, W. 1963. *The Man Who Fell to Earth*. London: Pan Books.

Todorov, T. 1975. *The Fantastic: A Structural Approach to a Literary Genre*. Translated by R. Howard. New York: Cornell University Press.

Trentini, G. 1997. *Oltre il potere. Discorso sulla leadership*. Milano: Franco Angeli Editore.

Venza, G. 2007. *Dinamiche di gruppo e tecniche di gruppo nel lavoro educativo e formativo*. Milano: Franco Angeli.

Zaleznik, A. 1977. "Manager and Leaders: Are They Different?" *Harvard Business Review*, May–June.

CHAPTER 7

Organizational Corruption in the Education System

Alessandro Hinna, Fabio Monteduro, and Sonia Moi

Department of Economics and Finance,
University of Rome Tor Vergata

Introduction

Corruption is a social plague that decreases social and economic wealth (Dela Rama 2011; Kaptein 2011; Lange 2008), limiting investment and growth and leading to ineffective government (Jain 2001; Langseth 1999; Lintjer 2000; Rose-Ackerman 1999; Schneider 2007; World Bank 2004a).

Over the years, many scholars have studied corruption, investigating and measuring its effects (Das and Parry 2011; Tanzi 1998; World Bank 2004a), causes (Ades and Di Tella 1996), and prevention strategies (Nielsen 2003).

Specifically, a country's corruption has been studied from different disciplinary perspectives, including psychology, sociology, economics, law, and political science. Each discipline has, therefore, investigated a country's corruption with a purpose, utilizing different analysis tools and creating a rather extensive knowledge of the phenomenon, which is, in part, still waiting to be systematized (Pinto, Leana, and Pil 2008).

Many sociological studies, for example, have investigated the correlation between a country's corruption and its democracy (i.e., Zhang, Cao, and Vaughn 2009) and between a country's corruption and political stability (Serra 2006). There are also a great number of political science studies that, over time, tried to understand what factors drive individual politicians to systematic corruption, discovering, for example, important correlations between the time mode of electoral process and the country's political corruption (Chang 2005; Ferraz and Finan 2011). In studies of an economic matrix, Klitgaard (1988) identified monopoly, discretion, and accountability as the three basic "ingredients" of corruption, finding a model considered valid (Mills 2012) for the analysis of the determinants of corruption.

As noted by several well-known contributions to the literature reviews of corruption, even if issues of corruption are widely discussed in scientific literature, little is known with respect to what feeds the occurrence of corruption episodes or illegal behavior within organizations, especially with regard to public organizations. Recently, organizational scholars investigated corruption at the organizational level of analysis, exploring causes, consequences, or possible strategies to reduce it (see, e.g., Aguilera and Vadera 2007; Argandona 2003; Den Nieuwenboer and Kaptein 2008; Lindgreen 2004; Matsumura and Shin 2005; Zahra, Priem, and Rasheed 2005). These studies typically refer to corporate organizations, while little is known about organizational determinants of corruption in the public sector, even if public sector corruption appears as one of the most severe obstacles to a country's development processes (U-Myint 2000). The importance of studying dynamics and causes of corruption in public sector organizations becomes even clearer if we refer to specific areas of activity. That is, for example, education. Assuming that:

> education, in addition to being an entitlement, is instrumental in promoting development, social justice, and other human rights. Education has the potential to instil hope in our children and encourage a spirit of common and shared responsibility for our planet and for humanity. (Transparency International 2013, xv)

We strongly believe that fighting and preventing corruption is related to the understanding of the causes of the same phenomenon, especially in the education system.

In particular, by tackling the problem of corruption in the education system, in addition to generating the potential economic and social impact of the sector, public organizations are also creating the basis for a policy of preventing and combating corruption at the country level.

In this scenario, starting from the differences between public and private organizations and taking into account peculiarities of an education system, the article's main object is to identify antecedents of corruption within school organizations. Therefore, this articles aims to: (1) identify a set of organizational variables that reflects the determinants of corruption within the private and public sectors; (2) identify a set of organizational variables that reflects the determinants of corruption within the education system; and (3) identify specific tools that can be put in place to fight corruption in the education system.

Drawing on a selective literature review, we use theories and theoretical considerations to define a model which aims to provide scholars and policy makers with measures capable of preventing corruption in the education systems. This chapter is divided into several sections. In the next first section, we focus on the meaning of corruption and provide a wide array of definitions in order to shed light on the definition adopted in academic literature. In the second section, we summarize the studies focusing on the analysis of the phenomenon from different points of view (macro-, meso-, and microlevel analysis). In the third section, we present the conceptual framework of the determinants of corruption in private and public sector organizations. In the fourth section, we provide a conceptual framework of the determinants of corruption in an education system (involving teachers, students, and administrative officers). In the fifth section, we propose a model, which may be used to fight and prevent corruption through the application of specific tools, such as codes of ethics and training activities. Directions for future research are discussed in the last section.

The Meaning of Corruption

It is not easy to define the concept of corruption in a clear and widely shared way. Basically, there is a certain consensus in defining corruption as the abuse of entrusted power for private gain (Pope 2000) and refer to the way in which the power of public office is used for personal gain in a manner that contravenes the rules of the game (Jain 2001). On this basis, for instance, corruption represents a behavior that deviates from the formal duties of conduct; in other words, the use of public authority for private interests such as wealth, power, and status (Khan 1996). Again, corruption refers to the agency theory and represents the use of public power for private gain, in which the official (the agent) entrusted by the public (principal) engages in some sort of malfeasance for private enrichment (Bardhan 1997) or occurs when there is an exchange of money for political decisions between a citizen and a public official. According to Rose-Ackerman (1978), corruption is an illegal payment to a public agent to obtain a benefit that may or may not be deserved in the absence of payoffs.

Moreover, a distinction exists between corruption and illegality: in the case of corruption, the central element is the abuse of "public power"; illegal acts, instead, do not necessarily require the use of public power. However, some illegal behaviors are closely linked to the concept of corruption, such as money laundering (Levi Dakolias and Greenberg 2007; Sharman and Chaikin 2009), fraudulent practices especially related to financial (Cheng and Ma 2009; Vinod 2008) or electoral mechanisms (Beaulieu 2014; McCann and Domínguez 1998).

It is important to note that corruption does not always result in bribery (Tanzi 1998), and corruptive conduct may lead not to just a private gain but also to a class, family, party, tribe gain, and so on (Tanzi 1998). Again, corruption is a phenomenon that affects public and private organizations; it can be domestic, international, administrative, or political.

For example, according to Heidenheimer and Johnson (2002), there are three different types of corruption: *black* corruption, which consists of serious violations of the legal system; *white* corruption, which consists of common social unethical behaviors that are tolerated by public opinion; and *grey* corruption, which occurs when some elements, usually elites, may want to see the actions punished, others not, and the majority may well be ambiguous (Heidenheimer and Johnson 2002).

Commonly, corruption is recognized to affect the political, administrative (or bureaucratic), and legislative system. The first type is often called *grand corruption* and concerns the way in which politicians exploit their power to make economic policies. Administrative (or bureaucratic) corruption, called *petty corruption*, occurs when citizens bribe a public official to receive a service to which they are entitled or to speed-up a bureaucratic procedure. Legislative corruption concerns the way in which actors can influence a legislator's behavior (Jain 2001).

From an organizational point of view, Pinto, Leana, and Pil (2008) focus on two dimensions of corruption in organizations: the first one occurs when organization's members act in a corrupt manner primarily for their personal benefit; showing that corruption is a behavioral phenomenon, related to the way in which individuals act (unethically) within the organization; the second refers to the way in which a group collectively acts in a corrupt manner for the benefit of the organization, showing that corruption involves an organization as a whole, through its management, who act illegally in order to gain benefits primarily for the same organization.

Considering the wide range of definitions, in this chapter we consider corruption as the various situations in which an abuse of power occurs in the education system to obtain private benefits, referring to corruption (as a bribe) or illegal acts.

Corruption in Private and Public Sector Organizations

Understanding the Determinants of Corruption in Organizations

As we stated in the introduction, a great number of scholarly contributions focus on causes and determinants of corruption. These studies offer an analysis of the phenomenon from three points of view: macro-, meso-, and microlevel analyses.

Many of these studies, however, concentrated their efforts on a macrolevel of analysis. In other words, they aim to investigate the determinants of corruption considering the "country level" in which social and economic issues are merged to identify the circumstances in which corruption may arise.

In particular, structural causes refer to a large number of variables. One of the most important ones seems to be the level of economic development of a country: some studies found a correlation between levels of corruption and economic development, noting that the higher the level of economic development and the lower the level of perceived corruption (Ades and Di Tella 1999; Treisman 2000). Other researchers refer to the political systems, in terms of institutions, democratic systems, or electoral system. For example, Treisman (2007, 228), "regressing perceived corruption indexes on FH political rights scores (lagged to reduce endogeneity), while controlling for economic development" found that "greater political rights are significantly related to lower perceived corruption in the World Bank ratings. Political rights remain significant when one controls for a variety of other possible determinants, including colonial heritage and religion." Furthermore, competitive environment is a relevant structural variable that may affect corruption at macrolevel (Ades and Di Tella 1999). In particular, these studies correlate levels of corruption with the degree of market openness, resources available in the market and the rents that could potentially be acquired by illegal transactions between private citizens and public officials.

Therefore, macrolevel characteristics mainly refer to the pressure that may result from the intersection between social, economic, or political interests along with the opportunities to corrupt that those characteristics may create.

Against this backdrop, the analysis of structural causes of corruption can be studied through Klitgaard's (1988) work. Using the agency theory framework, Klitgaard, Maclean-Abaroa, and Parris (2000, 35) states that an individual "will have the opportunity to garner corrupt benefits as a function of their degree of monopoly over a service or activity, their discretion in deciding who should get how much, and the degree to which their activities are accountable." Using a sort of a mathematical formula, he states that $C = M + D - A$ in which C is "corruption," M is "monopoly," D is "discretion," and A is "accountability."

The study of the macrolevel determinant of corruption may help policy makers in building anticorruption strategies, with the limit to act only on the pressure or the opportunity to corrupt. For example, as Persson, Rothstein, and Teorell (2010, 5) state, according to Klitgaard (1988):

> the principal should aim at negatively affecting the agent's motivations to engage in corrupt behaviour. This could most effectively be done through control instruments that decrease the level of discretion among agents, limit the monopoly of agents and increase the level of accountability in the system.

On the other hand, some studies focus on causes, mechanisms, and outcomes of corruption at the "mesolevel." These studies correlate organizational characteristics with corruption levels (or wrongdoing) within organizations and offer an analysis of corruption that comprises both cultural and social aspects from an organization's perspective.

In this context, organizational culture, namely the set of values, internal rules, and procedures, affects the way in which individuals act within an organization. In other words, each organization, by setting the stage for the identification of right or wrong conduct, may align individual behaviors toward a right or a corrupt conduct (Palmer 2012).

Within each organization, in fact, individuals act in order to achieve performance goals. In this scenario, the lack of capability to achieve performance goals may create an incentive to corrupt (or deviation from the correct behavior) in order to achieve the firm's objectives (Baucus 1994; Greve, Palmer, and Pozner 2010).

According to Baucus (1994), some organizational characteristics may push individual toward wrongdoing because of the need to guarantee a certain level of performance (or a certain number of outputs) which can generate misconduct problems in situation of poor financial performance or in the absence of slack resources.

The analysis of the determinant of corruption at mesolevel provide policy makers with some suggestions to identify anticorruption strategies, such as the promotion of transparent procedures and the improvement of regulation systems. However, this analysis is complicated by the great number of variables that intervenes into the system: organizational characteristics, environmental variables, cultural factors, and individual behaviors.

Finally, significant studies have been conducted on the determinants of corruption at microlevel (e.g., Collier 2002; Treviño 1986), taking into account antecedents of individual behaviors.

These studies addressed corruption problems while considering the rationality of individuals. In this context, corruption levels may arise depending on the specific characteristics of individuals and their integrity (Rose-Ackerman 1997). More specifically, the individual propensity to corrupt seems to be linked to the expected benefits of wrongdoing. In other words, an individual is more likely to corrupt, the higher the benefits of wrongdoing or the lower the potential penalty costs (if caught).

The issue of individual integrity, also, depends on other variables affecting the individual behavior, such as environmental characteristics in which individuals act, individual and collective culture and beliefs. In this scenario, a decision whether or not to corrupt depends on how the aforementioned variables affect cognitive processes at the individual level.

With respect to anticorruption strategies, these studies highlight the importance of the individual sphere, addressing the need to improve awareness on the corruption phenomenon through providing ethics training, strengthening recruitment processes, and resource management.

As aforementioned, these analyses present some limitations as they consider macro-, meso-, or microlevel individually; none of them integrates the three perspectives of analysis.

There are; however, some exceptions. Starting from the mesolevel analysis, some pioneering studies in corporate organizations have made important contributions by developing analytical models to investigate intentional and unintentional wrongdoing behaviors in corporate organizations, integrating theories and empirical contributions from economic, social, and psychological perspectives.

In particular, some of these studies focus on the particular configuration of the relationship between environment and organization, while others have focused on the relationship between the organization and individuals.

Among the first, a systematic contribution is offered from Baucus (1994), albeit in a context of particular reflection. The contribution of Baucus, in fact, is part of a series of studies that address factors that "can lead to an illegal act," stating that corporate wrongdoing can occur intentionally and unintentionally. This contribution, therefore, is not referring to the analysis of the corruption phenomena, as defined previously. However, it is of fundamental importance because of its multivariate model, which attempts to analyze the potential causes of wrongdoing behaviors. According to Baucus (1994), an illicit behavior derives from the combination of the right "pressure," "opportunity," and "predisposition," which can determine the specific characteristics of the competitive environment, legal and regulatory environment, and organizational characteristics (Figure 7.1).

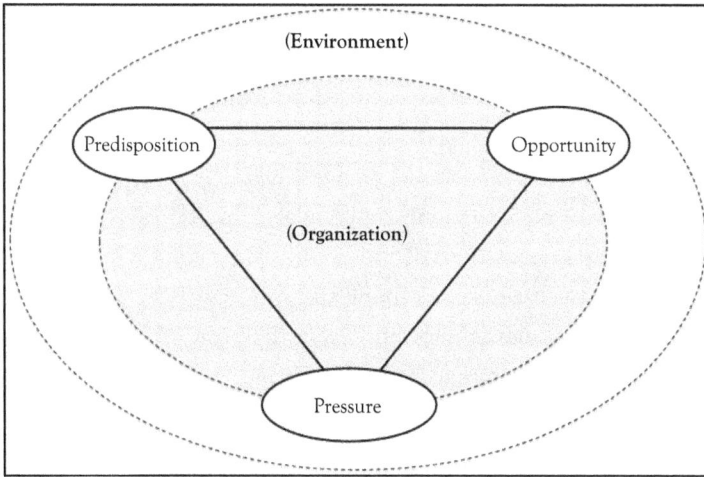

Figure 7.1 Environment–organization relationship: determinants of illicit behaviors

Source: Our elaboration.

In particular, referring to *pressure* or *need*, the cause of which can be found in an environment characterized by intense competition among companies, the heterogeneity of organization (suppliers, creditors, etc.), and the scarcity of essential resources. Similarly, the characteristics of legal and regulatory environment can be a source of pressure, given the high cost that the company has to bear to conform to regulation and to frequent changes in the law. On the other side, this may prove to be a source of pressure or need for certain organizational characteristics such as, for example, the degree of internal pressure or performance or the absence of slack resources.

Opportunity, for instance, can be created by environmental characteristics such as turbulence and munificence, as well as low intensity of rivalry. At the same time, it also creates the legal environment, where it is complex and ambiguous or features newly enacted legislation. On the other side, acts of opportunism can find themselves exhibiting characteristics of the organization, such as the firm's size or complexity. Finally, even the *predisposition* may find its sources in certain environmental characteristics, such as the consolidated level of illegal activity and the established relationships with regulatory agencies. At the same time, other sources of predisposition can be related to the level of employee commitment:

highly effective commitment can push employees to sacrifice their ethical values in the interest of the company, while a low commitment favors a low attachment to the workplace and, therefore, the pursuit of individual interests.

Thus, Baucus' (1994) model analyzes illegal acts of private organizations and integrates environmental and organizational characteristics, whose peculiar combinations define essentially the contest in which individuals act on the basis of their moral and ethical values.

However, the author does not define how the different combinations between organizational characteristics and individual characteristics can more or less explain the existence of wrongdoing behaviors. At this second type of analysis was instead interested, in parallel time, a second research path, which adopts sociological and psychological perspectives to advance—on the basis of the first works of Albrecht, Howe, and Romney (1984), Coleman (1987), and Cressey (1950, 1953, 1965)—a model of analysis known as "fraud triangle." According to this model, individual determinants of corruption in the workplace are to be found in the particular combination of opportunity-pressure, incentive, motivation-justification, and rationalization, where typically (Albrecht et al. 1984; Ashforth and Anand 2003; Comer 1985; Davies 2000; Gottfredson and Hirschi 1990; Hallier and Forbes 2004; Vardi and Weitz 2004; Wells 2004) *opportunity* refers to the context that makes a possible course of action; *motivation* refers to factors that prompt individuals to act in certain ways; and *rationalization* refers to the social constructed "adjustment" that violators use to legitimize their behavior (Figure 7.2).

In this research path, important steps have been made from Aguilera and Vadera (2007) and Den Nieuwenboer and Kaptein (2008), developing the model initially proposed by Cressey (1953), thus providing an important contribution to the development of management practices, which is, in fact, dedicated to the prevention of organizational corruption.

In particular, Aguilera and Vadera (2007) propose a theoretical contribution that systematically analyzes the simultaneous interaction of the three pillars of the "fraud triangle" model, as an antecedent to organizational corruption. With the aim of discovering managerial implications, they debate on corruption as "the abuse of authority for personal benefit" and they examine Weber's construct of authority (Weber [1922] 1978) as

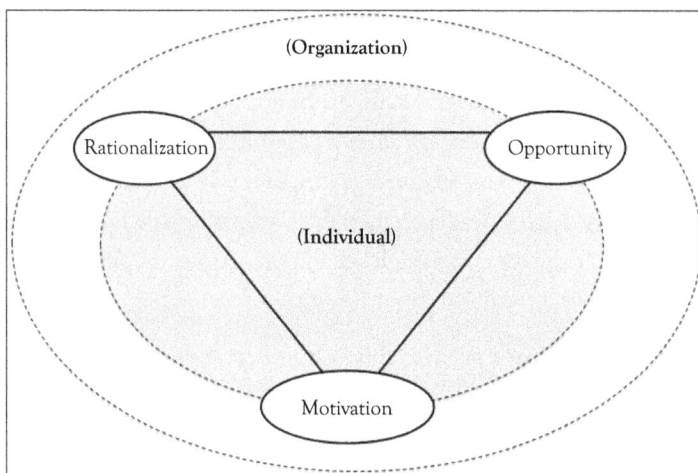

Figure 7.2 Organization–individual relationship: determinants of organization corruption

a contingent source of "opportunities" to conduct corruption of managers, driven by particular kind of motives (individualistic, collectivistic, or relational) and able to find particular justification (rationalization, socialization, or ritualism) for their own actions.

The authors states that three ideal types of authority (legal-rational, charismatic, or traditional) interact with different types of motivation and justifications, obtaining three distinct types of organizational corruption (procedural, schematic, and categorical), described as the abuse of authority for personal benefit.

As anticipated, a second important development of the fraud triangle arrives from Den Nieuwenboer and Kaptein (2008). Starting from a similar definition of corruption (the misuse of authority for personal, subunit, and organizational gain), they formulate three downward organizational spirals (the spiral of divergent norms, the spiral of pressure, and the spiral of opportunity) using social identity theory (Tajfel and Turner 1979). So, leaving a static vision of the fraud triangle, the authors propose a reflection on the dynamic nature of corruption, trying to understand how corruption develops over time in the interaction between the three sides of the fraud triangle and, therefore, in the last room, in a given context of interaction between individual and organization. In this frame, they formulate three downward organizational spirals: (a) the spiral of divergent norms, which starts when a progressive group's detachment from its sur-roundings and the increased conflict with the outside world; (b) the spi-ral of pressure, which starts because of the stress on performance, which might seduce people to engage in any type of corruption that increases one's performance or protects one's status; and (c) the spiral of opportu-nity, which starts when leaders refrain from imposing sanctions on some-one engaging in corruption, which becomes more prototypical over time.

Organization Corruption in Public Organizations

These contributions, built for the private sector, do not take into account the specific characteristics of the public sector, making the analysis more complex in that specific context. Therefore, in regards to the analy-sis of the phenomenon, we might understand the specificity of public sector organizations to translate, even in this context, the results of the researches thus far accomplished in the field of prevention of corruption organization.

As is known, there is vast literature devoted to the analysis of the differences and the similarities between public and private organiza-tions (i.e., Allison 1979; Antonsen and Jorgensen 1997; Bozeman 1987; Bozeman and Bretschneider 1994; Box 1999; Fottler 1981; Metcalfe 1993; Nutt and Backoff 1993; Perry and Porter 1982; Perry and Rainey 1988; Ring and Perry 1985; Stewart and Ranson 1988). Obviously, we do not wish to propose a review of such vast literature. Rather, we pro-pose a selective reading of it, according to the typical determinants of organization corruption as has been discussed until now. To do so, we will consider all the aspects connected to the relation of environment, organization, and individual, remaining consistent with the literature on organization corruption, we will even split the academic contributions according to the following pillars: pressure–motivation; opportunity; and predisposition–rationalization (Figure 7.3).

Pressure–Motivation

In his works, Cressey (1950, 1953, 1965) infers that pressure can be related to a perceived nonsharable problem that acts as a motivator to

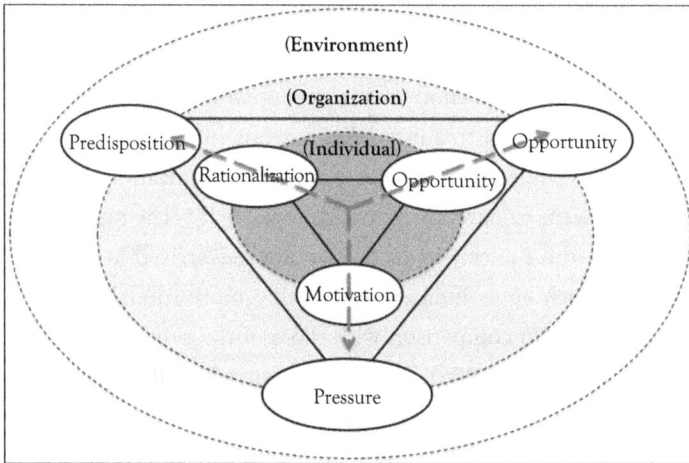

Figure 7.3 Environment, organization, and individual relationship: the integrated model of organization corruption determinants

commit a violation. According to Baucus (1994), pressure occurs when individuals or organizations place urgent demands or constraints on a firm, pushing until the firm's employees respond in some fashion. Corruption arises when individuals feeling pressured by someone or something, act in order to achieve the expected result. In the public sector, the complexity of the relationship between stakeholders and organizations can be considered from two different points of view: political influence and groups of interest influence. Both politician and interest groups can influence the managerial decision-making process (Caiden and Caiden 1977; Davis 2004; Rose-Ackerman 1978), bringing public managers to act illegally in order to respond to these requests. Considering the relationship with stakeholders, pressure can also create an incentive to behave legally, and this absence can increase corruption levels of public organizations. In other words, both literature and empirical evidence suggest that *social pressure* exercised through a sort of *social control* or through the *press* can affect corruption levels (Brunetti and Weder 2003; Freille, Haque, and Kneller 2007; Kalenborn and Lessmann 2013). In particular, independent press and qualitatively high reporting on corruption can exercise a strong pressure on public servants to act legally and in the public interest (Nogara 2009) due to the ability to increase public awareness and activate anticorruption values (Rose-Ackerman 1999). Social control, however, is not exclusively exercised through the *press*, but it is closely related to the concept of transparency and accountability. As Klitgaard (1998) states, corruption is also a function of the accountability level of the public administration, and fighting it requires a strong human involvement.

On the other side, the relationship between organization and employees does not seem to have any particular specificity. The numerous contributions on the subject, in fact, have not yet arrived at unequivocal conclusions, such as to indicate the specific motivational structures of public employees in comparison with those of the private sector (Lyons, Duxbury, and Higgins 2006). The only item on which the literature seems to agree is tied to value dimensions and, therefore, to organizational commitment. According to Boyne (2002), we consider as value variables those factors concerning attitudes and aspirations of staff.

In particular, main differences between public and private organizations concern the desire to serve the public results in a lower attention to financial rewards linked to a higher performance. In other words, according to Boyne (2002), public managers are believed to be less materialistic than private managers. As a consequence of the previous point, and the absence of a link between contributions of public servants and success of their organizations, public organizations have a lower managerial commitment than private organizations.

Opportunity

Opportunity represents "the presence of a favorable combination of circumstances that makes a possible course of action possible" (McKendall and Wagner 1997, 626) or, in other words, the possibility to have means or abilities to commit violations (Cressey 1950, 1953, 1965).

Condition of opportunity can also occur when there is no adequate punishment for illegal acts. As Den Nieuwenboer and Kaptein (2008) state, the main feature of the factor of opportunity is that the risk of getting caught and punished is such that it does not deter (potential) perpetrators.

As we state in the preceding, public managers are affected by higher regulatory constraints on procedures and difficulties of interpretation correlated to the proliferation of formal specifications and controls and external sources of formal influence and the greater fragmentation of those sources.

In this case, one of the possible consequences of the regulatory system is in regard to the occurrence of a kind of discretionary power in the design (Rose-Ackerman 1978), the application and the monitoring of rules that we can define as the "authority to design regulations as well as to administer them" (Jain 2001, 77). In fact, corruption can occur in cases of vagueness of rules, in its interpretation difficulties, or in case of high monitoring costs. The discretionary power principle can be easily explained by the agency theory (Bliss and Di Tella 1997).

In addition, conditions concerning legal constraints seem to be strictly linked with the previous considerations.

With regards to the regulatory environment, it is quite clear that public organizations are regulated by law and by internal regulation. The cases of frequent changes in regulation create a cost of conformation to them: the higher the cost to conform organizations to the regulation and the lower the cost of the penalty of no conformation, it can create the conditions to behave illegally.

Again, establishing a set of effective controls, functioning as a deterrent to corruption in a context of such uncertainty, is not easy because of the strong relationship with a plurality of factors such as penalty issues (Jain 2001). As Becker (1986) states, the occurrence of certain behaviors is related to the probability of getting caught and the probability (once caught) of getting punished. This can result in high monitoring costs related to the efforts made to uncover corruption and the efforts in the design of effective law enforcement (Jain 2001).

Public organizations have more formal procedures for the decision-making process and are less flexible than private organizations. This condition can be summarized into greater bureaucracy. As a consequence of this condition, public administrations are seen as obsessed by the formal respect of rules rather than results (Boyne 2002), which can lead to vague objectives of public organizations. In addition, as a consequence, a vague objective can create the opportunity to behave illegally in order to respond, in some fashion, to the planned activity. Moreover, the implementation of these activities through corruption without any type of punishment increases opportunities to commit illegal acts because of one's success in reaching targets (Den Nieuwenboer and Kaptein 2008).

Predisposition–Rationalization

Predisposition and rationalization are related to the specific characteristics of an organization or its surrounding environment that can lead workers to act illegally. In detail, predisposition acts with organizational factors, such as, according to Baucus (1994), the characteristics of the firm and the environment can predispose organizations to behave illegally, while rationalization involves cultural factors that induce individuals to act in ways that neutralize the strong ethical controls of society (Aguilera and Vadera 2007). Organizational characteristics are related to cultural factors, which can be typical of a country and affect perceived levels of corruption (Davis and Ruhe 2003) and, thus, predisposition to behave illegally. For instance, at the macrolevel, the Chinese guanxi represents a cultural factor that is a widespread business behavior (Luo 2008) in Chinese organizations. This embedded behavior creates conditions for the perpetration of illegal and corrupt behaviors. In the same way, cultural factors can lead public managers to behave illegally.

As aforestated, illegal activities can also be unintentional. Different contributions correlate the increase of ethical orientation and competences in training to a decrease of corruption levels (Cooper 2000; Johnson and Sharma 2004; Richter and Burke 2007). A recent work of Organisation for Economic Co-operation and Development (OCED 2003, 7) reinforces the importance of promoting ethical training among public servants, asserting that "ethics training for public officials is one of the instruments for building integrity in state institutions and ensuring good quality public governance."

Organization Corruption in the Education System

Types of Organizational Corruption

Education systems, in terms of organization, differ around the world and depend on the peculiarities of the territory and the social and cultural environment. In this context, education is provided by public and private organizations with a common aim, defined in the Universal Declaration of Human Rights (Article 26), that "everyone has the right to education."

Education represents an important expense for countries. In order to understand the relevance of the sector, we can take into account World Bank statistics on public spending on education. In particular, we consider public expenditures on education as a percentage of the gross domestic product (GDP); in other words, the total public expenditure (current and capital) on education expressed as a percentage of the GDP in a given year. Public expenditure on education includes government spending on educational institutions (public and private), education administration, and transfers or subsidies for private entities (students, households, and other private entities). The average of public spending on education for all countries in 2010 coincided to 4.9 percent of the GDP.

Since education represents a large component of the public sector and, also, of public expenditure, and it is seen as having a huge impact on cultural, social, and economic systems, malfunctions of the system or the proliferation of corruption phenomena within it represent a serious detriment to society as a whole.

As Chapman (2002, 3) states, education systems are particularly exposed to corruption. He identifies three reasons: (1) "as one of the few governmental agencies with high visibility representation all the way down to the community level, education is an attractive structure for patronage and manipulation of local sentiment"; (2) because of the fact that "decisions perceived to have significant consequences for people's lives are made by 'gatekeepers' who control decisions at each of those levels"; and (3) because of the great amount of funds spent in education system, and the way in which it is spent (small amounts).

As stated earlier, corruption can be defined as the abuse of entrusted power for private gain (Pope 2000). The same definition can be applied to the education system, enriched with other meanings. As a result, corruption in the education system can be defined as "the systematic use of public office for private benefit, whose impact is significant on the availability and quality of educational goods and services, and, as a consequence on access, quality or equity in education" (Hallak and Poisson 2002, 17). Some authors try to identify in which form corruption occurs in the education system.

In this sense, according to Chapman (2002), at the central or ministry level, corrupt behavior refers, for example, to kickbacks on construction and supply contracts, favoritism in hiring, appointments, and promotions decisions, diversion of funds from government accounts, ghost teachers and employees, requiring payment for services that should be provided free, and so on.

He states that, at the region or district level, corrupt behavior refers to, for example, overlooking school violations on inspector visits in return for bribes or favors, diversion of school supplies to private market, sales of recommendations for higher education entrance, and so on. Again, school level corrupt behavior refers to, for example, diversion of school fees, inflation of school enrolment data (if any), imposition of unauthorized fees, and so on. At the classroom or teacher level, instead, corrupt behavior refers to, for example, siphoning of school supplies and textbooks to the local market, selling test scores and course grades, selling change of grade, selling grade-to-grade promotion, or selling admissions.

Finally, according to Chapman (2002), at the international agencies level, corrupt behavior refers to, for example, the payment of bribes, payment of excessive or unnecessary fees to obtain services, or allocating (or acquiescing in the allocation of) project-related opportunities on the basis of candidate connections rather than on merit.

In addition, Chapman (2002) distinguishes between different types of corruption, such as blatantly illegal acts of bribery or fraud, actions to secure a modest income by people paid too little or too late, actions taken to get work done in difficult circumstances, differences in cultural perspectives, and behavior resulting from incompetence.

Corruption practices, especially in higher education, can involve or not involve students. In particular, "corruption that involves students as agents has a direct effect on their values, beliefs, and life chances, and corruption that does not involve students as agents has limited direct effect on them" (Rumyantseva 2005, 86).

According to Heyneman (2004), two main forms of corrupt practices exist in an education system: corruption in services and academic corruption.

Determinants of Organizational Corruption in an Education System

Starting from the peculiarity of the education system and, according to those studies and many other studies in the field (such as Tanaka 2001; Hallak and Poisson 2002, 2007; Transparency International 2013), we now consider the three macrovariables (pressure–motivation, opportunity, and predisposition–rationalization) for better understanding determinants of organization corruption in an education system (Figure 7.3).

Pressure–Motivation

In the previous section, we stated that pressure refers to a perceived nonsharable problem, which acts as a motivator to commit a violation (Cressey 1950, 1953, 1965) and occurs when individuals or organizations place urgent demands or constraints on a firm, pushing until the firm's employees respond in some fashion (Baucus 1994).

In general, in the private sector, pressure refers to competition among firms, high cost to conform to regulation, frequent changes in law or pressure on performance (Baucus 1994).

In the public sector, pressure refers to the complexity of the relationship between stakeholders and public organizations and to the regulatory environment. First, complexity has to be considered with reference to political influences and groups of interest influence; second, this also has to take into account the lack of social awareness about the functioning of the public administration and its results in terms of social pressure exercised through a sort of social control or through the press, which can affect corruption levels. Finally, frequent changes in regulations can create conformation, thus creating the conditions to behave illegally.

In an education system, pressure can be referred to the following variables:

- Access to information.
- Lack of "social" control.
- High competition into the education system.
- Rapid disbursement of funds.

The first variable is related to the access of information. That variable can be considered under the aspect of the absence of transparency on the selection process, admission to higher education, and so on. For example:

> students without sufficient information on financing options for higher education may find themselves overpaying so as to gain access to colleges or universities. For students who rely on federal, state or personal loans to pay for their education, unfair lending policies can drive up the price of education. (Osipian 2013, 151)

Again, the access to information can be reserved to a limited circle of people (Osipian 2008a).

The second variable, strictly related to the first one, is the absence of social and external controls (Hallak and Poisson 2002, 2007). In particular, the lack of information about the activity of the education system's organization related to the lack of social attention (media, press, or external authorities control), reducing the knowledge about how decisions are made, can also create an incentive to behave legally and, consequently, may increase the risk exposure of the organization and the system as a whole. Lacking access to information can be also seen as the:

> lack of knowledge of criteria for access to education institutions, lack of timely publication of data on enrolment, teachers' lists, examination results and financial flows including fees [*that can represent*] obstacles to information sharing and exposures to the public of the way the public sector operates. [Also,] the non-recognition of the right to information impedes them from exerting any social control. (Hallak and Poisson 2007, 69)

The third variable of pressure is the high competition among organizations of the education system. Especially in the context of higher education, organizations (in private and public sectors) can be considered as competitive companies, from different point of view, such as the admission process to higher education, university-ranking systems, the competition for funding, and, after education, the high competition for well-paid jobs. In relation to higher education, university-ranking systems, the competition for funding, pressure increased because of the increase in the number of students with different disadvantages (such as disabilities, social or economic disadvantages, etc.), for which organizations try to deal within a situation of lack of funds and scarce resources. "This highly competitive and under-resourced environment is situated in an increasingly competitive worldwide economy, as well as a social context that may encourage students to regard higher education primarily as a means to a vocational end" (Bretag 2013, 171). In relation to the high competition for well-paid jobs after education, responses to pressure results in illegal acts such as academic fraud, corruption on controllers and gatekeepers, and so on (Hallak and Poisson 2007).

The last variable of pressure is related to the rapid disbursement of funds. According to Hallak and Poisson (2007), in some countries, pressure on the rapid disbursement of funds can contribute to increased wrongdoing.

Opportunity

In the previous section, we stated that opportunity represents the presence of a favorable combination of circumstances that makes it possible to commit violations or wrongdoing that occurs when there is no adequate punishment for illegal acts.

In the private sector, opportunity refers to the lack of competition among firms, the rapid change of the environmental condition of industry, the complexity or ambiguously of the regulation, and the organizational complexity of the firm (Baucus 1994).

In the public sector, opportunity refers mainly to the higher regulatory constraints on procedures and difficulties in interpretation of norms. It is also related to the effectiveness of controls, functioning as a deterrent to corruption.

In the education system, opportunity can be explained by the following variables:

- Uncertainty of the regulation and the lack of transparency on procedures.
- The effectiveness of penalties.
- The discretionary power.

The first variable of opportunity is the uncertainty of the regulation and the lack of clarity and transparency on procedures regarding, for example, procurement processes (Chapman 2002) and human and financial resources management (Hallak and Poisson 2007). Vagueness and uncertainty, creating difficulties in the interpretation of the regulations, may result in intentional or unintentional wrongdoing. In fact, the absence of clear regulation can create, in certain situations, the opportunity to behave illegally. In this context, also, opportunities for corruption arise when a certain lack of clarity and transparency on procedures occurs. For example, in managing monetary resources, the lack of clear (and widespread) procedures can generate intentional and unintentional misallocation of funds (Chapman 2002). However, it is clear that the efficiency and transparency management of this resource is critical "in order to ensure that their output is of value to students and to society at large" (Kimeu 2013, 45). Again, the lack of clear procedure can increase the opportunity for the so-called teacher absenteeism (Hallak and Poisson, 2007). This phenomenon is considered one of the most representative of corruption in an education system, as shown by studies in developing countries. (Abadzi 2007; Adeyemi and Akpotu 2009; African Economic Research Consortium 2011; Benveniste, Marshall, and Araujo 2008; Benveniste, Marshall, and Santibañez 2008; Carneiro, Das, and Reis 2010; Center for Democratic Development 2008; Chaudhury et al. 2006; Das et al. 2005; Vermeersch and Kremer 2004; World Bank 2006, 2004b, 2001.) As commonly recognized, the problem of absenteeism is related to the loss of significant expenditures in education, which can be an obstacle to development of the sector as a whole.

The second variable of opportunity is the effectiveness of penalties. A clear, widely known and applied system of penalties against illegal behavior is the primary deterrent to prevent corruption phenomena. On the contrary, a system, although present but not applied, can create opportunities to experience corruption. Again, "harsh punishment for corruption also played a role of a serious deterrent" (Osipian 2008b, 3). Those can be analyzed from different points of view: those of administrative officers, teachers, and students. Every actor in the system may adopt illegal behavior. Empirical analysis shows that one cause of corruption in higher education is represented by the low effectiveness of penalties (Valentino

2007), which create opportunities for corruption because of the reduction of the costs of behaving illegally (and the benefits of those behaviors).

The last variable is discretionary power related to the question of the distribution in capacities and resources at the local level (Transparency International 2013). In particular, those of decentralization have represented an important issue, especially in countries such as the Russian Federation. Delegation of authority and discretionary power (also with reference to education system) may increase events of corruption, especially regarding the abuse of discretion (Osipian 2008b). This aspect can be seen as contrary to the principle of the encouragement of the decentralization:

> In order to develop participation, ownership, and social control. This can only be regarded as a step "in the right direction" if it is accompanied by significant capacity development at the central and local levels. If not, decentralization may boost opportunities for corrupt practices, as the experience of some countries. (Hallak and Poisson 2007, 70)

Predisposition–Rationalization

As we stated previously, predisposition and rationalization depends on the specific characteristics of an organization or its external or internal environments, which can lead workers to act illegally.

As well as in the public and private sectors, predisposition or rationalization in an education system can be referred to shared moral and ethical values. In this context, the code of conduct (or code of ethics) may represent the first instrument to be implemented. According to Boehm, Justice, and Weeks (2009), the absence of integrity and moral values in the education system results in high costs in terms of time loss of administrative and loss of respect within students' ethical and moral values, which increase corruption phenomenon. On the other hand, lack of moral and ethical values can be referred to the lack of training and communication within academic and, more in general, scholastic organizations (Boehm, Justice, and Weeks 2009). Also, it can be driven by the absence, not implementation or, at least, misapplication of ethic codes, or codes of conduct (Champan 2002; Hallak and Poisson 2007; Boehm, Justice, and Weeks 2009; Transparency International 2013).

The absence of a code of conduct, in fact, can create an incentive to behave illegally. Studies (see, e.g., Sirgy, Siegel, and Johar 2005) show that existence of an ethics code improves ethical behavior among teachers and administrative staffs.

Preventing and Fighting Corruption in the Education System

According to Heyneman (2004), an education system free of corruption is characterized by the equality of access to educational opportunity, the fairness in the distribution of educational curricula and materials, the fairness and transparency in the criteria for selection to higher and more specialized training, the fairness in accreditation in which all institutions are judged by professional standards equally applied and open to public scrutiny, the fairness in the acquisition of educational goods and services, the balance and generosity in curricular treatment of cultural minorities and geographical neighbors, and the maintenance of professional standards of conduct by those who administer education institutions and who teach in them, whether public or private.

In this context, the questions are, then, is it possible to eradicate, reduce, or prevent corruption in schools, universities, or, in general, public or private organizations? Which tools can we use? Can training play a key role in the fight against corruption?

There is no single answer to these questions. There is, however, a certain consensus toward the usefulness of training programs in preventing corruption (such as Biland and Vanneuville 2012; OECD 2012). In this sense, training can represent one of the main tools used to prevent corruption.

However, in the previous section we showed several factors that can affect levels of corruption within the education system. Can only training prevent the corruption phenomenon? Which other tools can be used to intervene on specific determinants of corruption in the various levels at which it occurs?

Taking into account the characteristics of corruption in the education system, we begin to suggest tools that can be used to prevent corruption, distinguishing between actors involved in the system that are mainly teachers, administrative officers, and students.

The Role of Teachers

Teachers play an important role in the education system, and the system can be affected by the possibility to behave illegally in order to achieve higher income (Valentino 2007).

As we stated in the preceding, determinants of corruption are divided into three categories of variables (Figure 7.3).

Referring to teachers, pressure can occur mainly in relation to the lack of the access to information or access to information only for certain categories of people (such as for some pupils, but not for all). Specific characteristics refer to lack information about selection criteria, examination criteria, and so on. Those characteristics also can be related to competition in the education system, creating pressure on teachers to behave illegally. Again, teacher pressure toward corruption can be driven by the creation, among students, of the necessity for private tutoring.

In this context, which instrument can be used in order to reduce pressure? According to Salmi and Helms (2013), governance can be adopted in order to reduce pressure and combat corruption. For example, ensuring clear and transparent information is accessible to all; in other words, the clarity, diffusion, and widespread knowledge about selection processes, criteria for passing exams, and so on, can help to reduce corruption levels. Or, again, the design of a well-structured accountability system, which involves the influence of the press and the sensibility of the public concern, as well as the engagement of citizens in order to push for ethical behavior in the education system (Chapman 2002). An example can be represented by the publication of corruption cases in university, schools newspapers, or local printed media in order to raising public awareness of corruption (Aleksanyan 2012).

Referring to opportunities (in terms of uncertainty of the regulation and the lack of transparency on procedures, effectiveness of penalties, and discretionary power), accountability systems and clear regulations can help to reduce the opportunities to behave illegally. Furthermore, opportunities can be reduced through an effective penalty system, which is regulated by a code of conduct that outlines behaviors believed to be correct and a disciplinary sanction system related to the illicit behaviors.

As stated earlier, lack of clear procedures and a clear system of applied punishment may create the opportunity for corruption; thus, the absenteeism of teachers as well as a correlated episode called "private tutoring." This, however, is a problem related to a further plurality of factors that affect not only the organizational sphere, but also the private, cultural, and motivational sphere of teachers. Acting on this issue, therefore, requires the implementation of integrated tools that take into account the various aspects related to absenteeism. Referring to the organizational point of view, the implementation of a code of ethics can help to clarify what is expected of the teacher's behavior. Again, it would seem appropriate to intervene with monetary (such as salary differentials) and nonmonetary incentives (such as professional growth, job stability, etc.) in order to improve teacher motivation and reduce the opportunity to behave illegally (Rogers and Vegas 2009).

The last variable is represented by rationalization or predisposition. As we stated earlier, they refer to cultural environment, which enable teachers to behave illegally. Tools can be used in order to combat (or, better, prevent) corruption, which need to be related to the creation of an unfavorable environment for corruption through the diffusion of ethical and moral values.

In this context, codes of ethics and training are believed to be effective in fighting corruption. A code of ethics or honor code systems (Boehm, Justice, and Weeks 2009) give teachers an important "self-monitoring tool, which (*is*) potentially more cost-effective than actions taken against offenders" (Hallak and Poisson 2007, 173), with the important aims to enhance teacher's commitment and to identify recognized standards of moral conduct.

In addition, training for teachers may become more valuable if related to ethics, integrity, and morality of actions' issues (a conceptual approach) in order to identify boundaries to which to apply those concepts and a practical approach, with the analysis of ethical dilemmas. This approach helps to promote an ethical culture, which is necessary to reduce teachers' motivation toward corruption.

These tools are not the only ones, but could serve as a pattern to be taken into account in the prevention of corruption in the education system, acting on the determinants that may affect the first category of actors: teachers.

The Role of Students

Students represent the second category of actors that intervene in the education system. In order to present an example of the phenomenon, a recent survey on cases of corruption in Armenia's education system shows that 72.5 percent of interviewed students answered "yes" to the question "are there any incidents of corruption at your university of which you are aware?" However, the more surprising result refers to the questions "have you ever had to give a bribe during your time at university?" and "how often did you give bribes during your time at university?" Referring to the first question, more than 45 percent of interviewed students admitted that they had given bribes, and, for second question, 47.6 precent admitted they had given bribes more than once (Aleksanyan 2012). This is a specific and particular situation, but is not an isolated problem—similar results were obtained in a survey conducted recently in Moldova (Valentino 2007)—and it is not a problem to underestimate from other realities.

Taking into account the determinants of corruption in the education system, which characteristics are assumed among students?

In this context, pressure toward corruption can occur mainly in cases that lack access to information and in relation to high competition in the education system.

In the first case, students are pressured toward corruption in order to achieve important information about their courses of studies. In the second case, we consider the high internal competition in the education system among students (in particular, related to the achievement of a well-paid job after education).

As well as in the case of a teacher being under pressure, the design of an accountability system can help to spread equal information to all students and, consequently, reduce corruption levels.

The education system is highly competitive. In many cases:

> students feel that they have to pay a bribe to be admitted to a particular university or programme. Mention is made of a common shadow price to particular institutions and programmes. In some parts of the world, bribery is so common that some students participate in it as a safety net. They pay a bribe on the grounds that, because everyone else is doing it, they do not want to be left behind for not participating. (Heyneman 2013, 102)

In this context, the equal access to education for all code of ethics for students, and the creation of an ethical environment with privileged collaboration among students can be considered as anticorruption measures.

The opportunity toward corruption for students can occur mainly referring to the effectiveness of penalties. The design of a regulation that includes severe penalties for corruption (such as the suspension of the school career) can be seen as good deterrents for the corruption phenomenon.

Finally, we take into account rationalization or predisposition, referring to a cultural environment that fosters unethical behaviors, in this specific case, among students.

Talking about culture, integrity, and moral values, training can represent an important tool to prevent corruption. This is important in order to "build values and develop capacities necessary to form the civic position of pupils against corruption" (Lithuanian Modern Didactics Centre 2006, 18). In drawing training programs for students, it is necessary to take into account the exploration of the concept of corruption and issues related to ethics, integrity, and morality of actions. In fact, the first approach needs to be conceptual in order to identify boundaries to which to apply those concepts. This approach helps to promote an ethical culture, which is necessary to reduce motivation or predisposition to corruption. Again, according to the Lithuanian Modern Didactics Centre (2006), programs should be "integrated"; that is, the integration of analysis of fundamental values and concepts related to the phenomenon of corruption into the disciplines that are already taught, paying special attention to aspects that did not receive previous attention. Finally, in terms of contents, training programs should cover the various issues related to the definition of corruption, integrity, ethics, and moral values and take into account moments of exercises, with the use of case studies and ethical dilemmas to solve in groups in the classroom.

The Role of Administrative Officers

The last category we analyze concerns administrative officers, which can be public officials (in a public education system) or private employers.

Referring to the pressure of administrative officers, corruption can occur, especially in relation to resource and funds' management and fraud (e.g., through false invoices, in relation to the rapid and inefficient disbursement of funds).

In this case, reducing or preventing corruption is possible, particularly with the design of adequate audit and control mechanisms and adequate punitive systems. A code of ethics, too, can be designed in order to underline integrity behaviors expected by officials; this can include (and as defined for teachers) the publication of corruption cases in university or schools newspapers or local printed media in order to raising public awareness of corruption (Aleksanyan 2012).

Opportunities for corruption can occur in cases of uncertainty of the regulation and the lack of transparency on procedures, the lack of effectiveness of penalties, and the discretionary power of officials. Especially referring to officials, the need of implementation (widespread among the organization) of clear rules and procedures as well as a code of conduct linked by an effective punitive system for unethical and corrupt conduct can help to reduce the opportunity toward corruption.

Finally, concerning rationalization or predisposition, tools can be implemented that are mostly the design and implementation of a code of ethics and training programs.

In this case, training programs need to be structured, taking into account the concept of ethics, corruption, integrity, and moral issues and, above all, training concerning the procedures (fund and resources management, procurement, and other procedures to help expose corruption) and behavior expected from employees.

Concluding Remarks

The issue of corruption has been widely debated, and it continues to be the center of attention in public policy, media, and public opinion. Scientific debate has focused on various aspects of corruption. Here, we focused on the determinant of corruption in the education system, after the analysis of the organizational determinants of corruption in the private and public sectors; thus, understanding of the phenomenon helps us to design a system of tools in order to prevent corruption.

This is particularly important in the education system, which is "instrumental in promoting development, social justice and other human rights. Education has the potential to instil hope in our children and encourage a spirit of common and shared responsibility for our planet and for humanity" (Transparency International 2013, xv).

We started the analysis by taking into consideration the theoretical contribution that gave important inputs to the study of organizational determinant of illegal behavior and corruption in the private sector. Then we have rearranged the model to the specific characteristics of the public sector in general and, specifically, to the education system.

Understanding the causes and determinants of corruption helps us to identify measures and instruments to combat and prevent corruption. In fact, a great number of tools, measures, and actions exist in order to help to reduce pressure or motivation to behave illegally, to decrease the opportunities that occur in the events of corruption, and to intervene on the predisposition or rationalization to act in a corrupt way.

As we stated, training can represent an important tool to implement in order to prevent motivations for corruption, along with setting up a favorable environment to the diffusion of ethical issues. However, it cannot be the unique tool.

Taking into account the entire system of relationship environment, organization, and individual, we referred to pressure–motivation, opportunity, and predisposition–rationalizations, as the macrodeterminants of corruption. We found that those variables in the education system can be explained as follows: referring to pressure, peculiarities of the education system refer to access to information, the lack of "social" control, the high competition in the education system, and the rapid disbursement of funds. In addition, in the education system, opportunity can explain uncertainty in regulations and the lack of transparency on procedures, the effectiveness of penalties, and the discretionary power. Finally, predisposition–rationalization refers to moral and ethical values, as well as the cultural environment in which the organization operates.

To identify anticorruption measures reflecting the specific problems outlined by the determinants of corruption in the education system, we first identified the specific actors involved in the system and to whom to extend anticorruption measures: teachers, students, and administrative employees.

We found that the main tools are divided into four categories: accountability systems, clear and specific rules (both procedures and penalty systems), implementation of a code of ethics and implementation of training programs.

In general, accountability systems helps to reduce pressure toward corruption; the design of clear and specific rules helps to reduce the opportunity toward corruption, and the implementation of a code of ethics and training programs helps to decrease motivation or predisposition to corruption.

In particular, those instruments can be implemented in a different way if we consider students, teacher, or employees.

Finally, this analysis aims to stimulate the scientific debate on the organizational determinant of corruption in an education system. We believe, in fact, that greater understanding of the phenomenon is the first step in fighting corruption is an important sector, such as an education system.

We hope this article raises a few open questions. Further studies regarding the causes of corruption in the education system should be undertaken along with empirical studies in order to identify the effectiveness of those instruments.

References

Abadzi, H. 2007. "Absenteeism and Beyond: Instructional Time Loss and Consequences." Policy Research Working Paper no. 4376. Washington, DC: World Bank.

Ades, A., and R. Di Tella. 1996. "The Causes and Consequences of Corruption: A Review of Recent Empirical Contributions." *Institute of Development Studies Bulletin* 27, no. 2, pp. 6–10.

Adeyemi, K., and N. Akpotu. 2009. "Cost Analysis of Teacher Absenteeism in Nigerian Secondary Schools." *Journal of Social Sciences* 21, no. 2, pp. 137–44.

African Economic Research Consortium. 2011. "Service Delivery Indicators: Pilot in Education and Health Care in Africa." AERC World Bank.

Aguilera, R.V., and A.K. Vadera. 2007. "The Dark Side of Authority: Antecedents, Mechanisms, and Outcomes of Organizational Corruption." *Journal of Business Ethics* 77, no. 4, pp. 431–49.

Albrecht, W.S., K.R. Howe, and M.B. Romney. 1984. *Deterring Fraud: The Internal Auditor's Perspective*. Altomonte Springs: The Institute of Internal Auditor's Research Foundation.

Aleksanyan, H. 2012. *Cases of Corruption and Its Prevention in Armenia's Education System*. Norwegian Institute of International Affairs (NUPI), Regional Competence-Building for Think-Tanks in the South Caucasus and Central Asia.

Allison, G. 1979. "Public and Private Management: Are They Fundamentally Alike in all Unimportant Respects?" In *Classics of Public Administration*, eds. J. Shafritz and A. Hyde. Belmont: Wadsworth.

Antonsen, M., and T. Jorgensen. 1997. "The Publicness of Public Organizations." *Public Administration* 75, no. 2, pp. 337–57.

Argandona, A. 2003. "Private-to-Private Corruption." *Journal of Business Ethics* 47, no. 3, pp. 253–67.

Ashforth, B.E., and V. Anand. 2003. "The Normalization of Corruption in Organizations." *Research in Organizational Behavior* 25, pp. 1–52.

Bardhan, P. 1997. "Corruption and Development: A Review of Issues." *Journal of Economic Literature* 35, no. 3, pp. 1320–46.

Baucus, M.S. 1994. "Pressure, Opportunity, and Predisposition: A Multivariate Model of Corporate Illegality." *Academy of Management Journal* 20, no. 4, pp. 699–721.

Beaulieu, E. 2014. "From Voter ID to Party ID: How Political Parties Affect Perceptions of Election Fraud in the U.S." *Electoral Studies* 35, pp. 24–32.

Becker, G.S. 1986. "Crime and Punishment: An Economic Approach." *Journal of Political Economy* 76, no. 2, pp. 169–217.

Benveniste, L., J. Marshall, and C. Araujo. 2008. *Teaching in Cambodia*. Washington, DC: World Bank.

Benveniste, L., J. Marshall, and L. Santibáñez. 2008. *Teaching in Lao PDR*. Washington, DC: World Bank.

Biland, E., and R. Vanneuville. 2012. "Government Lawyers and the Training of Senior Civil Servants. Maintaining Law at the Heart of the French State." *International Journal of the Legal Profession* 19, no. 1, pp. 29–54.

Bliss, C., and R. Di Tella. 1997. "Does Competition Kill Corruption?" *Journal of Political Economy* 105, no. 5, pp. 1001–23.

Boehm, P.J., M. Justice, and S. Weeks. 2009. "Promoting Academic Integrity in Higher Education." *The Community College Enterprise* 15, no. 1, p. 45.

Box, R. 1999. "Running Government Like a Business: Implications for Public Administration Theory and Research." *American Review of Public Administration* 29, no. 1, pp. 19–43.

Boyne, G.A. 2002. "Public and Private Management: What's the Difference?" *Journal of Management Studies* 39, no. 1.

Bozeman, B. 1987. *All Organizations Are Public*. London: Jossey-Bass.

Bozeman, B., and S. Bretschneider. 1994. "The Publicness Puzzle in Organization Theory: A Test of Alternative Explanations of Differences Between Public and Private Organizations." *Journal of Public Administration Theory and Research* 4, pp. 197–223.

Bretag, T. ed. 2013. "Short-Cut Students. From Academic Misconduct to Academic Integrity." In *Global Corruption Report: Education*. Transparency International. Routledge.

Brunetti, A., and B. Weder. 2003. "A Free Press Is Bad News for Corruption." *Journal of Public Economics* 87, no. 7, pp. 1801–24.

Caiden, G.E., and N.J. Caiden. 1977. "Administrative Corruption." *Public Administration Review* 37, no. 3, pp. 301–09.

Carneiro, P., J. Das, and H. Reis. 2010. *Estimating the Demand for School Attributes in Pakistan*. London: University College London.

Center for Democratic Development. 2008. *Tracking Leakage of Public Resource in Education: A Pilot Investigation of Teacher Absence in Public Primary Schools in Ghana*. Accra: Center for Democratic Development.

Chang, E.E. 2005. "Electoral Incentives for Political Corruption Under Open-List Proportional Representation." *Journal of Politics* 67, no. 3, pp. 716–30.

Chaudhury, N., J. Hammer, M. Kremer, K. Muralidharan, and H. Rogers. 2006. "Missing in Action: Teacher and Health Worker Absence in Developing Countries." *Journal of Economic Perspectives* 20, no. 1, pp. 91–116.

Chapman, D. 2002. *Corruption and the Education Sector*. Washington, DC, USA: Management Systems International.

Cheng, H., and L. Ma. 2009. "White Collar Crime and the Criminal Justice System: Government Response to Bank Fraud and Corruption in China." *Journal of Financial Crime* 16, no. 2, pp. 166–79.

Coleman, J.W. 1987. "Toward an Integrated Theory of White-Collar Crime." *American Journal of Sociology* 93, pp. 406–39.

Collier, M.W. 2002. "Explaining Corruption: An Institutional Choice Approach." *Crime, Law and Social Change* 38, no. 1, pp. 1–32.

Comer, M.J. 1985. *Corporate Fraud*. London: McGraw-Hill.

Cooper, T. 2000. *Handbook of Administrative Ethics*, 2nd ed. New York: Marcel Dekker.

Cressey, D.R. 1950. "The Criminal Violation of Financial Trust." *American Sociological Review* 15, no. 6, pp. 738–43.

Cressey, D.R. 1953. *Other People's Money: A Study in the Social Psychology of Embezzlement.* New York: Free Press.

Cressey, D.R. 1965. "The Respectable Criminal: Why Some of Our Best Friends Are Crooks." *Criminologica* 3, pp. 13–16.

Das, A., and M.M.B. Parry. 2011. "Greasing or Sanding? GMM Estimation of the Corruption-Investment Relationship." *International Journal of Economic Research* 2, no. 2, pp. 95–108.

Das, J., S. Dercon, J. Habyarimana, and P. Krishnan. 2005. "Teacher Shocks and Student Learning: Evidence from Zambia." Policy Research Working Paper no. 3602. Washington, DC: World Bank.

Davis, J. 2004. "Corruption in Public Service Delivery: Experience from South Asia's Water and Sanitation Sector." *World Development* 32, no. 1, pp. 53–71.

Davis, J.H., and J.A. Ruhe. 2003. "Perceptions of Country Corruption: Antecedents and Outcomes." *Journal of Business Ethics* 43, no. 4, pp. 275–88.

Davies, D. 2000. *Fraud Watch.* London: ABG Professional Information.

Dela Rama, M. 2011. "Corporate Governance and Corruption: Ethical Dilemmas of Asian Business Group." *Journal of Business Ethics* 109, no. 4, pp. 501–19.

Den Nieuwenboer, N.A., and S.P. Kaptein. 2008. "Spiraling Down into Corruption: a Dynamic Analysis of the Social Identity Processes That Cause Corruption in Organizations to Grow." *Journal of Business Ethics* 83, no. 2, pp. 133–46.

Ferraz, C., and F. Finan. 2011. "Electoral Accountability and Corruption: Evidence from the Audits of Local Governments." *American Economic Review* 101, no. 4, pp. 1274–311.

Fottler, M. 1981. "Is Management Really Generic?" *Academy of Management Review* 6, no. 1, pp. 1–12.

Freille, S., M.E. Haque, and R. Kneller. 2007. "A Contribution to the Empirics of Press Freedom and Corruption." *European Journal of Political Economy* 23, no. 4, pp. 838–62.

Gottfredson, M.R., and T. Hirschi. 1990. *A General Theory of Crime.* Stanford, CA: Stanford University Press.

Greve, H.R., D. Palmer, and J.E. Pozner. 2010. "Organizations Gone Wild: The Causes, Processes, and Consequences of Organizational Misconduct." *The Academy of Management Annals* 4, no. 1, pp. 53–107.

Hallak, J., and M. Poisson. 2002. *Ethics and Corruption in Education.* Policy Forum no. 15.

Hallak, J., and M. Poisson. 2007. *Corrupt Schools, Corrupt Universities: What Can Be Done?* Paris: International Institute for Educational Planning.

Hallier, J., and T. Forbes. 2004. "In Search of Theory Development in Grounded Investigations: Doctors' Experiences of Managing as an Example of Fitted and Prospective Theorizing." *Journal of Management Studies* 41, no. 8, pp. 1379–410.

Heidenheimer, A., and M. Johnson. 2002. *Political Corruption: Concepts and Contexts*. 3rd ed. New Brunswick: Transaction Publishers.

Heyneman, S.P. 2004. "Education and Corruption." *International Journal of Educational Development* 24, no. 6, pp. 637–48.

Heyneman, S.P. 2013. "Higher Education Institutions: Why They Matter and Why Corruption Puts Them at Risk." In *Global Corruption Report: Education–Transparency International*, eds. G. Sweeney, K. Despota and S. Lindner. 101–7. Oxon: Routledge.

Jain, A.K. 2001. "Corruption: A Review." *Journal of Economic Surveys* 15, no. 1, pp. 71–121.

Johnson, R.A., and S. Sharma. 2004. *About Corruption, in The Struggle Against Corruption: A Comparative Study*. Palgrave Macmillan.

Kalenborn, C., and C. Lessmann. 2013. "The Impact of Democracy and Press Freedom on Corruption: Conditionality matters." *Journal of Policy Modeling* 35, no. 6, pp. 857–86.

Kaptein, M. 2011. "Understanding Unethical Behavior by Unraveling Ethical Culture." *Human Relations* 64, no. 6, pp. 843–69.

Khan, M.H. 1996. "The Efficiency Implications of Corruption." *Journal of International Development* 8, no. 5, pp. 683–96.

Kimeu, S. 2013. "Misappropriation of Funds for Free Education in Kenya." In *Global Corruption Report: Education*, Transparency International. New York: Routhledge.

Klitgaard, R. 1988. *Controlling Corruption*. Berkeley, CA: University of California Press.

Klitgaard, R. 1998. *Combating Corruption*. United Nations Chronicle 35, no. 1, Department of Public Information.

Klitgaard, R., R. Maclean-Abaroa, and H.L. Parris. 2000. *Corrupt Cities: A Practical Guide to Cure and Prevention*. Oakland, CA and WA, DC: Institute for Contemporary Studies and the World Bank Institute.

Lange, D. 2008. "A Multidimensional Conceptualization of Organizational Corruption Control." *Academy of Management Review* 33, no. 3, pp. 710–29.

Langseth, P. 1999. *Prevention: An Effective Tool to Reduce Corruption. Report of Global Program Against Corruption*. Center for International Crime Prevention, Office of Drug Control and Crime Prevention, United Nations Office at Vienna.

Levi, M., M. Dakolias, and T.S. Greenberg. 2007. "Money Laundering and Corruption." In *The Many Faces of Corruption*, eds. G.E. Campos and

S. Pradhan. The International Bank for Reconstruction and Development the World Bank.

Lindgreen, A. 2004. "Corruption and Unethical Behavior: Report on a Set of Danish Guidelines." *Journal of Business Ethics* 51, no. 1, pp. 31–39.

Lintjer, J. 2000. "The Fight Against Corruption: How a Regional Development Bank Can Help. Progress in the Fight Against the Corruption in Asia and the Pacific." *Papers Presented at the Joint ADB-OECD Conference on Combating Corruption in the Asia-Pacific Region Seoul*, Korea, pp. 11–13.

Lithuanian Modern Didactics Centre & Ministry of Education and Science of the Republic of Lithuania. 2006. *Anti-corruption Education at School. Methodical Material for General and Higher Education Schools*. Vilnius: Garnelis Publishing.

Luo, Y. 2008. "The Changing Chinese Culture and Business Behavior: The Perspective of Intertwinement Between Guanxi and Corruption." *International Business Review* 17, no. 2, pp. 188–93.

Lyons, S.T., L.E. Duxbury, and C.A. Higgins. 2006. "A Comparison of the Values and Commitment of Private Sector, Public Sector, and Parapublic Sector Employees." *Public Administration Review* 66, no. 4, pp. 605–18.

Matsumura, E.M., and J.Y. Shin. 2005. "Corporate Governance Reform and CEO Compensation: Intended and Unintended Consequences." *Journal of Business Ethics* 62, no. 2, pp. 101–13.

McCann, J.A., and J.I. Domínguez. 1998. "Mexicans React to Electoral Fraud and Political Corruption: An Assessment of Public Opinion and Voting Behaviour." *Electoral Studies* 17, no. 4, pp. 483–503.

McKendall, M.A., and J.A.I. Wagner. 1997. "Motive, Opportunity, Choice, and Corporate Illegality." *Organization Science* 8, no. 6, pp. 624–47.

Metcalfe, L. 1993. "Public Management: From Imitation to Innovation." In *Modern Governance*, ed. J. Kooiman. London: Sage.

Mills, A. 2012. *Causes of Corruption in Public Sector Institutions and Its Impact on Development*. New York: United Nations Public Administration Network.

Nielsen, R.P. 2003. "Corruption Networks and Implications for Ethical Corruption Reform." *Journal of Business Ethics* 42, no. 2, pp. 125–49.

Nogara, M. 2009. "Role of Media in Curbing Corruption: The Case of Uganda Under President Yoweri K. Museveni During the 'No-Party' System." *DESA Working Paper Series* no. 72.

Nutt, P., and R. Backoff. 1993. "Organizational Publicness and its Implications for Strategic Management." *Journal of Public Administration Research and Theory* 3, no. 2, pp. 209–31.

OECD. 2003. *Ethics Training for Public Officials. A Study Prepared by the OECD Anti-Corruption. Network for Eastern Europe and Central Asia (ACN) and SIGMA, a Joint EU-OECD Initiative, Principally Financed by the EU, in*

Co-operation with the OECD Public Sector Integrity Network. www.oecd.org/corruption/acn/library/EthicsTrainingforPublicOfficialsBrochureEN.pdf

OECD. 2012. *Strengthening Integrity and Fighting Corruption in Education.* Serbia: OECD Publishing. http://dx.doi.org/10.1787/9789264179646-en

Osipian, A. 2007. "Corruption in Higher Education: Conceptual Approaches and Measurement Techniques." *Research in Comparative and International Education* 2, no. 4.

Osipian, A. 2008a. "Corruption in Higher Education: Does It Differ Across the Nations and Why?" *Research in Comparative and International Education* 3, no. 4.

Osipian, A. 2008b. "Corruption Hierarchies in Higher Education in the Former Soviet Bloc." *International Journal of Educational Development* 29, no. 3, pp. 321–30.

Osipian, A. 2013. "Recruitment and Admissions Fostering Transparency on the Path to Higher Education." In *Global Corruption Report: Education,* Transparency International: Routledge.

Palmer, D. 2012. *Normal Organizational Wrongdoing: A Critical Analysis of Theories of Misconduct in and by Organizations.* Demand: Oxford University Press.

Perry, J., and L. Porter. 1982. "Factors Affecting the Content for Motivation in Public Organisations." *Academy of Management Review* 7, no. 1, pp. 89–98.

Perry, J., and H. Rainey. 1988. "The Public–Private Distinction in Organization Theory: A Critique and Research Strategy." *Academy of Management Review* 13, no. 2, pp. 182–201.

Persson, A., B. Rothstein, and J. Teorell. 2010. "The Failure of Anti-corruption Policies. A Theoretical Mischaracterization of the Problem." QoG Working Paper Series 2010:19, The Quality of Government Institute, Department of Political Science, University of Gothenburg.

Pinto, J., C.R. Leana, and F.K. Pil. 2008. "Corrupt Organizations or Organizations of Corrupt Individuals? Two Types of Organization-Level Corruption." *Academy of Management Review* 33, no. 3, pp. 685–709.

Pope, J. 2000. *Confronting Corruption: The Elements of a National Integrity System (The TI Source Book).* Berlin & London: Transparency International.

Richter, W.L., and F. Burke. 2007. *Combating Corruption, Encouraging Ethics: A Practical Guide to Management Ethic.* Washington, DC: Rowman & Littlefield Publisher, Inch.

Ring, P., and J. Perry. 1985. "Strategic Management in Public and Private oOrganizations: Implications of DistinctiveContexts and Constraints." *Academy of Management Review* 10, pp. 276–86.

Rogers, F.H., and E. Vegas. 2009. "No More Cutting Class? Reducing Teacher Absence and Providing Incentives for Performance. The World Bank

Development Research Group Human Development and Public Services Team." Policy Research Working Paper no. 4847.

Rose-Ackerman, S. 1978. *Corruption: A Study in Political Economy*. Cambridge: Academic Press.

Rose-Ackerman, S. 1997. "The Political Economy of Corruption." *Corruption and the Global Economy* 31, p. 60.

Rose-Ackerman, S. 1999. *Corruption and Government. Causes, Consequences, and Reform*. Cambridge: Cambridge University Press.

Rumyantseva, N.L. 2005. "Taxonomy of Corruption in Higher Education." *Peabody Journal of Education* 80, no. 1, pp. 81–92.

Salmi, J., and R.M. Helms. 2013. "Governance Instruments to Combat Corruption in Higher Education." In *Global Corruption Report: Education*, Transparency International. Routledge.

Schneider, F. 2007. "Shadow Economies and Corruption All Over the World: New Estimates for 145 Countries." *Economics*.

Serra, D. 2006. "Empirical Determinants of Corruption: A Sensitivity Analysis." *Public Choice* 126, nos. 1–2, pp. 225–56.

Sharman, J.C., and D. Chaikin. 2009. "Corruption and Anti-money-laundering Systems: Putting a Luxury Good to Work." *Governance* 22, no. 1, pp. 27–45.

Sirgy, M.J., P.H. Siegel, and J.S. Johar. 2005. "Toward a Code of Ethics for Accounting Educators." *Journal of Business Ethics* 61, no. 3, pp. 215–34.

Stewart, J., and S. Ranson. 1988. "Management in the Public Domain." *Public Money and Management* 8, no. 2, pp. 13–19.

Tajfel, H., and J.C. Turner. 1979. "An Integrative Theory of Intergroup Conflict." In *The Social Psychology of Intergroup Relations*, eds. W.G. Austin and S. Worchel. Monterey: Brooks/Cole.

Tanaka, S. 2001. "Corruption in Education Sector Development: A Suggestion for Anticipatory Strategy." *The International Journal of Educational Management* 15, no. 4, pp. 158–66.

Tanzi, V. 1998. "Corruption Around the World. Causes, Consequences, Scope, and Cures." *International Monetary Fund Staff Papers* 45, no. 4.

Transparency International. 2013. *Global Corruption Report: Education*. Routledge.

Treisman, D. 2000. "The Causes of Corruption: A Cross-National Study." *Journal of Public Economics* 76, no. 3, pp. 399–457.

Treisman, D. 2007. "What Have we Learned About the Causes of Corruption from Ten Years of Cross-National Empirical Research?" *Annual Review of Political Science* 10, pp. 211–44.

Treviño, L.K., 1986. "Ethical Decision Making in Organizations: A Person-Situation Interactionist Model." *Academy of Management Review* 11, no. 3, pp. 601–17.

U-Myint. 2000. "Corruption: Causes, Consequences and Cures." *Asia-Pacific Development Journal* 7, no. 2, pp. 33–58.

Valentino, V. 2007. *Managing Corruption in Higher Education in Moldova* [master thesis]. John F. Kennedy School of Government, Harvard University.

Vardi, Y., and E. Weitz. 2004. *Misbehavior in Organizations: Theory, Research, and Management.* Mahwah, NJ: Lawrence Erlbaum.

Vermeersch, C., and M. Kremer. 2004. "School Meals, Educational Achievement, and School Competition: Evidence from a Randomized Evaluation." Policy Research Working Paper no. 3523. Washington, DC: World Bank.

Vinod, H. 2008. "Fraud and Corruption." In *Governance, Risk, and Compliance Handbook: Technology, Finance, Environmental, and International Guidance and Best Practices*, ed. A. Tarantino. Wiley.

Weber, M. [1922] 1978. *Economy and Society.* Berkeley: University of California Press.

Wells, J. 2004. *Corporate Fraud Handbook: Prevention and Detection.* New York: John Wiley & Sons.

World Bank. 2001. *Honduras: Public Expenditure Management for Poverty Reduction and Fiscal Sustainability.* Washington, DC: World Bank.

World Bank. 2004a. *Mainstreaming Anti-corruption Activities in World Bank Assistance–A Review of Progress Since 1997.* Washington, DC: World Bank.

World Bank. 2004b. *Papua New Guinea: Public Expenditure and Service Delivery (PESD).* Washington, DC: World Bank.

World Bank. 2006. *Mongolia: Public Financing of Education: Equity and Efficiency Implications.* Washington, DC: World Bank.

Zahra, S.A., R.L. Priem, and A.M.A. Rasheed. 2005. "The Antecedents and Consequences of Top Management Fraud." *Journal of Management* 31, no. 6, pp. 803–28.

Zhang, Y., L. Cao, and M.S. Vaughn. 2009. "Social Support and Corruption: Structural Determinants of Corruption in the World." *Australian and New Zealand Journal of Criminology* 42, no. 2, pp. 204–17.

CHAPTER 8

Human Resource Management in UK Higher Education: Business Schools and Their Dark Side

Thomas F. Burgess

Leeds University Business School

Introduction

This chapter examines the dark side of management (Neider and Schriesheim 2010; Griffin and O'Leary-Kelly 2004) in higher education (HE) by focusing on the management of academics in management and business schools in UK universities.[1] In particular, the chapter concentrates on wrongdoing perpetrated by managers while managing academics; that is, the human resource management (HRM) process. Much is spoken in UK universities about wrongdoing in such human resource processes, but little is published on this topic. Academics often hear comments about situations where the processes are suspected to be biased, for example, where an individual might be appointed as professor[2] as a result

---

[1] Hereafter, the term "business school" is used to encompass both business and management schools.

[2] Note in the UK, although things are changing, the term professor is still used differently from the way it is used in the more widespread U.S.-type of system. In such U.S.-type systems, members of both senior and junior staff have the title professor—although in the latter cases it is qualified by "assistant" and "associate". The UK tradition was that only the senior person was accorded the title professor—the junior staff might be termed lecturer or senior lecturer.

of patronage (Martin 2009) rather than meritocratic practices. However, given the covert nature of this type of wrongdoing, it is not surprising that concrete evidence of such happenings is rarely available. In this evidential vacuum, some might argue that such organizational misconduct, if it does occur, is rare and the results of "one bad apple in the barrel." This chapter takes an alternative view and applies the approach of Palmer (2013) in which he states that "wrongdoing perpetrated in and by organizations" is normal and widespread (2013, 1). The type of wrongdoing investigated here concerns management's unilateral modification of the academic's psychological contract. Modifications which become manifest in the day-to-day HRM processes and the particular activities of appointment, development, and promotion; and their flip side of reprimanding, demoting, and encouraging staff to leave. The chapter allies this normal organizational-wrongdoing approach with the general contextual frame of liquid modernity as promulgated in the work of Bauman (Elliott 2007a). The paucity of evidence for organizational wrongdoing, and the theoretical stance adopted, leads to a conceptual and notional view of the subject matter rather than to one that relies on reporting results of an empirical study. However, methodologically the chapter capitalizes on secondary data and, in particular, presents a case study of events at one business school constructed from secondary data reported in the higher educational press. The case is taken to be an extreme occurrence that, in the spirit of Starbuck (2006), illuminates other less extreme situations.

The chapter proceeds as follows. The next section introduces the theory of normal organizational wrongdoing and relates this to UK universities. The contextual framework of liquid modernity is outlined followed by some introductory remarks on universities, new public management (NPM), and business schools. A key societal pressure impinging on the HE environment is discussed next; namely, the government research assessment exercises (RAEs). The chapter then focuses on the detail of wrongdoing in the management of academics and an illustrative case study is presented of events in a UK business school. The case study is discussed and concluded.

Organizational Wrongdoing: The Normal and Abnormal Views

Palmer (2013) identifies two perspectives on organizational wrongdoing: the dominant and alternative perspectives. In the dominant perspective, wrongdoing is conceptualized as unusual, abnormal behavior; while in the alternative perspective, wrongdoing is normal and ubiquitous. Palmer proposes two contrasting approaches to explain the causes of wrongdoing; approaches that map to the two perspectives. In the first approach the wrongdoers are likely to be individuals who deliberately pursue the wrongdoing knowingly—this approach links with the abnormal wrongdoing perspective. The alternative approach is where wrongdoers, influenced by their social context, fall in to their wrongdoing without apparently thinking their actions through.

In addition, Palmer delineates eight specific accounts or explanations which he associates with the two approaches. The first two accounts, the rational choice and the culture accounts, are closely associated with the abnormal perspective. The third account, the ethical decision account, can be linked to both the normal and abnormal perspectives. The remaining five accounts are associated with the normal organizational wrongdoing perspective. The last of these five accounts, the social control of wrongdoing, is a more comprehensive account that is marked out by its clear inclusion of the role of social control agents in creating wrongdoing.

This chapter applies Palmer's alternative perspective of normal organizational wrongdoing to the conduct of management in UK business schools. In particular, we concentrate on wrongdoing by managers when managing academics and acknowledge how this has increased because of changes over the last three decades. Interestingly, in the past, many managers of academics were likely to be academics themselves since professors often assumed managerial roles for a limited period on a rota basis. However, nowadays the senior managers of business schools are much more likely to be external appointments, including from business, rather than academics taking their turn at managing their school. Palmer differentiates between wrongdoing by individuals and wrongdoing by collectives.

The chapter proceeds on the basis that although wrongdoing may be primarily laid at the door of an individual; often, as Palmer acknowledges, it requires the compliance—whether tacitly or not—of others. More and more, collectives of managers can be identified in universities that operate according to an increasingly managerial view articulated by government, university senior management, and related bodies.

Normal Organizational Wrongdoing and UK Universities

It is worthwhile observing that Palmer mainly applies his approach to private sector organizations, whereas here we are dealing with (UK) universities—organizations that are virtually all located in the public sector. However, in the last three decades universities have been subjected to an environment where HE is seen increasingly as a private, rather than a public, good. Consistent with Palmer's focus on the private sector, he defines organizational wrongdoing as "any behavior that organizational participants perpetrate in the course of fulfilling their organizational roles ... that the state judges to be wrongful" (Palmer 2013, 35). In general he defines wrongdoing from a sociological standpoint where social control agents are the valid arbiters of what passes for wrongdoing. Although many such control agents can be discerned, he accords greatest primacy to the state. Given the UK state's role in human resource issues it might seem appropriate to use the state as the key social agent in the context of university employment. The state is accorded custodianship of matters such as human rights and employment-related issues, for example, adherence to equal opportunities and antidiscriminatory practices. However, wrongdoing goes beyond infringement of legal minima defined by state legislation; Palmer identifies three underlying criteria for determining wrongdoing: legal, ethical, and socially responsible.

This chapter argues, differently to Palmer, that the state is not an impartial arbiter but is, in fact, a major player with responsibilities for the wrongdoing in universities. The argument, which is developed in more depth later, is that the state has overseen an unethical reshaping of work within universities that is manifested in the shattering of academics' psychological contracts (Rousseau 1990; Dabos and Rousseau 2004). The principal agency for this state-sponsored reshaping is university manage-ment. Therefore, since the state is, perhaps, the prime mover in generating the major pressures that are driving societal change in the UK HE sector, then its role as a social control agent is questionable. In the circumstances, other social control agents can be legitimately identified in the UK, such as the main university trade union.

Before focusing closely on business schools and applying Palmer's framework; the chapter considers the current context of universities and makes some comments on how the UK HE sector has got to where it is now. Although the chapter considers the UK context; there are similar social pressures at work in other parts of the globe. To frame the contex-tual discussion, the broad theory of liquid modernity (Bauman 2000) is used.

Liquid Modernity

It seems that many today would accept that universities are institutions embedded within a society that is subject to substantial change. One view of this extensive change has been articulated by the eminent sociologist Zygmunt Bauman who contemplated societal change and developed his theory of liquid modernity (Bauman 2000; Elliott 2007a). He refers to "liquidization" whereby the social processes arising from global capitalism fuel the undermining of pre-existing institutions and place increased pres-sures on the individual who is cast adrift in a sea of insecurity. According to Bauman (2000), the precariousness experienced by the individual can be captured in the concepts of: "*insecurity* (of position, entitlements and livelihood), of *uncertainty* (as to their continuation and future stability) and of *unsafety* (of one's body, one's self and their extensions: possessions, neighbourhood, community)" (161). However, Poder (2007) argues that the theory of liquid modernity is a view of the future rather than one that is "already empirically predominant" (136).

A key concern of liquid modernity relevant to this chapter's treatment of relationships between managers and academic employees within public sector institutions can be highlighted: "the outsourcing of public politi-cal functions to non-political, deregulated market forces" (Elliott 2007b, 49). A key element of liquid modernity that this paper attends to is the role of management; a role which has changed in general but in particular has been reconstructed in the public sector. The public sector has been overwhelmed by the introduction of business ideas and practices; including the introduction of deregulation, outsourcing, privatization, and performance management (see the following comments on NPM). According to Bauman, one of the key facets of the general transformation to liquid management is that it forces the individual to indulge more in self-management to achieve objectives set by managers; who then do not need to manage individuals as tightly as before. However, just because managers do not need to manage tightly, does not mean they will refrain from *tight management*. The evidence in the HE sector points to managers becoming more involved in managing individuals with the adoption of performance management systems. The tendency for managers to pursue micromanagement alongside of increased expectations for individuals to self-manage is part of the new HE environment.

Despite the emphasis on self-management, the power and status of professionals are eroded under liquid modernity. Conversely, the power of management has grown such that they (managers) can be seen as *the* professional class. Their power has grown such that it is now common for managers to systematically subvert the legitimate contributions of owners, employees, and other stakeholders; a phenomenon that is labeled managerialism by some (Locke and Spender 2011).

UK Universities in the 21st Century

Collini (2012) points out that universities have been around for some time but, in practice, the modern university is a product of the 19th century. These more modern times have been marked out by a state of flux rather than robust, little-changing institutions. The classical, Humboldtian, view of the university as a self-governing community of scholars has given way to the "highly managerial corporate enterprises" (Collini 2012, 22) that we see today. Conversion to a hotbed of managerialism impacts both on the university's goals and on how it is managed. The changing goals of the university can be seen as varying the mission of the university from that of being the knowledge creator and repository for society, to that of being a vehicle for increasing a country's gross domestic product

(GDP). As Harley, Muller-Camen, and Collin (2004, 330) comment "The university is no longer expected to fashion a cultured elite, but to fuel the engines of economic competitiveness and survival."

Within the flux of change buffeting universities, a number of major strands can be identified: massification, marketization, and NPM. Massification, that is the expansion, of UK HE in the latter part of the 20th century from elite to mass system is documented by Halsey (1992). More recent commentaries are provided by Bryson and Barnes (2000) and Collini (2012). The crisis generated by moving to a mass system has been added to by the ideologically motivated drive by various governments for marketization; that is the commodification of HE by means such as recognizing students as consumers and customers, and charging full-price fees for courses. The phenomenon of NPM has appeared as a mechanism for inserting the market into the public sector, including HE. According to Hood (1995), NPM seems to entail a shift in emphasis from policy-making to management skills, from a focus on process to output, from orderly hierarchies to more competitive provision of public services, from fixed to variable pay, from a uniform and inclusive public service to variations in structure with more emphasis on contract provision. The rise of NPM can be linked to four administrative megatrends: (i) attempts to slow down or reverse public expenditure, (ii) shift to privatization, (iii) development of technology such as information technology, and (iv) internationalization (Hood 1991). In the past, the ethical ethos of universities and HE in general, has often been seen as quite different from that of business; however, the recent trend for managerialism to be brought to bear in the public sector, for example, the NPM movement, has challenged such traditional ethical perspectives. Importing managerialism in to education can be used to "manufacture consent" (Menter et al. 1997, 65) and threatens to exacerbate the dark side of management.

Oxenham (2013) has applied the concepts of liquid modernity to HE while Lorenz (2012) critically analyzed the impact of NPM on universities, albeit with an emphasis on their teaching mission rather than their research mission. Lorenz sees the impact of NPM in four tendencies: (i) a worsening of the Faculty or student ratio with increased student numbers and increased teaching loads for Faculty; (ii) the substitution of flexible and cheap staff for expensive, tenured full-time professors leading to a shrinking core Faculty surrounded by a growing periphery of inse-cure teaching staff; (iii) the disassociation of teaching and research—with research also being outsourced and commodified; and (iv) increased prices for education coupled with decreases in resource inputs.

The transition to a mass, marketized HE system coincident with the introduction of NPM has led to the erosion of academic staff's profes-sional status and the shattering of the academic's psychological contract; a phenomenon that is prevalent in current organizations (Robinson and Brown 2004; Benmore 2002). The undermining of the academic's profes-sional status has been associated with increased uncertainty due to factors such as the removal of tenure (Dnes and Seaton 1998), intensification of workload (Willmott 1995), imposition of new performance management systems (Deem 2004), increased reliance on line management (Enders, De Boer, and Leisyte 2008), commodification of the teaching process (Willmott 1995), increased reliance on casual and zero hour labor con-tracts (Halcomb et al. 2010), erosion of salaries (Deem 2004), reduced pension provision, imposition of new job roles based on the U.S. pro-fessorial system, and other related factors. The academic's job satisfac-tion has reduced, increased stress levels and bullying have been reported, and burnout of university teaching staff is on the increase (Watts and Robertson 2011; Tookey 2013; Kinman and Court 2010).

One of the key aspects that the chapter later focuses on is the impo-sition on academics of performance management systems that align with the government-instituted national assessment of research performance by universities. It can be argued that performance management systems suitable for the factory floor, which rely on approaches similar to the dis-credited management by objectives (Armstrong 2000), have been inap-propriately applied to the knowledge work of professionals. One factor that can explain the rapid adoption of such performance management systems in universities is that university vice-chancellors and principals have readily accepted the neoliberal ideologies underlying change in HE (Smith and Adams 2008). This factor is then exacerbated by the doctrine that applies in large organizations; namely that what is right is what the top person wants (Jackall 2010).

Business Schools

This section examines business schools and their university context. The first business schools originated in the United States in the 1880s while the famous Harvard Business School was founded in 1908 (Locke and Spender 2011). Although the United Kingdom was slow to adopt the business school concept, UK business schools have undergone impressive growth since the 1960s (Williams 2010, 109), in both number and size. The number of business schools in the UK is near to 150 (Williams 2010, vii), indicating that virtually all UK universities now house a business school. In fact business schools have grown more than many other academic fields reflecting their popularity with students; now activity on business and management programs forms the largest group in UK HE whether measured by numbers of Faculty or undergraduate students (Mills et al. 2006). This higher-than-average growth in business schools has meant that some of the pressures on their academics have been more acute than in non-business schools.

A UK business school can be defined as "a high-level educational institution in which students study subjects relating to business and commerce, such as economics, finance, and management" (Oxford Dictionaries 2014). A more stringent definition, particularly applied in the United States, is that a business school is a graduate school that offers a Master in Business Administration (MBA). Sometimes the growth of business schools coupled with their ability to recruit students to high-priced programs, such as MBAs, can unduly color their relationship with the center of the university where business schools can be seen as "cash cows" to be milked (Pfeffer and Fong 2004). Students of business schools tend to be characterized as more instrumental in their approach to HE than students in other subject areas (Burgess 2012).

This impressive growth of business schools could not have been achieved without one of their key features; specifically in the university they are the largest "importers" of Faculty from other academic fields and disciplines (Mills et al. 2006). Also, business schools are more likely than other university faculties to recruit people who have had careers outside of HE. While providing benefits, these heterogeneous features also mean that the Faculty could be less cohesive than other fields or disciplines and more susceptible to managerial rhetoric. Business schools also have one of highest attrition rates for early career staff which may reflect this lack of homogeneity.

In past decades, the growth in the size of business schools has been accompanied by their growth in influence within universities. However, obtaining academic recognition within universities has not always been easy since some Faculty outside of business schools have been slow to accept the academic standing of business and management subjects. Unfortunately the adverse reaction of academics, in general, to managerialism's encroachment on universities sometimes means that non-business school Faculty identify business schools with this encroachment and direct some of their bad feelings in the direction of business schools. However, it may be that business school managers, and academics, tend to accept performance management approaches from business more readily than non-business school Faculty.

Business schools also have an uneasy relationship with business (Zell 2001); and business people can be quite strong in their criticism of business schools. This type of criticism is perennial and has lasted nearly as long as business schools have existed (Khurana 2007). Business leaders criticize schools for not teaching the right knowledge and skills needed by business, and condemn them for carrying out irrelevant research (Bennis and O'Toole 2005). Governments in the United States and the United Kingdom have also reflected such adverse comments; however, it is worth observing that business school academics (Hamel 2007; Mintzberg 2004; Parker 2002) have also provided major critiques of business school activities—but often of a different nature. The global financial crisis that struck in 2008 has added to the already evident concerns about modern capitalism and its business ethics. Questions have been raised once more about the adequacy of what is taught to managers in business schools; and whether business ethics should feature more strongly in the curriculum of such schools. However such concerns are the latest installment of pressures on HE, and business schools in particular, to change the way that they manage themselves.

The Research Assessment Exercises

Without doubt one of the areas of performance management that has had a major impact on UK universities has been the sequence of government-mandated national research evaluation exercises; formerly these were called RAEs while the latest incarnation was termed the Research Excellence Framework (REF). The primary purpose of these exercises was declared as a means of determining public funding for universities' research; however, the published results have become a key factor in shaping a university's reputation through such as the various ranking systems that apply. The REF's guidelines (2015) specified that departments choosing to submit academics to the exercise should do so via a profile comprised up to four outputs[3] obtained over the qualifying period of 2008 to 2013. Subjects were organized in to four main panels containing 36 units of assessment, with business schools in Unit 19 (Business and Management Studies) of Panel C (www.ref.ac.uk/panels/unitsofassessment/). The government would appoint panel members to assess submitted publications against a four point scale where one star (1*) represents national level of quality and the highest score (4*) world-leading quality.

In the years leading up to the deadline for entry of submissions, academics in the high-status universities were under pressure to achieve management-established targets such as a minimum of four publications with each scored at a minimum of 3*. The general view was that such a profile was deemed necessary as an entry threshold given the way that government financing would be connected to quality scores. Although each submitted publication was to be assigned a quality rating by the appropriate REF evaluation panel, this score would not be known in advance and therefore this became part of the uncertainty surrounding

---

[3] The concentration here is on outputs connected to individual researchers—these comprised 65 percent of the weighting for the submission's overall score. Usually an output is a publication and we prefer to use this term rather than output in the following text. Aspects other than outputs were to be assessed such as cases demonstrating impact of research (20 percent) and the research environment of the submitting department (15 percent).

the whole REF endeavor. In business schools the yardstick that found favor to reduce uncertainty was to score publications based on the ranking that the Association of Business School's Journal Quality Ranking assigned to the journal that the article was published in.

Leaving aside the doubt over the outcome of the assessment of a publication's quality, the process of obtaining a publication is, in itself, something that has many uncertainties attached. Thus, in line with Bauman's theory, we can see the focus on REF performance as a ratcheting up of uncertainty for the individual. This uncertainty attached to REF performance has loomed large in various areas of academic work activity including day-to-day management and recruitment, career development and promotion, and other human resource processes that are dealt with next.

Human Resource Management Processes

As indicated earlier, the day-to-day management of academics and the HRM processes of recruitment, career development, and promotion provide opportunities for managers to indulge in wrongdoing. As outlined earlier, managers have imposed new performance management systems in an attempt to achieve goals such as the organization performing well in the REF. Examples of HRM processes are discussed briefly next, before concentrating on the flip side of HRM processes via a case study that illustrates, as a key theme, management actions taken to prepare a business school for the 2014 REF.

Recruitment processes can be, and are, circumvented by such methods as writing job specifications to fit a targeted individual, and advertising posts with the minimum of notice and through limited channels. Targeting posts to individuals is a practice that is suspected to be used particularly during such as reorganizations when existing staff are required to reapply for posts. By judicious choice of the composition of shortlisting and interviewing panels, managers can bring undue influences to bear. The decision-making literature shows that people tend to search for evidence that supports their desired outcomes, that is confirmation bias (Connolly and Ordóñez 2003), rather than making the rational, unbiased decisions that formal HRM systems describe. One of the particular impacts of the REF has been the emphasis on external recruitment of research stars and, as a consequence, universities have been compared with football clubs buying in star players (Butler and Mcallister 2011).

Managers, and powerful professors, are often in the position to channel opportunities for career enhancement and development in the direction of their preferred individuals and so set things up to fast-track them through promotion panels (Martin 2009). Such opportunities include, but are not limited to, inclusion in grant applications and coauthorship of high status publications. The influence of patronage is often discussed in academic circles but, as with much of wrongdoing, is seldom researched or publicized. In the United Kingdom, as in other countries, promotion to professor has no doubt been influenced by patronage, and the ambiguity around promotional criteria opens up the potential for bias. For example, emphasizing potential helps to reinforce the in-built bias against mature individuals looking for internal promotion.

The preceding comments concentrate on the potential for wrongdoing associated with such as recruitment, development, and promotion; next we use the medium of a case study to examine the flip side of these processes by looking at managerial wrongdoing in the context of censuring, demoting and encouraging staff to leave as preparation for the REF. Clearly, the obverse and flip-side of these HRM aspects are related, in that demoting and encouraging staff to leave creates opportunities for recruitment and promotion of other staff.

Case Study

As an illustrative case study, we take the reported events at Swansea University's School of Management that appeared in the press from the middle of 2013. In the 2008 RAE, the School had submitted 22 Category A staff (out of approximately 60 staff) and the mean score they had received was 2.35*. This "poor" performance, as described in the reports referred to in the following, formed part of the catalyst for senior management of the university to make new management appointments to the School in 2013.

In February 2013, Niall Piercy took up his role as deputy dean for operations in the School of Management. In May, he was joined by his father, Nigel Piercy, who was announced as dean while his father's partner was appointed as a reader (Jump 2013b). A spokesman described the dean as "an academic with a global reputation" and that his son and partner were appointed after an "open recruitment process." These comments were presumably made as a reaction to suspicions that had been aired that there was some element of undue influence at work in these appointments. The gist of Jump's (2013b) report was that non-early-career-research academics would be moved to teaching only contracts if they did not have four papers deemed to be of at least 3* quality for the REF. As a consequence they would be faced with teaching for up to 18 hours per week in comparison to six hours a week for their REF-submissible colleagues (Jump 2013a). An anonymous informant said that the policy had been introduced without consultation and stated "The lack of collegiality and dismissive attitude to current faculty by the new regime is going to have an adverse effect on staff retention, recruitment and the student experience" (Jump 2013b). In the article in October 2013, Jump commented on the situation at Swansea and connected it to a wider-ranging report of the situation in UK universities where academic staff at a sample of eight universities had been threatened with redundancy for non-submission to the REF.

In July 2014 Jump referred to a document dated February in which Professor Niall Percy (the pro dean) claimed that the school "has a legacy of 20 to 30 staff (of 70) who are not up to standard" and "Large scale severance, redundancy or early retirement" was considered the solution (Jump 2014a). Professor Nigel Piercy (the dean) was reported to have further upset staff in March 2014 when a spreadsheet of student satisfaction scores was circulated and modules with low scores were threatened with "special measures." Twenty-two academics submitted a formal grievance claiming that the spreadsheet undermined their "professional credibility." In a school survey of academics conducted anonymously in April, many complained of management disrespect and low morale. According to Jump's report, the dean commented that the survey results should be taken "with a pinch of salt" since they represented a small number of staff who "had a cosy lifestyle doing whatever they wanted for years." He was quoted as saying "This is not a commune. This is a managed institution pursuing goals that are closely aligned with the university's. It is not a rest home for refugees from the 1960s, with their ponytails and tie-dyed T-shirts."

In a letter published in the *Times Higher* of July 24, Guillam (2014, 30–31) commented on Jump's July report as follows:

> The underlying story of discontent and aggressive management at Swansea University's School of Management … is, sadly, becoming all too common in UK HE—and business schools seem to be especially prone to it. What is unusual in this case is the sheer contempt and naked ideological agenda of those involved. Insults about hippy-dippy communes and tie-dyed T-shirts seem more like comments on the Daily Mail website than something you would expect from a senior manager in a university.

The School was again in the news in August (Jump 2014c) and again in September (Jump 2014b); this time the focus was on a dispute that had broken out over an attempt by the dean to upgrade student's examination marks. An external examiner had complained about what he saw as a substantial upgrading of marks, describing this as a "gross debasing of standards" and an attempt by "the management team to increase league table performance by manipulation of degree outcomes." The dean responded that rescaling examination marks is a "completely acceptable practice" and he asserted that the need for adjustment sprung from politically inspired deliberate low marking by disgruntled staff. The dean also called in to question the external examiner's record and alleged his behavior followed from "close personal links" to members of the school whose area (Labour Economics) was being shut down. He also accused members of School staff and a pro vice-chancellor of being "Internet trolls."

In the September article the dean reflected on the overall situation. He said he felt "sympathetic" toward those who "have been sitting there for 30 years … with no one interfering with them and then some jerk comes along from outside and upsets the apple cart." He said 21 staff had left since he arrived and he had recruited "sensational" new staff that comprised 65 percent of the current school staff.

Discussion

The case study is clearly unusual in the sense of the story being played out in the national press; the reports cited here were in the *Times Higher Education* which is the national weekly magazine for UK HE. UK universities are renowned for their use of gagging orders (Parr 2014a) and so the appearance of such matters in the press tends to be few and far between. The case appears an extreme outlier—in the sense of the outspokenness of the School's management and in the values articulated—but it can be argued as highlighting typical elements of the business school, and the general university, environment. It is also an outlier in the sense of reports appearing in the press despite the normal secrecy arising from gagging and other practices. In the spirit of Starbuck's (2006) insight that extreme cases are often more revealing than run-of-the-mill situations, this extreme case is taken to be informative of the wrongdoing that takes place within business schools; wrongdoing perpetrated by managers on employees. The case can be interpreted as displaying a management that is intent on enforcing what it sees as the changed requirements for performance within the organization. No evidence is present that the management considers that a major restructuring of the academic's psychological contract has taken place; and certainly no genuine expressions of sympathy or empathy are apparent. Indeed what seems evident is scornful disregard for any difficulties that individuals might face in trying to adjust to the new circumstances. What is apparent is the flip side of recruitment, development, and promotion; that of censure, threat of demotion, and of dismissal.

As indicated, the appointment of the new dean and the actions he took with the intention of improving performance, were justified implicitly by reference to the School's poor performance in the last RAE and the desire to advance results in the forthcoming 2014 REF. This rationale reflects how thoroughly these research evaluation exercises have penetrated in to the university psyche and how, despite the sometimes-voiced rebellious thoughts, senior management in universities have accepted these research-related yardsticks as key performance measures to demand of academics. Unfortunately exhortation too frequently tips over in to bullying, a major problem adding to increased stress levels in HE (University and College Union 2012a).

The teaching developments in universities apply countervailing pressures to the emphasis on research arising from the REF and other measures. These developments include the National Student Survey and similar bespoke initiatives in universities to measure students' satisfaction with teaching and assessment. The case study reflects these developments in the publication of module scores and their use to punish those seen as poorly performing. Unfortunately evidence does not show that satisfaction is a useful predictor of learning (Abrami, d'Apollonia, and Rosenfield 2007); yet the emphasis on students as customers had led to satisfaction supplanting the idea of education being about knowledge transfer. The erosion of these *traditional* ideas are apparent in the previous case study with the issue of the upgrading of student marks; and the associated phenomenon of grade inflation that, although more prevalent in the United States, is making its impact felt in the United Kingdom. Academics who decide that student achievement is below standard are often cast by management in the role of *enemies* of the student and of the university.

Over recent times university management have developed and introduced performance management systems that reflect the influx of NPM and the neoliberal agenda. Both research and teaching dimensions figure prominently in such systems; although other areas such as good citizenship do also feature, they do so to a lesser extent. It seems that too often management uses these performance management systems to pressure and coerce individuals (see coercive accountability [Shore and Wright 1999]) who they see as not performing to the required level. The use of performance management as a blunt instrument is evident in the studied case in both areas of research and teaching. What the case illustrates is how the concentration on performance metrics has taken place gradually but inexorably in universities and is systematically undermining the academic as a professional.

As a consequence of this undermining, bias and discrimination have grown within universities and business schools. It is well known that UK universities are class-biased with regard to student composition; a lot of attention is paid to trying to improve the representation of lower classes in the student population. What is not so well-remarked on is that since many academics are recruited from students who have travelled through to the higher echelons of the HE system; then this class bias is also a feature of Faculty. It is not clear what impact such bias has on university operations. Gender bias is well-recognized in UK academia (Knights and Richards 2003) and evidence of racist incidents can also be found (University and College Union 2012b). Not so obvious is the discrimination on age grounds that can take place (Strike and Taylor 2009). One of the facets of the case is what might be construed as implicit age discrimination. The use of language where the *underperformers* are characterized as being around for a long time and being rooted in the 60s is surely aimed at mature individuals who have travelled well-down their career paths. Age discrimination is one of the insidious values that prosper within HE.

Age is usually correlated with employment tenure. Given that one of the key concerns in this chapter is the shattering of the psychological contract, it is worthwhile reflecting on the influence of tenure[4] on the perception of this contract in a fast-changing environment. Academics with long tenure are, perhaps, the ones who notice more acutely the erosion of the psychological contract given that they have been exposed longer and to more of the adverse changes that have occurred. New entrants to the profession are inclined to establish their psychological contracts in line with management's current view of what is required. Gammie (2006) provides some evidence that new entrants to the profession imported from business do display a more positive view of the psychological contract. In general, new entrants may be more prone to accept management's views including that long-tenured staff are "soldiering,"[5] to use the scientific management term (Taylor 1911). Given the preceding, it is not surprising management may be happier working with newer entrants who they no doubt see as more favorably disposed to performing in line with management's desires; that is, they provide a more flexible workforce.

Despite paying lip-service to equality by such as the eradication of politically incorrect language (e.g., the substitution of early-career in place of the adjective young when describing new academic staff), promotion and progression systems are too often geared to promoting youth

---

[4] I am using tenure here in the general sense of time in an organization and not in the more specific academic sense of meaning employment security.

[5] The term encapsulates the view that workers, unless they were closely monitored and controlled, would limit their productivity.

by emphasizing euphemistic criteria such as potential, that is, potential to perform in line with management's worldview. Patronage is an important force within HE (Martin 2009) whereby the powerful, senior individual (e.g., professor) can help the less-experienced individual (e.g., new career entrant) to advance by ensuring that opportunities are placed in their path and by promoting their potential. However, patronage by management rather than senior academics is becoming more influential.

If, as the chapter advocates, organizational wrongdoing is widespread in universities, one could ask why there is not more reported evidence than the limited amount available. It is useful to remember the popular aphorism that "absence of evidence is not evidence of absence." Little evidence stems from wronged individuals themselves; this is not surprising given the climate of fear which means that individuals are very reluctant to speak up; also the earlier remarked-on climate of gagging clearly has a major influence. However other more subtle pressures are at work. In their study of the impact of NPM in UK business schools Clarke et al. state that "academic identities have been rendered even more fragile by the intense pressures on academics to perform" (Clarke, Knights, and Jarvis 2012, 6). As Clarke, Knights, and Jarvis (2012, 7) quote (Humphreys 2005, 852) it is "unusual for academics to expose their doubts, fears and potential weaknesses." Another reason for tacit acceptance is that observers of wrongdoing might believe that if they turn a blind eye to the biased processes then they, in their turn, might benefit. Whistle blowing does not occur that frequently in general and particularly not in HE. One reason for this is the widespread use of suspensions and gagging orders by management when issues do surface in HE (Parr 2014a).

However, other more subtle reasons can be discerned. One of the key messages of Lorenz's critique is that the academic is disenfranchised and caught within a logic which denies the legitimacy of academic criticism of management (Lorenz 2012). A further factor that Clarke, Knights, and Jarvis (2012) identify is that when business school academics adopt a professional perspective of seeing their work as a "labor of love" then this predisposes them to be complicit with accepting recent adverse changes in the work environment. Academic research that examines wrongdoing and takes a critical line on the management is actively discouraged. Clark et al. cite the comments of Alvesson et al. (2008, 7) that "it is rare that academics study the 'lived realities' of their own organizations" and they reason that there is a "reluctance to expose 'backstage' behaviours to outside audiences." Other factors militate against academics airing their discontent. The competition between individuals is high and is often sustained by high self-confidence; where admission of doubts about abilities to achieve the performance targets expected of them would be seen as a major weakness.

Conclusion

Rather than viewing organizational wrongdoing perpetrated on UK business school academics as infrequent, this chapter has taken the view that it is a normal practice. The limited empirical evidence of such wrongdoing means that the narrative relies on theoretical arguments and secondary data including a case study culled from reports in the HE media. Notwithstanding such restrictions, the chapter has sought to illuminate the darker side of organizational life. The chapter aims to increase awareness of the widespread nature of the phenomena of wrongdoing within business schools; this is a first step down the path that could help to understand, prevent, and mitigate such wrongdoing. More theorizing and empirical research would be useful to support further steps down this path.

References

Abrami, P.C., S. d'Apollonia, and S. Rosenfield. 2007. "The Dimensionality of Student Ratings of Instruction: What We Know and What We Do Not." In *The Scholarship of Teaching and Learning in Higher Education: An Evidence-Based Perspective*, eds. R.P. Perry and J.C. Smart, 385–456. Netherlands: Springer.

Alvesson, M., L. Ashcraft, and R. Thomas. 2008. "Identity Matters: Reflections on the Construction of Identity Scholarship in Organi-zation Studies." *Organization* 15, no. 1, pp. 5–28.

Armstrong, M. 2000. "The Name Has Changed but Has the Game Remained the Same?" *Employee Relations* 22, no. 6, pp. 576–93.

Armstrong, M., and S. Taylor. 2014. *Armstrong's Handbook of Human Resource Management Practice*. London: Kogan Page.

Bauman, Z. 2000. *Liquid Modernity*. Cambridge: Polity Press.

Benmore, G. 2002. "Perceptions of the Contemporary Academic Employment Relationship." *International Studies in Sociology of Education* 12, no. 1, pp. 43–58.

Bennis, W.G., and J. O'Toole. 2005. "How Business Schools Lost their Way." *Harvard Business Review* 83, no. 5, pp. 96–104, 154.

Bryson, C., and N. Barnes. 2000. "Working in Higher Education in the Unitied Kingdom." In *Academic Work and Life: What It Is to Be an Academic, and How This Is changing,* ed. M. Tight, 147–85. Bingley, UK: Emerald Group Publishing Ltd.

Burgess, T.F. 2012. "How Business School Research Values Shape the Student Experience." In *Handbook of Research on Teaching Ethics in Business and Management Education,* eds. C. Wankel and A. Stachowicz-Stanusch, 606–18. Hershey, PA: Information Science Research.

Butler, L., and I. Mcallister. 2011. "Evaluating University Research Performance Using Metrics." *European Political Science* 10, no. 1, pp. 44–58.

Clarke, C., D. Knights, and C. Jarvis. 2012. "A Labour of Love? Academics in Business Schools." *Scandinavian Journal of Management* 28, no. 1, pp. 5–15.

Collini, S. 2012. *What Are Universities for?* London: Penguin Books Ltd.

Connolly, T., and L. Ordóñez. 2003. *Judgment and Decision Making.* Wiley Online Library.

Dabos, G.E., and D.M. Rousseau. 2004. "Mutuality and Reciprocity in the Psychological Contracts of Employees and Employers." *Journal of Applied Psychology* 89, no. 1, pp. 52–72.

Deem, R. 2004. "The Knowledge Worker, the Manager-Academic and the Contemporary UK University: New and Old Forms of Public Management?" *Financial Accountability & Management* 20, no. 2, pp. 107–28.

Dnes, A.W., and J.S. Seaton. 1998. "The Reform of Academic Tenure in the United Kingdom." *International Review of Law and Economics* 18, no. 4, pp. 491–509.

Elliott, A., ed. 2007a. *The Contemporary Bauman.* Abingdon, Oxon: Routledge.

Elliott, A., ed. 2007b. "The Theory of Liquid Modernity: A Critique of Bauman's Recent Sociology." In *The Contemporary Bauman,* 46–61. Abingdon, Oxon: Routledge.

Enders, J., H. De Boer, and L. Leisyte. 2008. "On Striking the Right Notes: Shifts in Governance and the Organisational Transformation of Universities." In *From Governance to Identity,* eds. A. Amaral, I. Bleiklie, and C. Musselin, 113–29. Netherlands: Springer Science + Business Media BV.

Gammie, R.P. 2006. *Psychological Contracts in a Business School Context* [Thesis]. Doctor of Education (EdD), University of Stirling: Scotland.

Griffin, R.W., and A.M. O'Leary-Kelly. eds. 2004. *The Dark Side of Organizational Behavior.* San Francisco: Jossey-Bass.

Guillam, P. 2014. "Manage Expectations." *Times Higher Education*, July 24, pp. 30–31.

Halcomb, E.J., S. Andrew, K. Peters, Y. Salamonson, and D. Jackson. 2010. "Casualisation of the Teaching Workforce: Implications for Nursing Education." *Nurse Education Today* 30, no. 6, pp. 528–32.

Halsey, A.H. 1992. *Decline of Donnish Dominion: The British Academic Professions in the Twentieth Century*. Oxford: Oxford University Press.

Hamel, G. 2007. *The Future of Management*. Boston, MA: Harvard Business School Press.

Harley, S., M. Muller-Camen, and A. Collin. 2004. "From Academic Communities to Managed Organisations: The Implications for Academic Careers in UK and German Universities." *Journal of Vocational Behavior* 64, no. 2, pp. 329–45.

Hood, C. 1991. "A Public Management for all Seasons?" *Public Administration* 69, no. 1, pp. 3–19.

Hood, C. 1995. "The 'New Public Management' in the 1980s: Variations on a Theme." *Accounting, Organisations and Society* 20, nos. 2/3, pp. 93–109.

Jackall, R. 2010. *Moral Mazes: The World of Corporate Managers*. Oxford: Oxford University Press.

Jump, P. 2013a. "Some Face High Price for Failure to Hit REF Targets." *Times Higher Education*, October 3, p. 8.

Jump, P. 2013b. "Swansea's REF Plan Diet Hard to Swallow." *Times Higher Education*, September 5, p. 8.

Jump, P. 2014a. "Academic Staff are Accused of Enjoying 'Lovely Cosy Lifestyle'." *Times Higher Education*, July 10, p. 11.

Jump, P. 2014b. "'No Regrets' says Swansea Dean, Unperturbed by Acrimony Over Reforms." *Times Higher Education*, September 4, pp. 6–7.

Jump, P. 2014c. "Upscaling Dean Claims his Actions Compensated for Disgruntled Swansea staff." *Times Higher Education*, August.

Khurana, R. 2007. *From Higher Aims to Hired Hands*. Princeton, NJ: Princeton University Press.

Kinman, G., and S. Court. 2010. "Psychosocial Hazards in UK Universities: Adopting a Risk Assessment Approach." *Higher Education Quarterly* 64, no. 4, pp. 413–28.

Knights, D., and W. Richards. 2003. "Sex Discrimination in UK Academia." *Gender, Work & Organization* 10, no. 2, pp. 213–38.

Locke, R.R., and J.C. Spender. 2011. *Confronting Managerialism: How the Business Elite and Their Schools Threw Our Lives Out of Balance*. London: Zed Books.

Lorenz, C. 2012. "If You're so Smart, Why Are You Under Surveillance? Universities, Neoliberalism, and New Public Management." *Critical Inquiry* 38, no. 3, pp. 599–629.

Martin, B. 2009. "Academic Patronage." *International Journal for Educational Integrity* 5, no. 1, pp. 3–19.

Menter, I., Y. Muschamp, P. Nicholls, J. Ozga, and A. Pollard. 1997. *Work and Identity in the Primary School: a Post-Fordist Analysis.* Buckingham: Open University Press.

Mills, D., A. Jepson, T. Coxon, M. Easterby-Smith, P. Hawkins, and J. Spencer. 2006. *Demographic Review of the UK Social Sciences.* Swindon: Economic and Social Research Council.

Mintzberg, H. 2004. *Managers not MBAs: A Hard Look at the Soft Practice of Managing and Management Development.* London: Prentice Hall.

Molesworth, M., R. Scullion, and E. Nixon, eds. 2011. *The Marketisation of Higher Education and the Student as Consumer.* Abingdon, Oxon: Routledge.

Neider, L.L., and C.A. Schriesheim. eds. 2010. *The Dark Side of Management.* Charlotte, NC: Information Age Publishing.

Oxenham, M. 2013. *Higher Education in Liquid Modernity.* Abingdon, Oxon: Routledge.

Oxford Dictionaries. 2014. www.oxforddictionaries.com/definition/english/business-school (accessed October 23, 2014).

Palmer, D. 2013. *Normal Organizational Wrongdoing: A Critical Analysis of Theories of Misconduct in and By Organizations.* Oxford: Oxford University Press.

Parker, M. 2002. *Against Management.* Cambridge: Polity Press.

Parr, C. 2014. "Attempts to 'Gag and Silence' are Commonplace." *Times Higher Education*, September 11, p. 9.

Pfeffer, J., and C.T. Fong. 2004. "The Business School 'Business': Some Lessons From the US Experience." *Journal of Management Studies* 41, no. 8, pp. 1501–20.

Poder, P. 2007. "Relatively Liquid Interpersonal Relationships in Flexible Work Life." In *The Contemporary Bauman*, ed. A. Elliott, 136–53. Abingdon, Oxon: Routledge.

REF's guidelines. 2014. "REF 2014: Research Excellence Framework." www.ref.ac.uk/ (accessed April 27, 2015).

Robinson, S.L., and G. Brown. 2004. "Psychological Contract Breach and Violation in Organizations." In *The Dark Side of Organizational Behavior*, eds. R.W. Griffin and A.M. O'Leary-Kelly, 309–337. San Francisco: Jossey-Bass.

Rousseau, D.M. 1990. "New Hire Perceptions of Their Own and Their Employer's Obligations: A Study of Psychological Contracts." *Journal of Organizational Behavior* 11, no. 5, pp. 389–400.

Shore, C., and S. Wright. 1999. "Audit Culture and Anthropology: Neo-Liberalism in British Higher Education." *Journal of the Royal Anthropological Institute*, pp. 557–75.

Smith, D.N., and J. Adams. 2008. "Academics or Executives? Continuity and Change in the Roles of Pro-Vice-Chancellors." *Higher Education Quarterly* 68, no. 4, pp. 340–57.

Starbuck, W.H. 2006. *The Production of Knowledge: The Challenge of Social Science Research*. Oxford: Oxford University Press.

Strike, T., and J. Taylor. 2009. "The Career Perceptions of Academic Staff and Human Resource Discourses in English Higher Education." *Higher Education Quarterly* 63, no. 2, pp. 177–95. doi:10.1111/j.1468-2273.2008.00404.x

Taylor, F.W. 1911. "The Principles of Scientific Management." In: Project Gutenberg www.gutenberg.org/ebooks/6435 (accessed April 24, 2015).

Tookey, M. 2013. *The Impact of the Academic Psychological Contract on Job Performance and Satisfaction* (Doctoral dissertation). Norwich Business School, University of East Anglia.

University and College Union 2012a. 2012 *Occupational Stress Survey*. London.

University and College Union 2012b. *The Position of Women and BME Staff in Professorial Roles in UK HEIs*. London.

Watts, J., and N. Robertson. 2011. "Burnout in University Teaching Staff: A Systematic Literature Review." *Educational Research* 53, no. 1, pp. 33–50.

Williams, A.P.O. 2010. *The History of UK Business and Management Education*. Bingley: Emerald.

Willmott, H. 1995. "Managing the Academics: Commodification and Control in the Development of University Education in the UK." *Human Relations* 48, no. 9, pp. 993–1027.

Zell, D. 2001. "The Market-Driven Business School: Has the Pendulum Swung Too Far?" *Journal of Management Inquiry* 10, no. 4, pp. 324–38.

About the Authors

Thomas F. Burgess, after 25 years of working full-time for Leeds University Business School, branched out in 2014 as an Independent Researcher but retaining a role as Visiting Senior Research Fellow at LUBS. He continues to research collaboratively with established partners in academia and to edit the *International Journal in Productivity and Performance Management*. However, this change allows him to set his own priorities and to spend more time on his research projects. His research interests remain in innovation, technology, performance management, and social networks.

Francesco Cannia is a clinical psychologist, group analyst, and human resources consultant by public administration and private companies. He has over 5 years experience in training and practice in analysis, evaluation, and organizational design, human resources development, and change management. He works at SNA—Scuola Nazionale dell'Amministrazione as Designer, Researcher, and Trainer in different programmes and laboratories, such as Leadership and Public Management and Conflict Management.

Debabrata Chatterjee is a Professor in organizational behavior at the Indian Institute of Management, Kozhikode, India. His research interest spans the fields of institutional theory and innovation. He is particularly interested in studying institutions and institutional change that impact on innovations in emerging economies. Currently, he is researching the role of Indian higher educational institutions in developing innovations for emerging markets. He teaches core courses on organization theory, and elective courses on organizational change and the management of innovation at the postgraduate and doctoral levels.

Dorina Chicu is a Postdoctoral Researcher in the Department of Business Management at the University Rovira i Virgili (URV), having previously completed Master's Degree in Strategic Management at the same University. She has a degree in economics at the Academy Studii Economice in

Moldova. After working for several years in private companies, she joined the URV as a full-time PhD student in November 2011. In 2015 she completed her doctoral thesis. She is part of the FHOM group (Factor Humà, Organitzacins i Mercats) and has recently completed a research stay at the Kemmy Business School, Limerick, Ireland.

Giorgia Cioccetti is a Group Analyst, trained and graduated in Clinical Psychology at La Sapienza University in Rome. She has over 5 years of professional experience in training and practice in various private and public organizations. She worked in human resources consulting and organizational design, she is still working as Designer, Researcher, and Trainer in the School of Public Administration (SNA) in Rome.

Maria del Mar Pàmies Pallisé is Assistant Professor in the Department of Business Management at the Universitat Rovira i Virgili (URV). She studied business administration (URV) and marketing research (University of Barcelona) and has a Master's Degree in Strategic Management (URV). In 2011 she completed her doctoral thesis on consumer behavior in situations of waiting services for which she was awarded the Best Doctorate Thesis Award by the URV. She teaches at the University in the area of marketing and market research, and previously she worked in sales and marketing in several private companies.

Gilda María Hernández Maskivker is a Postdoctoral Researcher in the Department of Business Management at the University Rovira i Virgili (URV). She has a Degree in Tourism and Master's Degree in Analysis Techniques and Innovation in Tourism. In 2015, she completed her doctoral thesis. She has developed teaching tasks (undergraduate) and research in the field of marketing and consumer behavior. Her main research line is on waiting time in tourist services. She recently completed a research stay at California State University Long Beach (United States).

Alessandro Hinna, PhD, is Associate Professor of Organization Studies at Tor Vergata University of Rome, where he currently teaches Organization Theory, Organization and Change in Public Organization, and People Management. He also is Professor of Public Management at the Italian School of Public Administration. He is Chair of the "Organizational Behavior" Strategic Interest Group and Officer of the "Public

Management" Strategic Interest Group, at the European Academy of Management. He has done research activity on topics related to organization and change management in public organizations, behavioral dimensions in public governance, organizational design, individual behavior, public service motivation, and human resource management.

Stephan Leixnering is Senior Scientist at the Research Institute for Urban Management and Governance at WU Vienna University of Economics and Business. He previously held research and teaching positions at the Institute for Public Management and the Institute for Organization Studies at WU. His research focuses on the governance and organization of the public sector. He also works on the emergence of organizational forms and ethical aspects of organization and management.

Sandro Mameli is full-time Professor of Public Management at the National School of Administration, Italy, and Head of the Management, Organization and Human Resources Department of the School. His research activities focus on the organizational impact of private-like reforms in public sector, critical discourse analysis, and the clinical approach in organization studies.

Maria Gisa Masia is Dynamic and Clinical Psychologist, with a specialization in Group Analysis and a Master in Marketing and communication. She has over 5 years experience in human resources recruiting and selection as well as change management through the use of CAF (Common Assessment Framework) in Public Administration (Ministry of Justice). She has more than four years collaboration with SNA ("Public Management" Strategic Program headed by Prof. Sandro Mameli) on Organizational Analysis, Training programmes and Research. She is specialized in innovative and participative training methodologies (Case Study Design, Leadership and Managerial Laboratories).

Wolfgang Mayrhofer is Full Professor and Head of the Interdisciplinary Institute of Management and Organisational Behaviour, Department of Management, WU Vienna University of Economics and Business, Austria. He previously has held research and teaching positions at the University of Paderborn, Germany, and at Dresden University of Technology, Germany, after receiving his diploma and doctoral degrees in

Business Administration from WU. He conducts research in comparative international human resource management and leadership, work careers, and systems theory and management.

Sonia Moi is a PhD student in Public Management and Governance at the University of Rome "Tor Vergata," where she holds a Master's Degree of Science in Economics and completed an MPhil in Engineering for the Public Administrations. Her research topics include corruption and risk management, governance (especially in public and nonprofit organizations).

Fabio Monteduro, PhD, is an Assistant Professor of "Business Administration" at the University of Rome "Tor Vergata." At the same university, he is Faculty Member of the PhD in "Public Management and Governance" and Board Member of the Bachelor of Science in Business and Economics. He is actively involved in international scientific networks such as the European Academy of Management and the International Research Society for Public Management. His main research topics are: accountability and control in organizations; performance management; and public and nonprofit governance.

Gerard Ryan is an Associate Professor in marketing at the Universitat Rovira i Virgili and Visiting Professor at Cornell University, with over 20 years experience in teaching, research, and management in university education. A native of Ireland, Gerard was a full-time Tenured Lecturer and Head of the Masters Program in Marketing at Middlesex University Business School in London (1995 to 1997) before joining the EUM of the Universitat Pompeu Fabra in Barcelona where he was an International Consultant before becoming Head of the Department of International Relations and Coordinator of Studies in Business Logistics (1997 to 2003). He joined the Rovira i Virgili University in 2003 where he was a founding member of FHOM, which is part of the Catalan Government's map of official research groups. Gerard has also collaborated on a continuous basis with the following institutions and universities: University of Limerick, Waterford IT, Limerick IT, University of North London, Royal College of Nursing of the UK, The Open University of Catalonia, ESADE Barcelona and Madrid, University of Barcelona, Polytechnic

University of Catalonia, the University of Castellon, and the National University of the South of Argentina.

Mireia Valverde Aparicio is an Associate Professor in the Department of Business Management at the Universitat Rovira i Virgili (URV) and Visiting professor at Cornell University, United States. She studied at the University of Barcelona, University of Limerick (Ireland), Cranfield School of Management (United Kingdom), and URV, where she read her doctoral thesis on the roles of the various actors involved in managing people in organizations. She has worked in several universities in different countries and is currently in the URV since 2000 to 2001, where she is performing tasks of teaching (undergraduate, postgraduate, and doctorate), management (area coordinator, secretary, and director of the department) and research, heading the group FHOM, recognized by the Government.

Duncan Waite is a Professor of Education and Community Leadership, Texas State University. He is Editor of The International Journal of Leadership in Education (Routledge), and coeditor of The International Handbook of Leadership in Education (forthcoming, Wiley-Blackwell). He has published extensively on school leadership, qualitative research methods, and the sociocultural forces surrounding education, schooling, and leadership. He has keynoted conferences in Norway, Turkey, Spain, Russia, Chile, Israel, and more.

Index

This book is a publication in support of the United Nations Principles for Responsible Management Education (PRME), housed in the UN Global Compact Office. The mission of the PRME initiative is to inspire and champion responsible management education, research and thought leadership globally. Please visit www.unprme.org for more information.

The Principles for Responsible Management Education Book Collection is edited through the Center for Responsible Management Education (CRME), a global facilitator for responsible management education and for the individuals and organizations educating responsible managers. Please visit www.responsiblemanagement.net for more information.

—Oliver Laasch, University of Manchester, Collection Editor

Announcing the Business Expert Press Digital Library

Concise e-books business students need for classroom and research

This book can also be purchased in an e-book collection by your library as

- a one-time purchase,
- that is owned forever,
- allows for simultaneous readers,
- has no restrictions on printing, and
- can be downloaded as PDFs from within the library community.

Our digital library collections are a great solution to beat the rising cost of textbooks. E-books can be loaded into their course management systems or onto students' e-book readers. The **Business Expert Press** digital libraries are very affordable, with no obligation to buy in future years. For more information, please visit **www.businessexpertpress.com/librarians**. To set up a trial in the United States, please email **sales@businessexpertpress.com**.

www.ingramcontent.com/pod-product-compliance
Lightning Source LLC
Chambersburg PA
CBHW070505200326
41519CB00013B/2718